READY-TO USE READING ACTIVITIES FOR THE ELEMENTARY CLASSROOM

Sue Jones Erlenbusch

Illustrations by the Author

THE CENTER FOR APPLIED
RESEARCH IN EDUCATION
West Nyack, New York 10995

Library of Congress Cataloging-in Publication Data
Erlenbusch, Sue Jones.
Ready-to-use reading activites for the elementary classroom.

Includes index.
1. Individualized reading instruction. 2. Reading (Elementary) --
United States--Language experience approach. 3. Activity programs
in education--United States. 4.Holidays--United States. I. Title.
LB 1050.38.E75 2000 372.4'147 00-24973

Printed in the United States of America

10 9 8 7 6 5 4 3 2 1

ISBN: 0-13-054983-5

**THE CENTER FOR APPLIED RESEARCH
IN EDUCATION
West Nyack, NY 10994**

www.phdirect.com

Contents

About This Book

Reading Activities for Every Month of the School Year contains material for a wide variety of reading skills on various reading levels. The reproducible activity sheets are designed to act as a supplement to the basal reading program and to help you provide for the often broad range of reading abilities found in every classroom.

Some of the skills stressed include following written directions, color recognition, fine motor coordination, visual discrimination, phonics, sequencing, creative writing, and vocabulary development.

The Activities

The activity sheets can be reproduced as many times as needed for use with your students. Here are several suggestions for using these activity sheets.

1. Use the language experience approach with the story starter activity sheets. Beginning readers can dictate their story endings for you to write for them, and older children can write them on their own. All of the children, however, should illustrate their own stories. After the stories are finished and illustrated, they can be mounted on construction paper and displayed on a story wall. Use the wall outside your classroom to allow other students and staff members to read your classes' stories.

For instance, a very attractive story wall can be made using the "Snow" and "Ice" story starters in January. The "Snow" stories can be mounted on dark blue construction paper and displayed together, while the "Ice" stories can be mounted on light blue construction paper and displayed together. You can use a poster in the center of the display to tie it all together, as shown here.

Story walls attract a lot of attention and compliments for your students. You may want to invite parents to come to the classroom so that your students can show off their efforts. You may be able to arrange for your school district's photographer to take a picture of the story wall and some of your students for the district's newspaper.

2. If you don't use the stories to make a story wall, you might make arrangements with another teacher to have your students make a guest appearance to read their stories to new audiences.

3. If you have a principal who wants to encourage young readers personally, you might arrange for each student to go to the office and read his or her story to the principal.

4. The story starters and other activity sheets can be used to make a personal book for each student to take home at the end of a unit. This lets parents see some of the activities the students have been working on.

Vocabulary

Vocabulary is an important part of this book. Here are suggestions for helping your students learn the words covered on the activity sheets.

1. The vocabulary words in each unit can be used to make word cards for a bulletin board display. You can turn the daily review of the words into a game to see who can say all of the words without missing one and "striking out," For example, your October bulletin board might look something like this:

2. You can type each vocabulary word on a small card and put these word cards on a key ring so that two students can work together to review the words.

3. If you have a Bell & Howell Language Master Card Reader, or similar machine, you can put each vocabulary word on a card so that each child can work independently to review the words.

4. If you have some students who need to use a tactile approach, you can write the words on cards using a felt-tip pen and then go over each word with an all-purpose white glue that dries clear.

5. You can also make a set of vocabulary cards for each student. In a shoe box, each student will have sections divided into "Words I Know" and "Words I Am Learning." During the review session, each time a child tells you a word on sight, you place a check on the card and file it appropriately at the end of the session. When a child has a specified number of checks, he or she is allowed to take the word card home.

6. For children who are just learning to read, you can make sentence strips by cutting long strips of paper. As shown here, you can write the sentence and let the child draw a picture of the vocabulary word to help him or her learn the new word.

After the child has learned all of the words on the sentence strip and can read it easily and consistently, he or she may take the sentence strip home.

7. You can use the vocabulary words to make a bingo game for each unit. In the center of each card, draw a holiday picture as the free square. Make at least six cards with the words arranged in a different order on each card. One person may use a card to call the words while the other players place chips on each word as it is called. The winner calls the next game.

8. Game boards on cardboard pizza circles and posterboard can also be made to accompany each unit. Two children may play a game that helps reinforce vocabulary words. Game boards might look something like the two shown here.

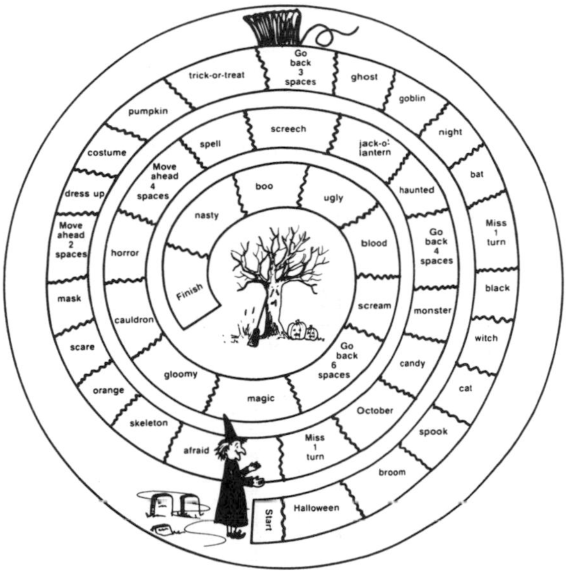

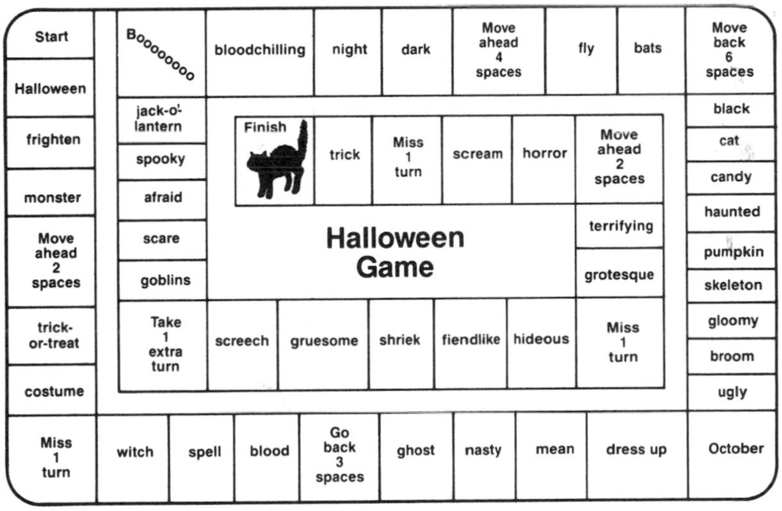

Skills Index

A special feature of *Reading Activities for Every Month of the School Year* is the Skills Index that indicates all of the reading skills covered by each activity.

Keep these skills in mind when using the activity sheets so that you can choose the appropriate activities for each student.

Sue Jones Erlenbusch

Skills Index

Activity Number and Title	Capitalization	Categorizing	Comprehension	Creative Writing	Fine Motor Coordination	Phonics	Punctuation	Recognition of Colors	Sequencing	Sequencing Days of the Month	Sequencing Letters	Sequencing Special Days	Visual Discrimination	Vocabulary Development
1-1 Labor Day			X											
1-2 A Picture to Color					X			X						
1-3 Same or Different													X	
1-4 Alphabet Scramble											X			
1-5 Who Is It?											X			
1-6 What Is It?											X			
1-7 The Lost Book														X
1-8 Back to School Maze														X
1-9 Word Match														X
1-10 Word Hunt														X
1-11 Missing Consonant Puzzle						X								
1-12 Missing Vowel Puzzle						X								
1-13 Color Word Scramble								X	X					
1-14 Word Scramble									X					X
1-15 Scrambled Days									X					X
1-16 Order! Order!									X					X
1-17 Sentence Completion			X											
1-18 Make a Word														X
1-19 Crossword Puzzle			X											
1-20 School Days				X										
1-21 The New Student				X										

Activity Number and Title	Capitalization	Categorizing	Comprehension	Creative Writing	Fine Motor Coordination	Phonics	Punctuation	Recognition of Colors	Sequencing	Sequencing Days of the Month	Sequencing Letters	Sequencing Special Days	Visual Discrimination	Vocabulary Development
1-22 Schoolmarms and Schoolmasters			X											
1-23 Country Schoolhouse			X											
1-24 The Hickory Stick			X											
1-25 School Tools			X											
1-26 Schoolhouse Word Hunt														X
1-27 Schoolhouse Scramble									X					X
2-1 Columbus Day			X											
2-2 Columbus Day Maze														X
2-3 Columbus Day Word Hunt														X
2-4 A Picture to Color					X									
2-5 Same or Different													X	
2-6 Alphabet Scramble											X			
2-7 Who Is It?											X			
2-8 The Lost Broomstick														X
2-9 Halloween Maze														X
2-10 Jack-o'-Lantern Puzzle		X												
2-11 Halloween Word Match														X
2-12 Trick-or-Treat														X
2-13 Halloween Word Hunt														X
2-14 A Bloodchilling Story			X											
2-15 Sh! It's a Secret!			X											

Activity Number and Title	Capitalization	Categorizing	Comprehension	Creative Writing	Fine Motor Coordination	Phonics	Punctuation	Recognition of Colors	Sequencing	Sequencing Days of the Month	Sequencing Letters	Sequencing Special Days	Visual Discrimination	Vocabulary Development
2-16 Missing Consonant Puzzle						X								
2-17 Missing Vowel Puzzle						X								
2-18 Who Needs It?			X											
2-19 Make a Word														X
2-20 The Unfinished Spell				X										
2-21 A Halloween Story				X										
2-22 Look Who's Cooking				X										
2-23 Halloween Word Scramble									X					X
2-24 Halloween Divination			X											
2-25 Halloween Spirits			X											
2-26 Word Hunt														X
3-1 Veterans Day			X											
3-2 Turkey Time					X			X						
3-3 Same or Different													X	
3-4 Alphabet Scramble											X			
3-5 Who Is It?											X			
3-6 The Lost Feast														X
3-7 Thanksgiving Maze														X
3-8 Thanksgiving Puzzle		X												
3-9 Thanksgiving Word Match														X

Activity Number and Title	Capitalization	Categorizing	Comprehension	Creative Writing	Fine Motor Coordination	Phonics	Punctuation	Recognition of Colors	Sequencing	Sequencing Days of the Month	Sequencing Letters	Sequencing Special Days	Visual Discrimination	Vocabulary Development
3-10 Give Thanks														X
3-11 Thanksgiving Feast														X
3-12 Thanksgiving Word Hunt														X
3-13 The First Thanksgiving Day			X											
3-14 Sh! It's a Secret!			X											
3-15 Missing Consonant Puzzle						X								
3-16 Missing Vowel Puzzle						X								
3-17 Thanksgiving Word Scramble									X					X
3-18 Who Needs It?			X											
3-19 Make a Word														X
3-20 My Thanksgiving Day				X										
3-21 Thanksgiving Story				X										
3-22 Thanksgiving			X											
3-23 Thanksgiving Customs			X											
3-24 Word Hunt														X
4-1 A Picture to Color					X									
4-2 Same or Different													X	
4-3 Alphabet Scramble											X			
4-4 Who Is It?											X			
4-5 What Is It?											X			

Activity Number and Title		Capitalization	Categorizing	Comprehension	Creative Writing	Fine Motor Coordination	Phonics	Punctuation	Recognition of Colors	Sequencing	Sequencing Days of the Month	Sequencing Letters	Sequencing Special Days	Visual Discrimination	Vocabulary Development
4-6	Christmas Eve Maze														X
4-7	Christmas Maze														X
4-8	Christmas Puzzle		X												
4-9	Christmas Match														X
4-10	A Christmas Wish														X
4-11	Christmas Word Hunt														X
4-12	Sh! It's a Secret!			X											
4-13	Christmas Consonant Puzzle						X								
4-14	Christmas Vowel Puzzle						X								
4-15	Christmas Word Scramble									X					X
4-16	Who Needs It?			X											
4-17	Make a Word														X
4-18	A Letter to Santa				X										
4-19	A Christmas Story				X										
4-20	What's Cooking?				X										
4-21	Saint Nicholas			X											
4-22	Christmas			X											
4-23	Word Hunt														X
4-24	Hanukkah			X											
5-1	A Picture to Color					X			X						

Activity Number and Title	Capitalization	Categorizing	Comprehension	Creative Writing	Fine Motor Coordination	Phonics	Punctuation	Recognition of Colors	Sequencing	Sequencing Days of the Month	Sequencing Letters	Sequencing Special Days	Visual Discrimination	Vocabulary Development
5-2 Find the Hidden Mitten													X	
5-3 Same or Different													X	
5-4 Alphabet Scramble											X			
5-5 What Is It?											X			
5-6 The Hidden Sled														X
5-7 Guess What														X
5-8 New Year's Eve Puzzle		X												
5-9 Word Match														X
5-10 Winter Fun														X
5-11 Word Hunt														X
5-12 Sh! It's a Secret!			X											
5-13 Missing Consonant Puzzle						X								
5-14 Missing Vowel Puzzle						X								
5-15 Make a Word														X
5-16 Make a Word														X
5-17 Order! Order!												X		
5-18 The Snowball Fight				X										
5-19 Snow				X										
5-20 Ice				X										
5-21 Martin Luther King, Jr. Day			X											

Activity Number and Title	Capitalization	Categorizing	Comprehension	Creative Writing	Fine Motor Coordination	Phonics	Punctuation	Recognition of Colors	Sequencing	Sequencing Days of the Month	Sequencing Letters	Sequencing Special Days	Visual Discrimination	Vocabulary Development
5-22 Martin Luther King, Jr. Word Hunt														X
6-1 Groundhog Day			X											
6-2 Groundhog Day Word Hunt														X
6-3 A Picture to Color					X									
6-4 Same or Different													X	
6-5 Alphabet Scramble											X			
6-6 A Secret Pal											X			
6-7 What Is It?											X			
6-8 Valentine Maze														X
6-9 Valentine Maze														X
6-10 A Valentine Puzzle		X												
6-11 Valentine Match														X
6-12 Word Hunt														X
6-13 Sh! It's a Secret!			X											
6-14 Word Scramble									X					X
6-15 Make a Word														X
6-16 Valentine Puzzle			X											
6-17 Sentence Completion			X											
6-18 A Valentine Party				X										
6-19 A Love Note				X										

Activity Number and Title		Capitalization	Categorizing	Comprehension	Creative Writing	Fine Motor Coordination	Phonics	Punctuation	Recognition of Colors	Sequencing	Sequencing Days of the Month	Sequencing Letters	Sequencing Special Days	Visual Discrimination	Vocabulary Development
6-20	Surprise! Surprise!				X										
6-21	A Love Potion				X										
6-22	What's Cooking?				X										
6-23	Saint Valentine			X											
6-24	Love Lore			X											
6-25	Abraham Lincoln			X											
6-26	Lincoln's Birthday														X
6-27	George Washington			X											
6-28	Washington's Birthday														X
6-29	Missing Consonant Puzzle						X								
6-30	Missing Vowel Puzzle						X								
7-1	A Picture to Color											X			
7-2	Same or Different													X	
7-3	Alphabet Scramble											X			
7-4	Who Is It?											X			
7-5	What Is It?											X			
7-6	Shamrock Maze														X
7-7	Saint Patrick's Day Puzzle		X												
7-8	Word Match														X
7-9	Shopping Spree														X

Activity Number and Title	Capitalization	Categorizing	Comprehension	Creative Writing	Fine Motor Coordination	Phonics	Punctuation	Recognition of Colors	Sequencing	Sequencing Days of the Month	Sequencing Letters	Sequencing Special Days	Visual Discrimination	Vocabulary Development
7-10 March Calendar										X				
7-11 Word Hunt														X
7-12 Sh! It's a Secret!			X											
7-13 Missing Consonant Puzzle						X								
7-14 Missing Vowel Puzzle						X								
7-15 Word Scramble									X					X
7-16 Rhyme Time														X
7-17 Make a Word														X
7-18 My Three Wishes				X										
7-19 The Pot of Gold				X										
7-20 Legend of the Leprechaun				X										
7-21 Saint Patrick			X											
7-22 The Last Snake			X											
8-1 April Fool's Day			X											
8-2 Arbor Day			X											
8-3 Arbor Day Word Hunt														X
8-4 A Picture to Color					X									
8-5 Same or Different													X	
8-6 Alphabet Scramble											X			

Activity Number and Title		Capitalization	Categorizing	Comprehension	Creative Writing	Fine Motor Coordination	Phonics	Punctuation	Recognition of Colors	Sequencing	Sequencing Days of the Month	Sequencing Letters	Sequencing Special Days	Visual Discrimination	Vocabulary Development
8-7	Who Is It?											X			
8-8	The Lost Bonnet														X
8-9	Easter Maze														X
8-10	Easter Puzzle		X												
8-11	Easter Puzzle		X												
8-12	Easter Match														X
8-13	Easter Word Hunt														X
8-14	Easter Sentences	X						X							
8-15	Sh! It's a Secret!			X											
8-16	Easter Consonant Puzzle						X								
8-17	Easter Vowel Puzzle						X								
8-18	Word Scramble									X					X
8-19	Word Scramble									X					X
8-20	Make a Word														X
8-21	An Easter Story				X										
8-22	Easter Morning				X										
8-23	New Clothes for an Old Witch				X										
8-24	Easter			X											
8-25	Word Hunt														X

Activity Number and Title	Capitalization	Categorizing	Comprehension	Creative Writing	Fine Motor Coordination	Phonics	Punctuation	Recognition of Colors	Sequencing	Sequencing Days of the Month	Sequencing Letters	Sequencing Special Days	Visual Discrimination	Vocabulary Development
9-1 May Day Customs			X											
9-2 May Day Superstitions			X											
9-3 Mother's Day			X											
9-4 Memorial Day			X											
10-1 Father's Day			X											
10-2 Flag Day			X											
11-1 Independence Day			X											
11-2 Independence Day Word Hunt														X
12-1 Columbus Sails			X											

SEPTEMBER

A	B	C				

Creative Writing • 3
Phonics Workbooks • 3
Vocabulary • 5
Game Board • 6

Activity Number and Title		Special Day
1-1	Labor Day	Labor Day
1-2	A Picture to Color	Back to School
1-3	Same or Different	Back to School
1-4	Alphabet Scramble	Back to School
1-5	Who Is It?	Back to School
1-6	What Is It?	Back to School
1-7	The Lost Book	Back to School
1-8	Back to School Maze	Back to School
1-9	Word Match	Back to School
1-10	Word Hunt	Back to School
1-11	Missing Consonant Puzzle	Back to School
1-12	Missing Vowel Puzzle	Back to School
1-13	Color Word Scramble	Back to School
1-14	Word Scramble	Back to School
1-15	Scrambled Days	Back to School
1-16	Order! Order!	Back to School
1-17	Sentence Completion	Back to School
1-18	Make a Word	Back to School
1-19	Crossword Puzzle	Back to School
1-20	School Days	Back to School
1-21	The New Student	Back to School
1-22	Schoolmarms and Schoolmasters	Back to School
1-23	Country Schoolhouse	Back to School
1-24	The Hickory Stick	Back to School
1-25	School Tools	Back to School
1-26	Schoolhouse Word Hunt	Back to School
1-27	Schoolhouse Scramble	Back to School

Creative Writing

This is a good time to introduce the idea of doing a first draft, making corrections, and then doing a final draft for the creative writing activities. On the first draft, ask the children to just tell their stories without worrying about spelling, punctuation, capitalization, grammar, and sentence construction. After they get their stories down on paper, you can help each child make the necessary corrections. When a story is ready for the final draft, ask the child to use his or her very best handwriting and then make an illustration. When this final draft and illustration are completed, the story is ready to be mounted and displayed on the story wall, put in a personal book, read to a new audience, or taken home.

Children readily accept the idea of doing a first draft, making corrections, and then doing a final draft because they want their best work displayed for others.

Phonics Workbooks

September is also a good time to introduce phonics workbooks that have been made by you and the students. To make a consonant workbook, take twenty-one sheets of ruled paper and print one of the consonants in both capital and lower case form in the lower right-hand corner of each sheet. Behind each of these sheets place a sheet with the subheadings "Sentences That Tell You Something" and "Sentences That Ask You Something." There should be enough space for six sentences under each subheading. Place all of these pages between two pieces of construction paper and staple them together. Print the title of the book on the front cover. You may illustrate the cover or ask each child to draw and color a picture on his or her own book. Write the child's name on the front of the workbook in the lower right-hand corner.

Here is a sample layout for a consonant workbook.

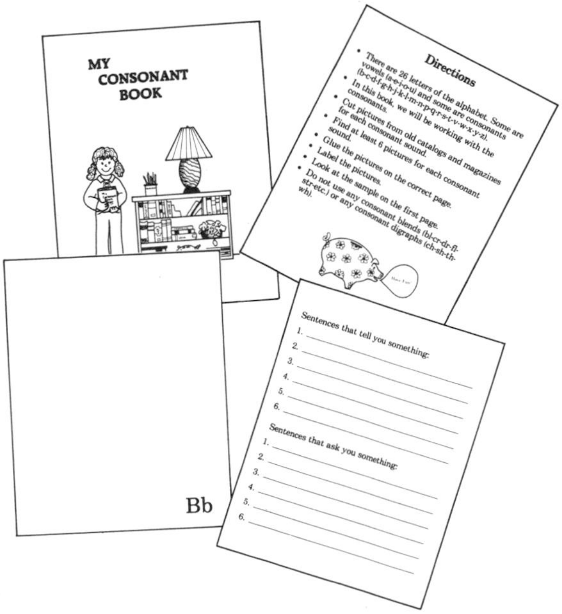

Bring a wide variety of monthly magazines and catalogs to class. The larger editions of the major catalogs are excellent for teaching students to use an index as they look up pictures for each page of the book. Christmas catalogs and the December issues of the monthly magazines are so popular that it's hard to get enough copies to use!

Ask students to find at least six pictures for each consonant page. (Work on only one page at a time.) The pictures should be cut out and glued onto the correct page of the book; then each picture should be labeled. Next, the student must use each of the six labeled words in both a telling and an asking sentence. Correct spelling, grammar, capitalization, and punctuation should be stressed.

Students can also be encouraged to make consonant blend, consonant digraph, and vowel workbooks, as shown in the sample layouts here.

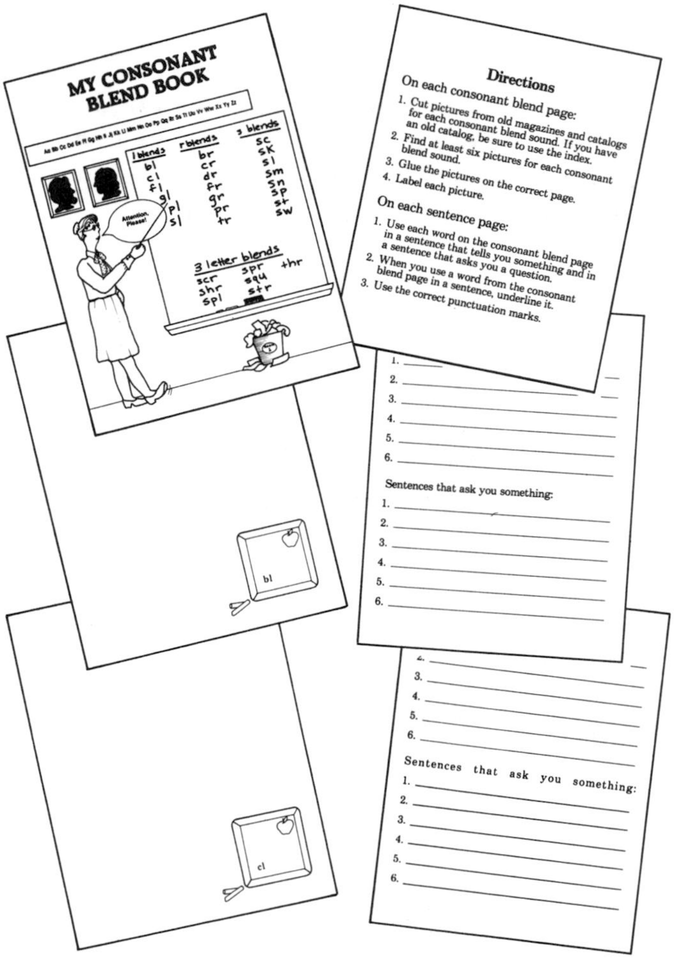

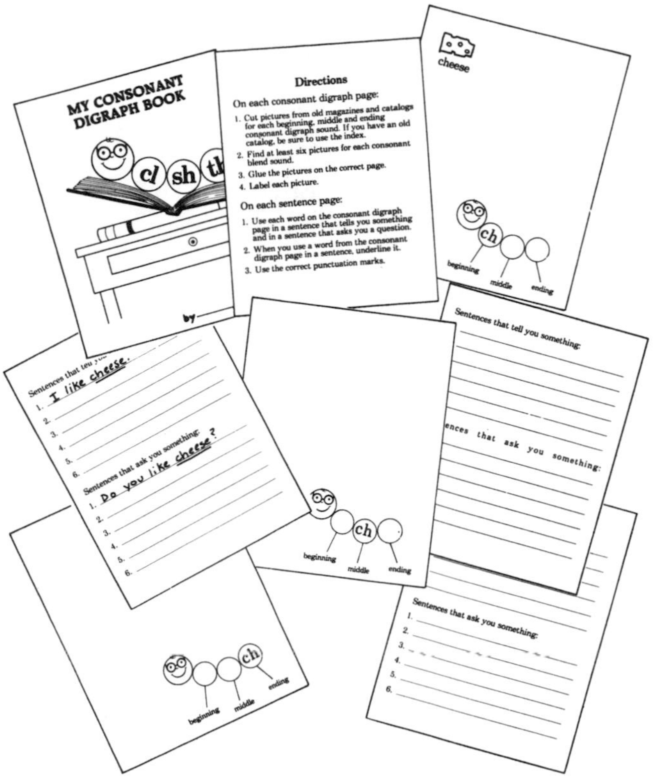

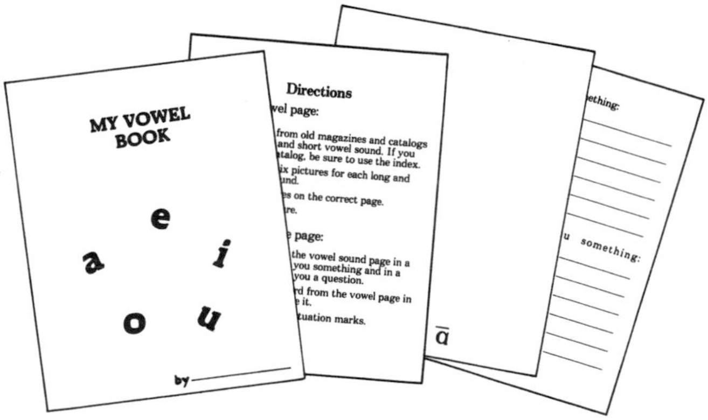

Vocabulary

The following four word lists will help develop your students' vocabularies in September.

Labor Day Word List	**Back to School Word List 1**	**Back to School Word List 2**	**Back to School Word List 3**
celebrated	schoolhouse	math	schoolmarms
Monday	chalkboard	custodian	graduate

Labor Day Word List	Back to School Word List 1	Back to School Word List 2	Back to School Word List 3
symbolize	crayons	language	discipline
observed	pencils	secretary	grades
city	paper	physical education	quill
year	schedule	music	ink
holiday	blocks	science	written
school	apple	geography	chalkstone
summer	books	semester	foolscap
September	reading	ruler	taught
bill	teacher	eraser	received
state	desk	spelling	copybook
signed	education	art	schoolmasters
legal	student	social studies	patience
Oregon	cafeteria	pupil	chalk
person	lunch	subject	punish
President	principal	parents	supervisor
honor	dictionary	nurse	terms
national	encyclopedia	cooks	stick
working	recess	writing	hickory

Game Board

Here is a game board pattern for you to use in September.

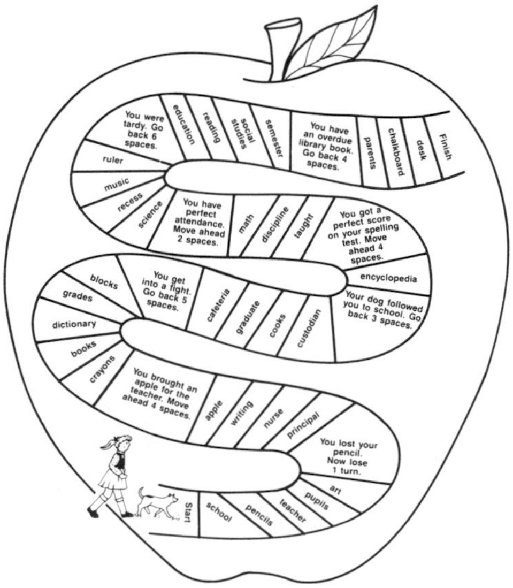

Name ______________________________

LABOR DAY

Directions: Fill in the blanks with words from the list at the bottom of this sheet.

Labor Day is (1) ________________ on the first (2) ________________ in (3) ________________. Peter J. McGuire was the person who first (4) ________________ the need for a holiday to (5) ________________ all (6) ________________ people. The first Labor Day (7) ________________ took place in New York (8) ________________ in 1882. In 1887, Oregon became the first (9) ________________ to make Labor Day a (10) ________________ holiday. In 1894, (11) ________________ Grover Cleveland signed a bill making Labor Day a (12) ________________ holiday.

Since it is the last (13) ________________ before the (14) ________________ of the new school year, Labor Day has come to (15) ________________ the end of (16) ________________ and the beginning of (17) ________________.

suggested fall Monday
symbolize City
celebration observed
state President start summer
holiday national
working September legal honor

Name ______________________________

A PICTURE TO COLOR

Directions: Use the color chart to help you choose the right colors to color the picture.

Name ______________________________

SAME OR DIFFERENT

Directions: Look at the word on the left. Circle the word on the right that is like the one on the left.

pencils	penculs	pencols	pencils	pincels
apple	apple	appel	apperl	appele
crayons	croyans	crayons	crayuns	crayans
paper	papur	papor	papers	paper
teachers	teacher	teachers	techers	teachurs
books	book	boaks	books	dooks
reading	reeding	reading	reabing	raeding
recess	recuss	recees	recass	recess
school	schul	shool	school	schuul
chalk	chalk	cholk	chaulk	choalk

Name ________________________

ALPHABET SCRAMBLE

Directions: Write the letters of the alphabet in the correct order. The first three are done for you.

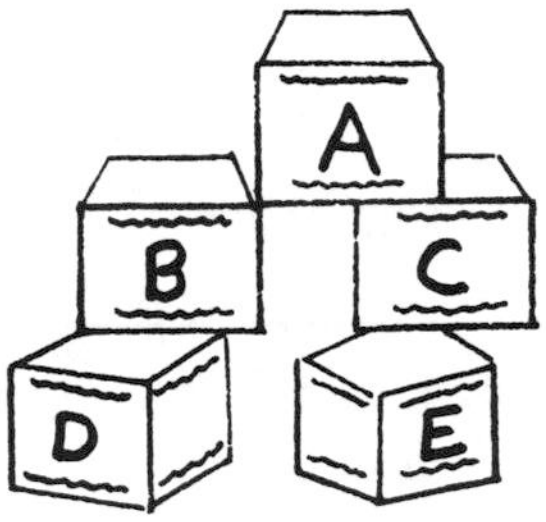

A	B	C				

WHO IS IT?

Directions: Connect the dots to find out who is in this picture. Start with the first letter of the alphabet. First, connect the lower case letters. Then, connect the capital letters.

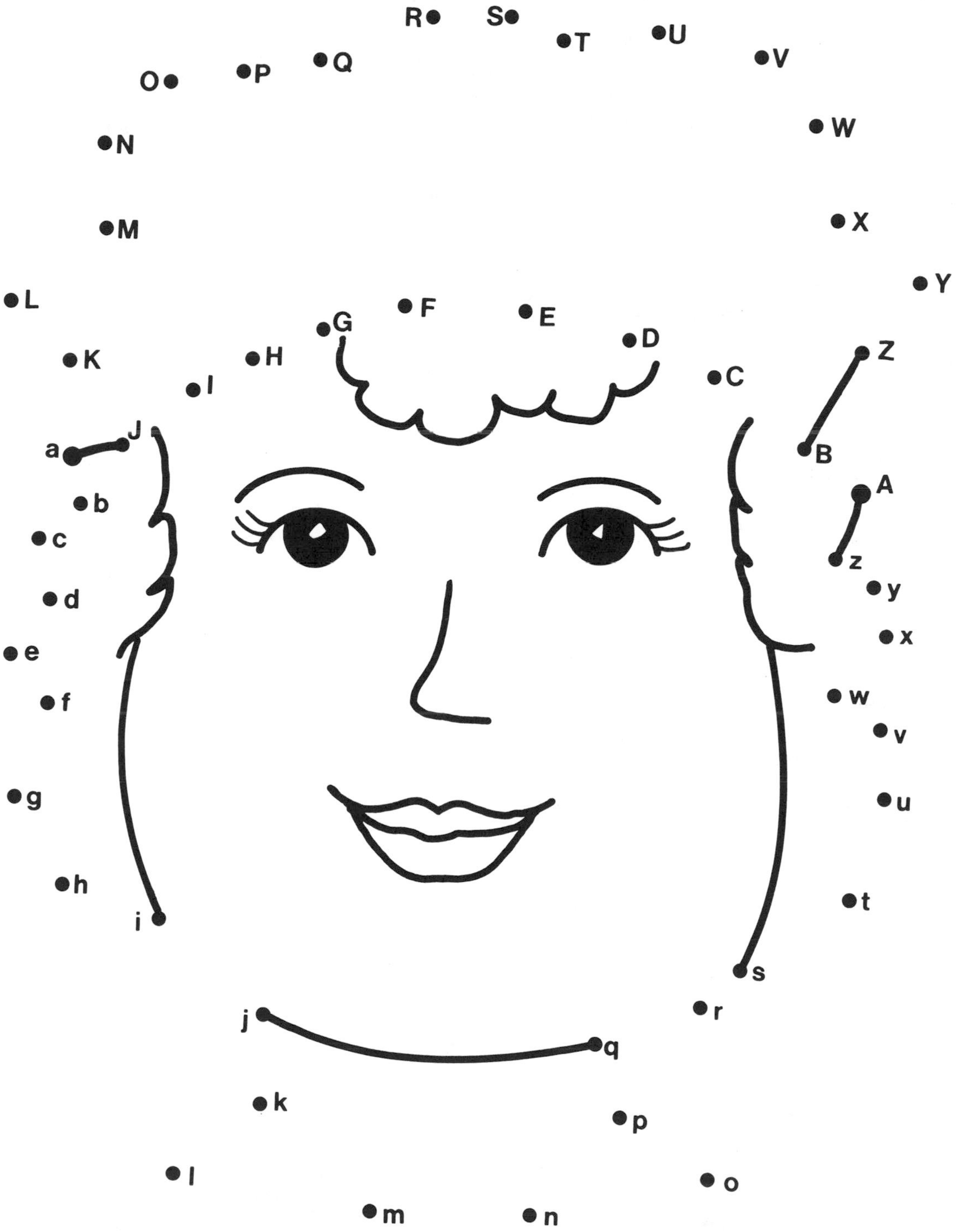

Name ______________________________

WHAT IS IT?

Directions: Connect the dots to find out what is in this picture. Start with the first letter of the alphabet. First, connect the lower case letters. Then, connect the capital letters.

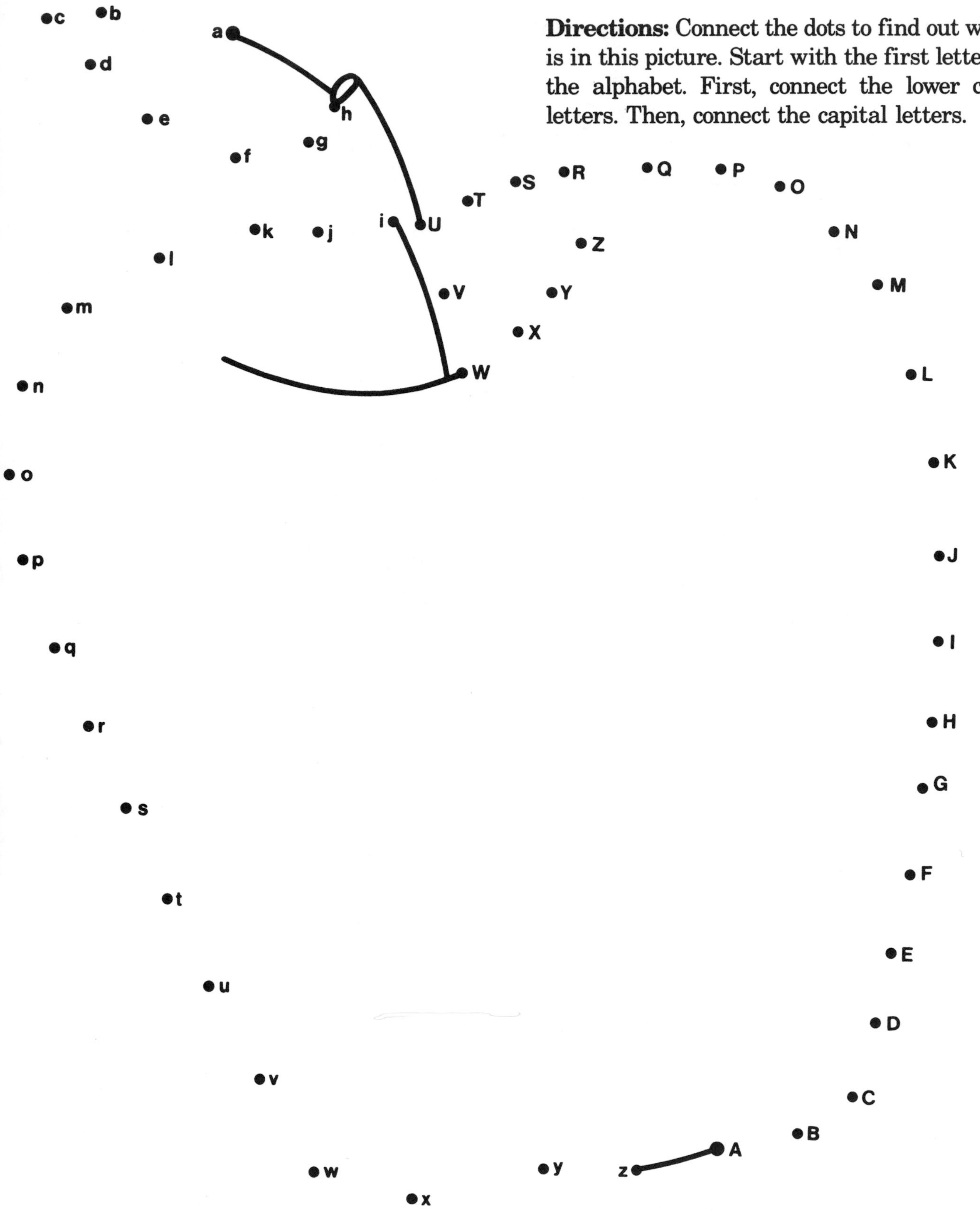

Name ______________________________ 1-7

THE LOST BOOK

Directions: Mugs has hidden Susie's book. Help her find it by drawing a line through all of the September words. Start near Susie.

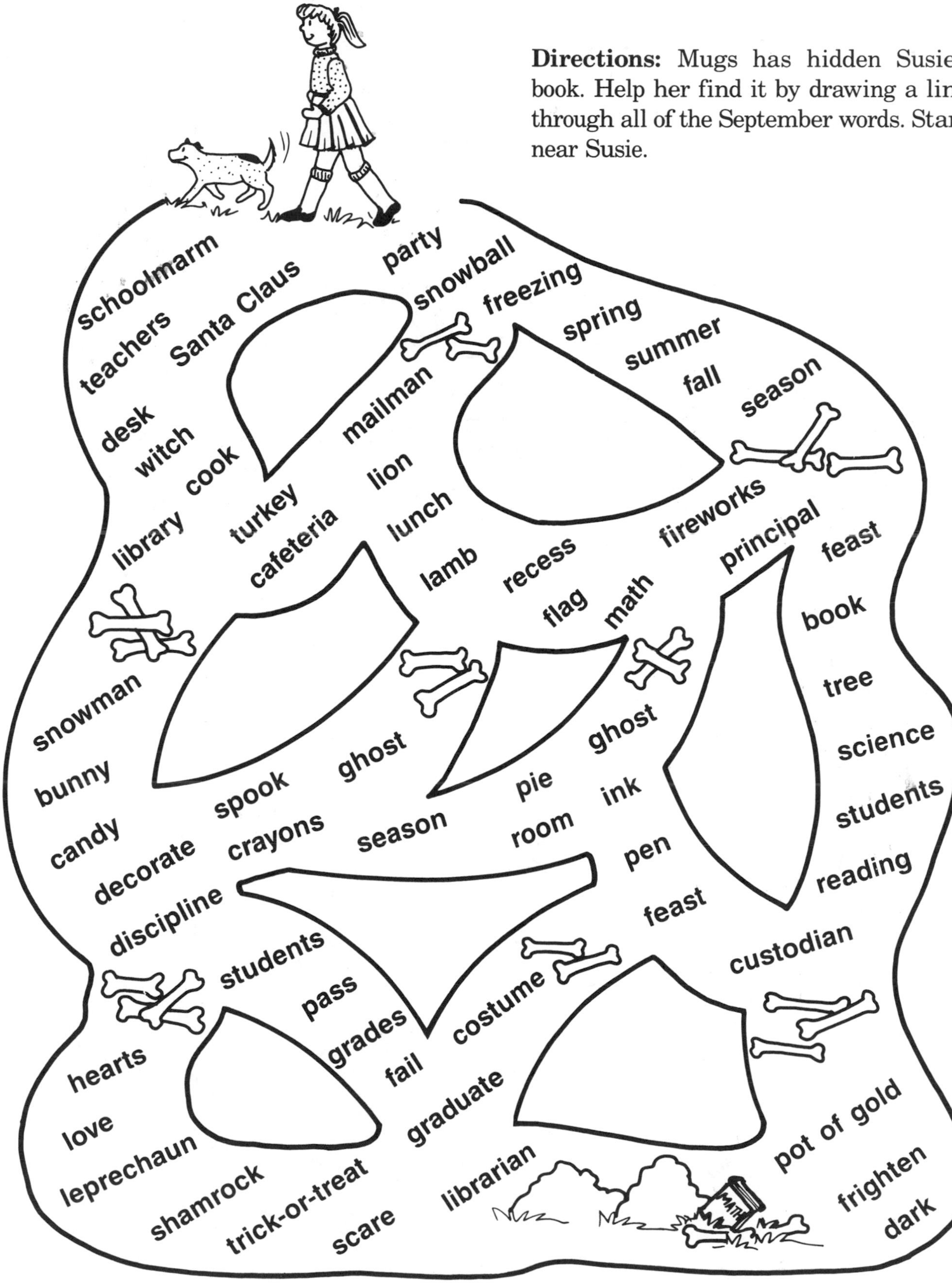

Name ______________________________

BACK TO SCHOOL MAZE

Directions: Freddy is lost. Help him find the schoolhouse by drawing a line from him through all of the September words.

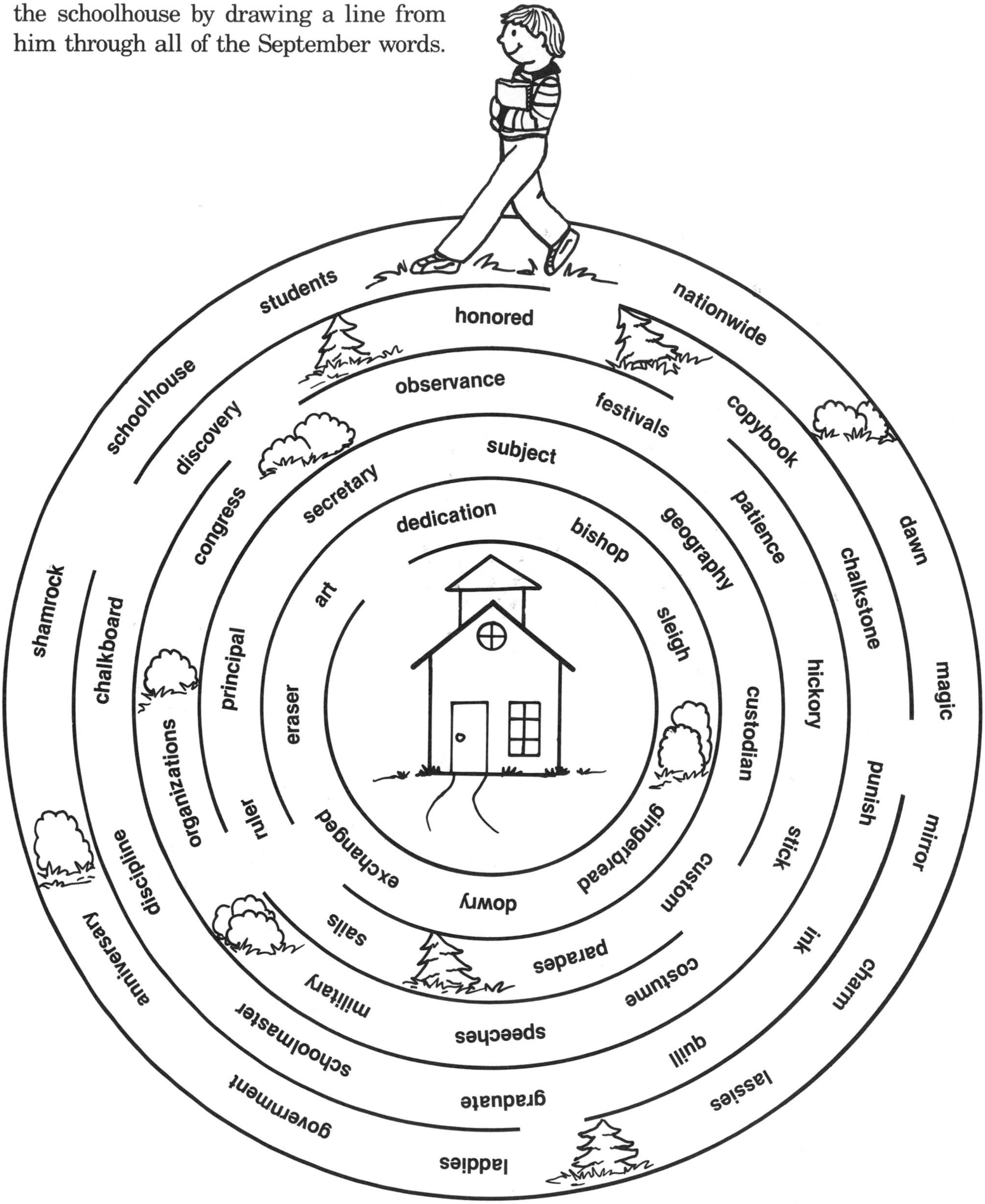

Name ____________________

WORD MATCH

Directions: Draw a line to match the pictures to the correct words.

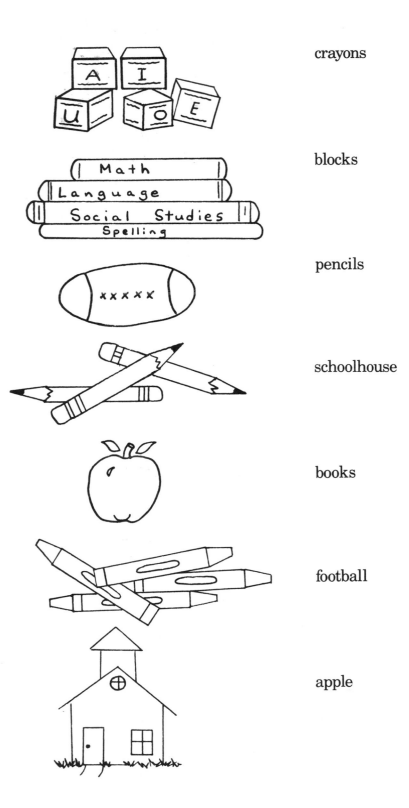

crayons

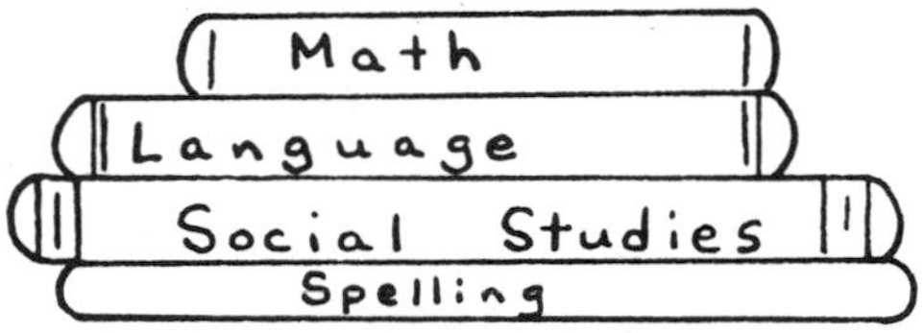

blocks

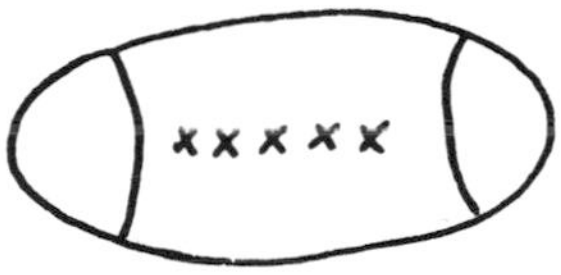

pencils

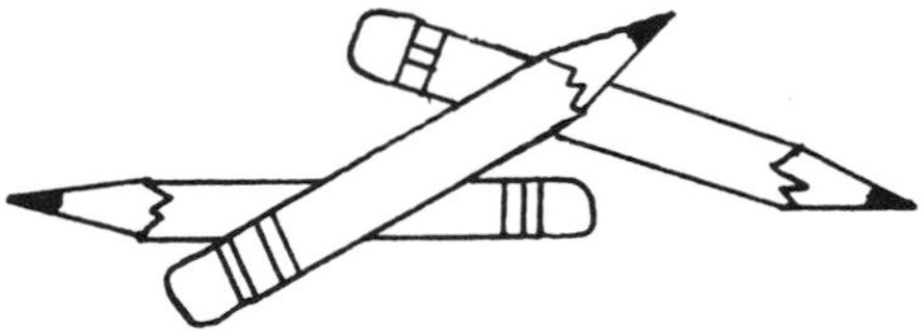

schoolhouse

books

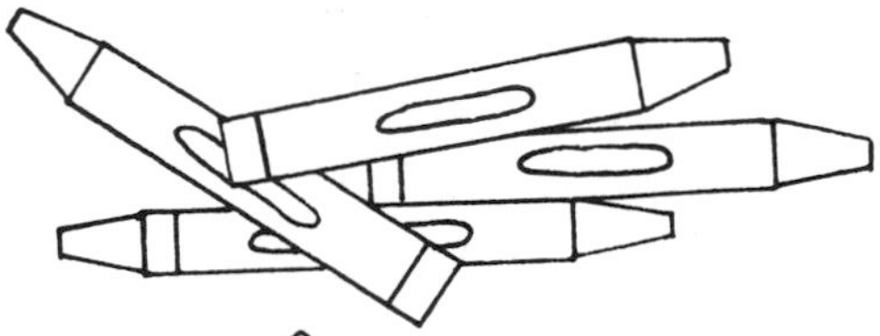

football

apple

Name ______________________________

WORD HUNT

Directions: Circle the hidden words. You may go across and down.

p	h	y	s	i	c	a	l	e	d	u	c	a	l
m	g	h	e	t	e	d	u	c	a	t	i	o	n
q	r	e	w	y	a	e	n	s	r	a	z	r	i
w	r	i	t	i	n	g	c	p	i	l	a	t	g
a	s	v	o	s	r	p	h	e	t	q	l	s	h
m	u	s	i	c	p	s	t	l	h	i	a	p	e
r	e	a	d	i	n	g	x	l	m	w	n	e	a
e	w	c	m	e	o	s	b	i	e	r	g	l	l
c	f	g	k	n	h	n	w	n	t	x	u	l	t
e	d	e	y	c	t	m	a	g	i	n	a	i	h
s	u	l	j	e	s	v	r	d	c	z	g	n	c
s	o	c	i	a	l	s	t	u	d	i	e	s	e

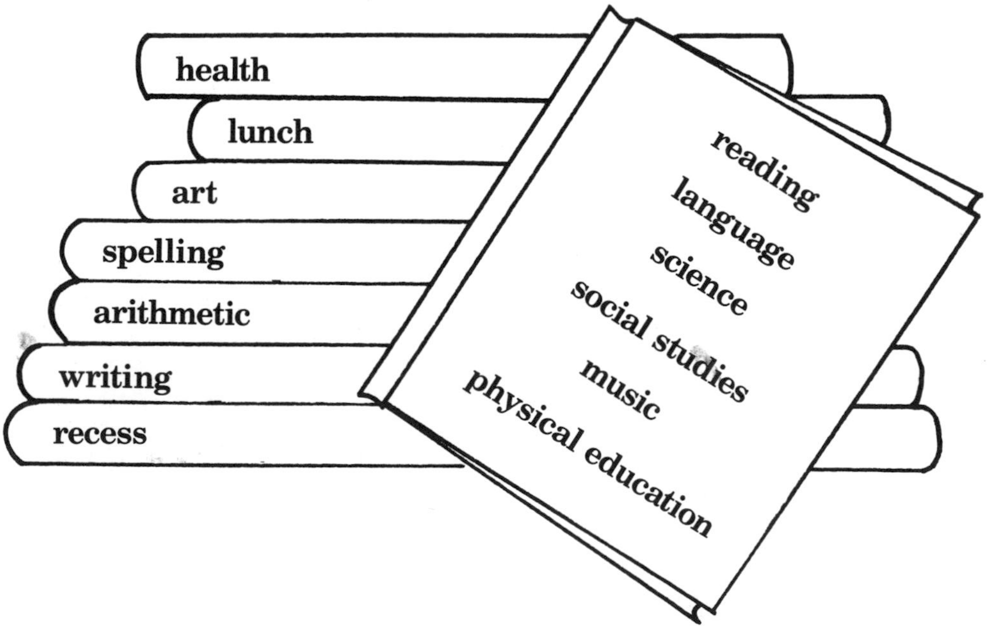

MISSING CONSONANT PUZZLE

Directions: Fill in the missing consonants.

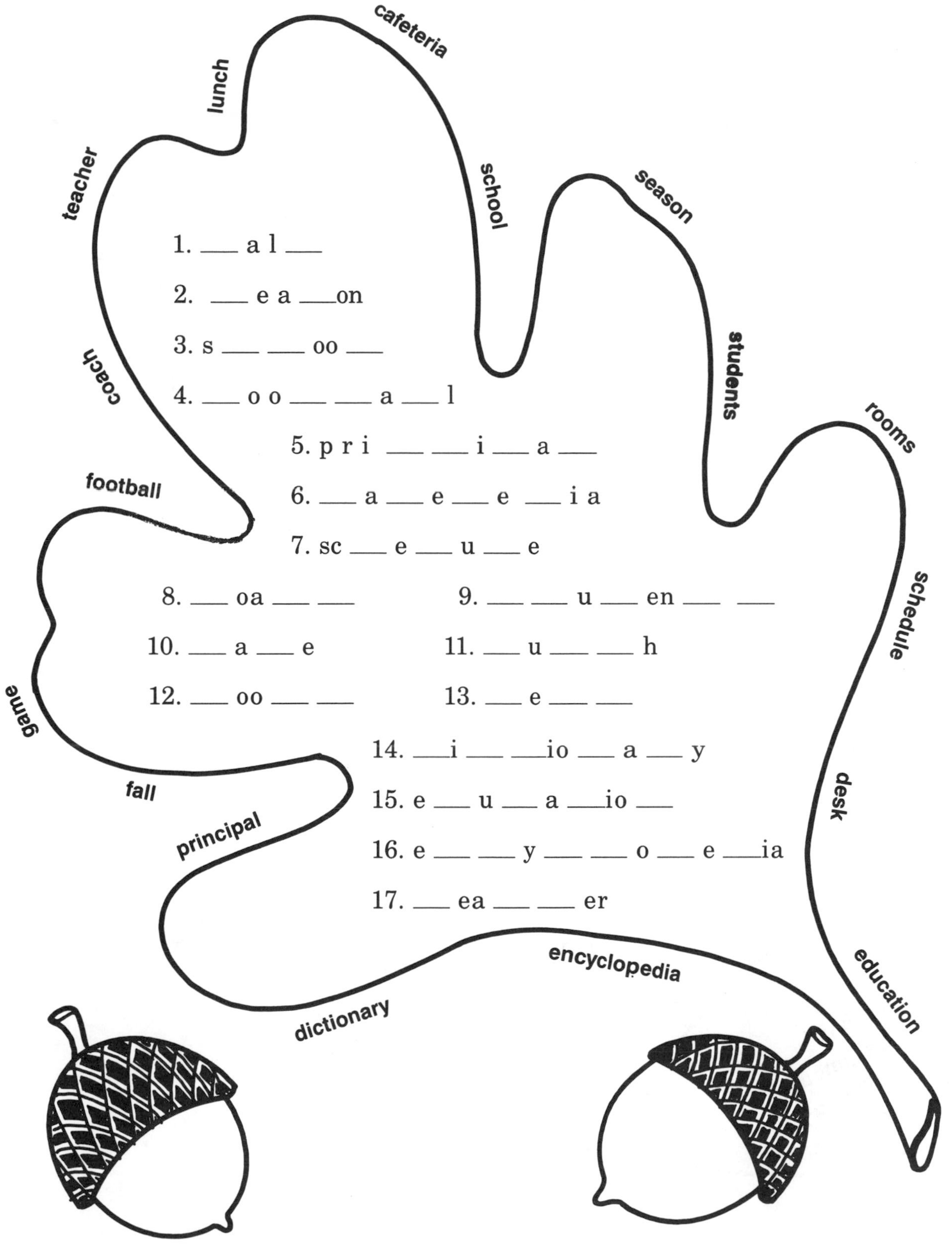

1. ___ a l ___
2. ___ e a ___on
3. s ___ ___ oo ___
4. ___ o o ___ ___ a ___ l
5. p r i ___ ___ i ___ a ___
6. ___ a ___ e ___ e ___ i a
7. sc ___ e ___ u ___ e
8. ___ oa ___ ___
9. ___ ___ u ___ en ___ ___
10. ___ a ___ e
11. ___ u ___ ___ h
12. ___ oo ___ ___
13. ___ e ___ ___
14. ___i ___ ___io ___ a ___ y
15. e ___ u ___ a ___io ___
16. e ___ ___ y ___ ___ o ___ e ___ia
17. ___ ea ___ ___ er

Name ______________________________

MISSING VOWEL PUZZLE

Directions: Fill in the missing vowels.

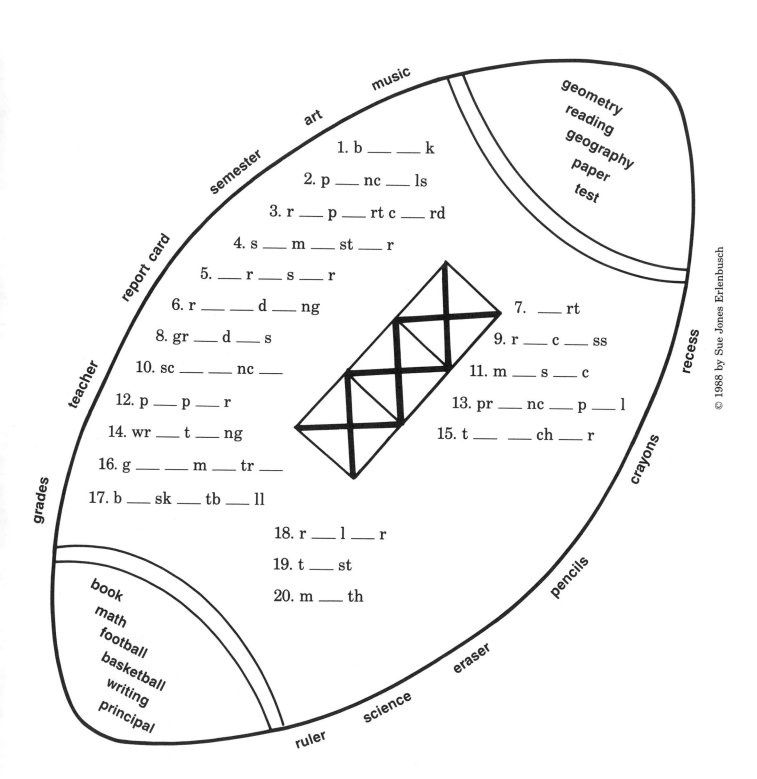

1. b ___ ___ k
2. p ___ nc ___ ls
3. r ___ p ___ rt c ___ rd
4. s ___ m ___ st ___ r
5. ___ r ___ s ___ r
6. r ___ ___ d ___ ng
7. ___ rt
8. gr ___ d ___ s
9. r ___ c ___ ss
10. sc ___ ___ nc ___
11. m ___ s ___ c
12. p ___ p ___ r
13. pr ___ nc ___ p ___ l
14. wr ___ t ___ ng
15. t ___ ___ ch ___ r
16. g ___ ___ m ___ tr ___
17. b ___ sk ___ tb ___ ll
18. r ___ l ___ r
19. t ___ st
20. m ___ th

music
art
semester
report card
teacher
grades

geometry
reading
geography
paper
test

recess
crayons
pencils
eraser
science
ruler

book
math
football
basketball
writing
principal

Name ______________________

COLOR WORD SCRAMBLE

Directions: Unscramble the names of the colors.

dre ___ ___ ___

lcbak ___ ___ ___ ___ ___

lwyole ___ ___ ___ ___ ___ ___

ebul ___ ___ ___ ___

worbn ___ ___ ___ ___ ___

eurplp ___ ___ ___ ___ ___ ___

regen ___ ___ ___ ___ ___

egnaro ___ ___ ___ ___ ___ ___

thwei ___ ___ ___ ___ ___

ikpn

atn

eiovtl ___ ___ ___ ___ ___ ___

Name ____________________________

WORD SCRAMBLE

Directions: Directions: Unscramble the words.

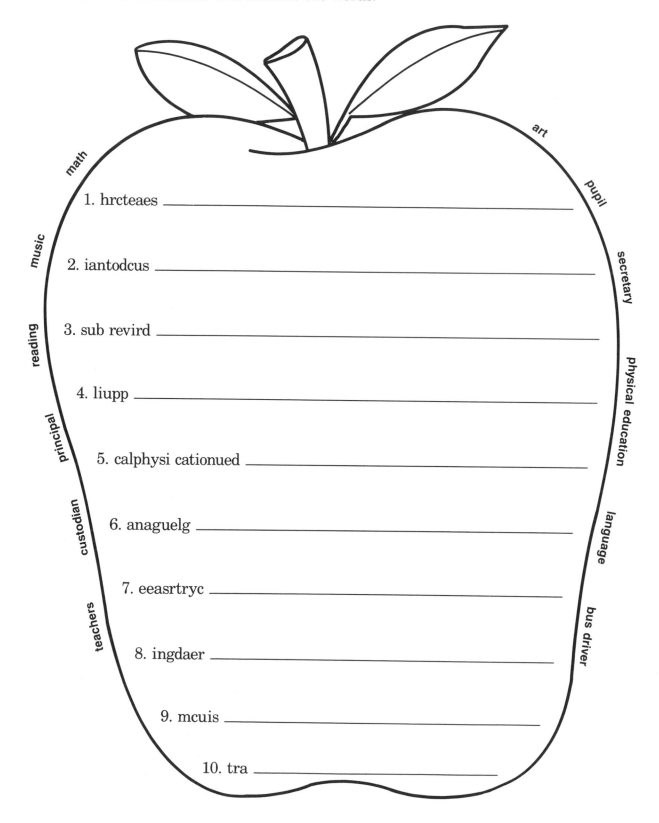

math
music
reading
principal
custodian
teachers
art
pupil
secretary
physical education
language
bus driver

1. hrcteaes ____________________
2. iantodcus ____________________
3. sub revird ____________________
4. liupp ____________________
5. calphysi cationued ____________________
6. anaguelg ____________________
7. eeasrtryc ____________________
8. ingdaer ____________________
9. mcuis ____________________
10. tra ____________________

Name ________________________________

SCRAMBLED DAYS

Directions: Unscramble the names of the days. Write the seven days of the week in the correct order.

Aa Bb Cc Dd Ee Ff Gg Hh Ii Jj Kk Ll Mm Nn Oo Pp Qq Rr Ss Tt Uu Vv Ww Xx Yy Zz

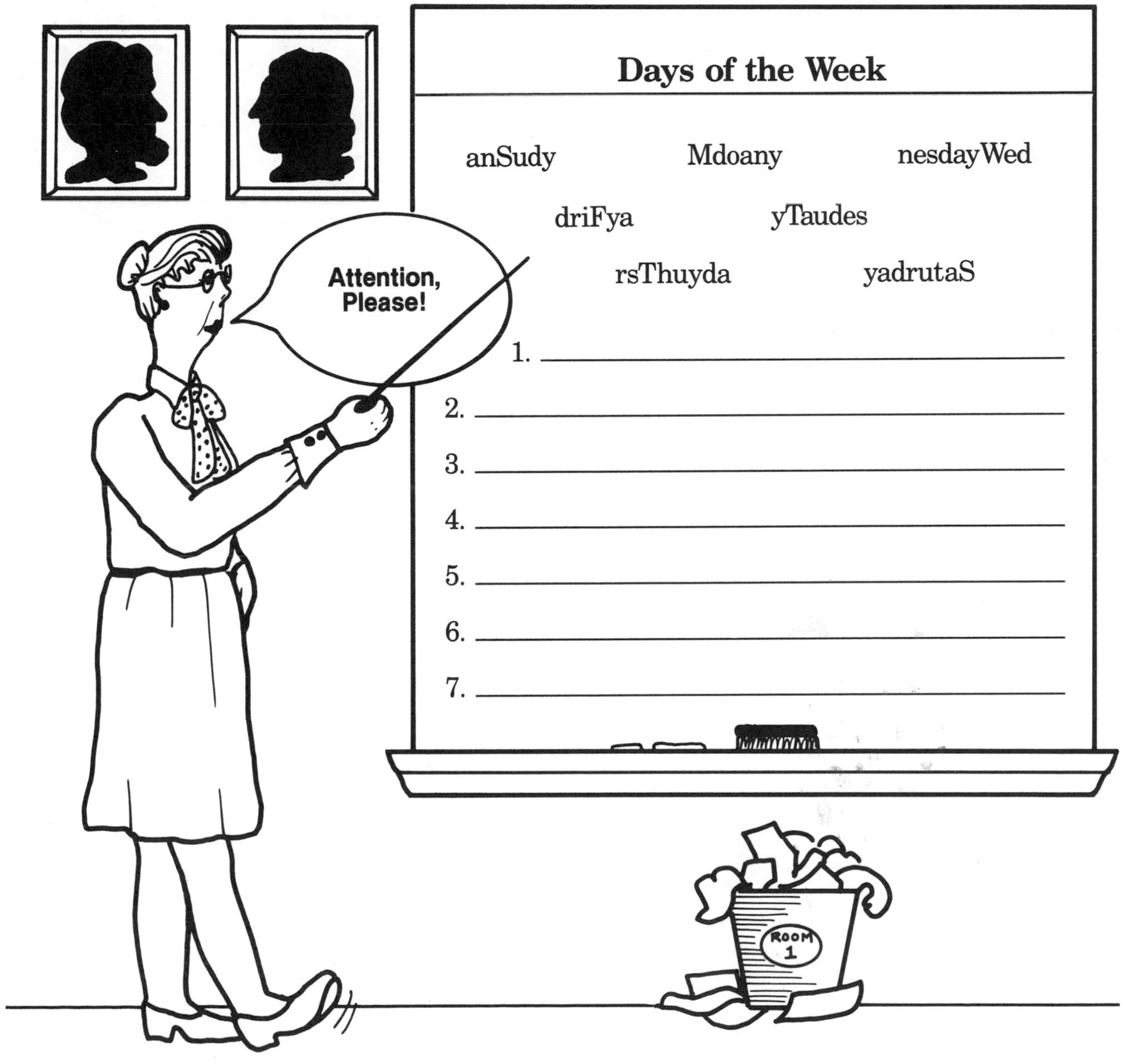

Days of the Week

anSudy   Mdoany   nesdayWed

driFya   yTaudes

rsThuyda   yadrutaS

1. ______________________
2. ______________________
3. ______________________
4. ______________________
5. ______________________
6. ______________________
7. ______________________

Name ________________________________

ORDER! ORDER!

Directions: Unscramble the names of the months. Write the twelve months of the year in the correct order.

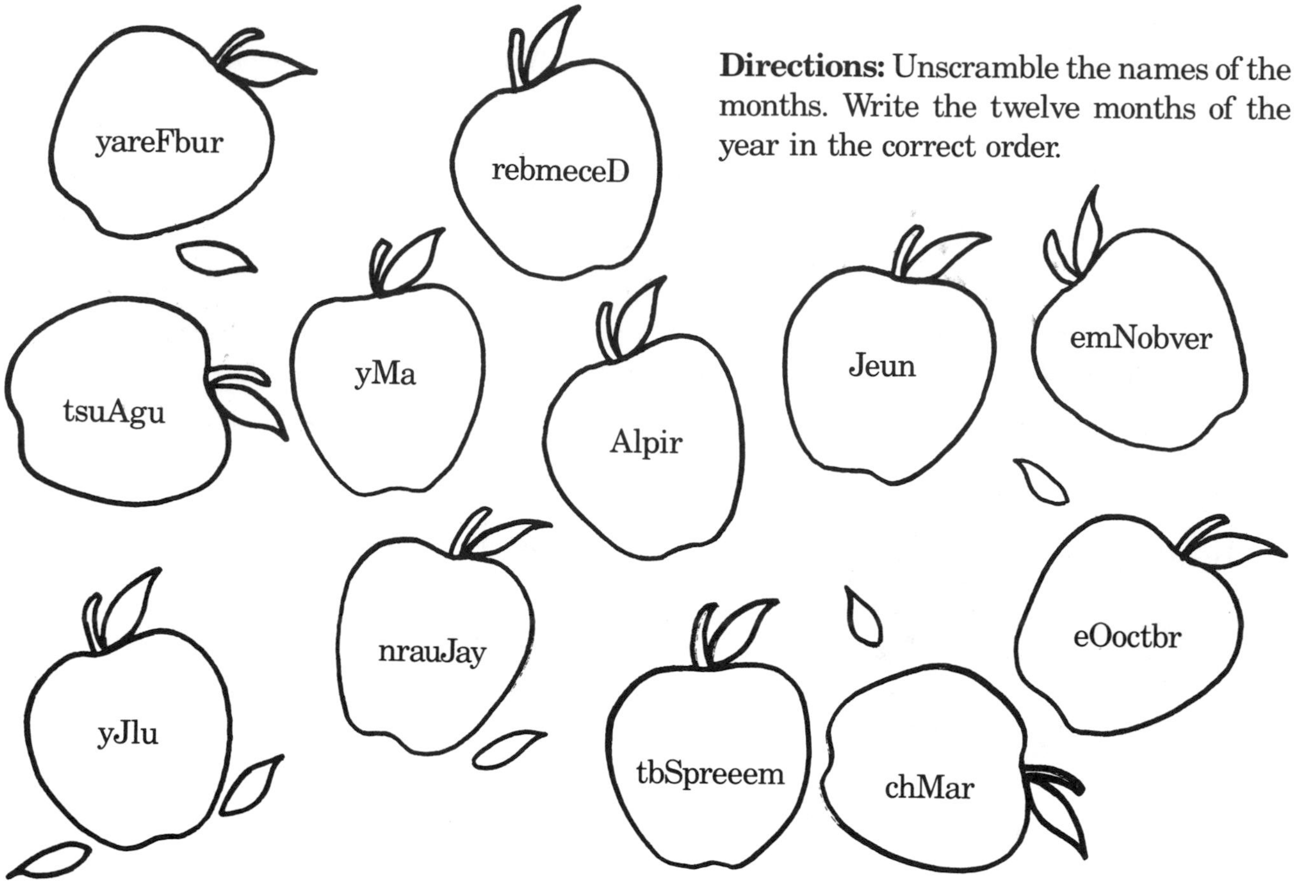

1. ________________________________
2. ________________________________
3. ________________________________
4. ________________________________
5. ________________________________
6. ________________________________
7. ________________________________
8. ________________________________
9. ________________________________
10. ________________________________
11. ________________________________
12. ________________________________

Name ______________________________

SENTENCE COMPLETION

Directions: Read each sentence. Write a word on each blank to complete each sentence.

1. School begins in the month of ______________________.

2. My new teacher seems very ______________________.

3. My favorite subject is ______________________.

4. My least favorite subject is ______________________.

5. I wish my mother wouldn't put ______________ in my lunch.

6. My best friend is ______________________.

7. When my best friend and I were __________, we __________.

8. At recess, I like to play ______________________.

Name ______________________________

MAKE A WORD

Directions: Use the letters in the words "Back to School" to make as many different words as possible.

Back to School

Name ________________________________

CROSSWORD PUZZLE

Directions: Write the answers in the correct places.

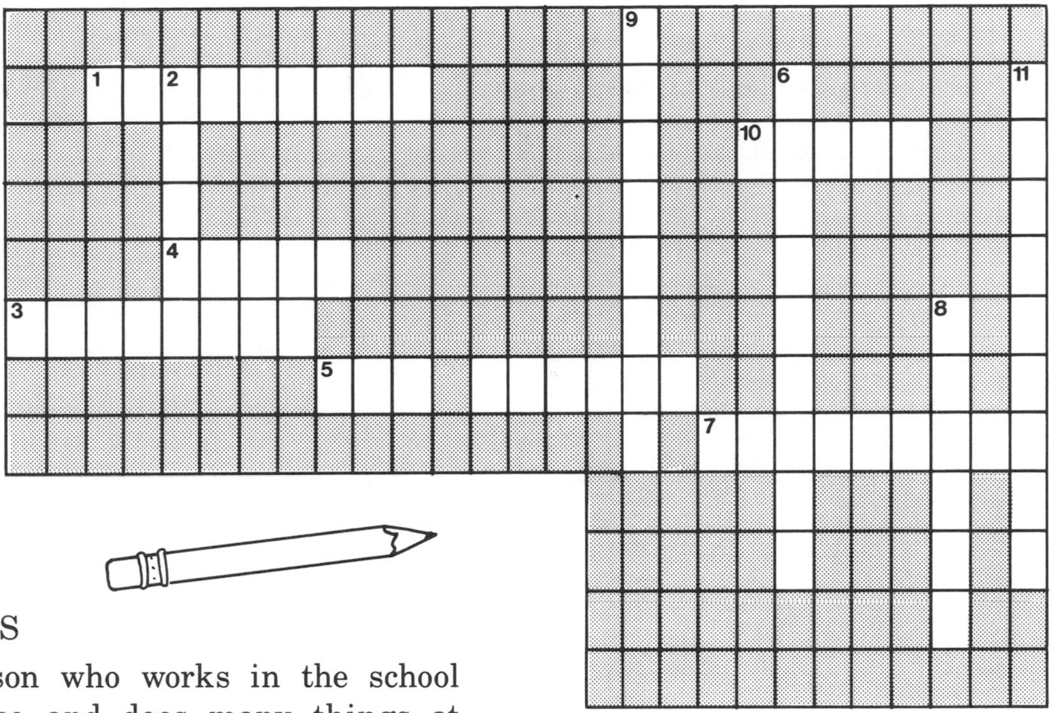

ACROSS

1. Person who works in the school office and does many things at once.
3. People who help us learn new things.
4. People who fix our lunch.
5. Person who brings many children to school.
7. Person who is in charge of the school.
10. Person who helps us if we get hurt.

DOWN

2. Person who teaches us how to play many sports.
6. Person who keeps the school neat and clean.
8. People who try to learn more every day.
9. People who attend school.
11. Person who helps us if we have a problem.

WORD BANK	
secretary	cooks
pupils	bus driver
parents	children
coach	counselor
teachers	students
nurse	janitor
custodian	instructor
principal	assistant
librarian	

Name ______________________________

SCHOOL DAYS

Directions: Complete the story. Illustrate your story in the space below.

Sometimes when I'm getting ready to go to school, I wish ____________________

Name ______________________________

THE NEW STUDENT

Directions: Complete the story. Illustrate your story in the space below.

Susie, Freddy, and Ricky have a dog named Mugs. Mugs likes to go everywhere with them. One morning when they were walking to school, he ______________________________

Name ______________________________

SCHOOLMARMS AND SCHOOLMASTERS

Directions: Fill in the blanks with words from the apple.

In the 1700s and 1800s, (1) ______________________ teachers were known as schoolmarms and male teachers were known as (2) ______________________. These teachers received very little (3) ______________ training. If they were sixteen, an eighth grade (4) ______________, and could pass a teaching (5) ______________, they could become a teacher.

Teachers were expected to teach children on many different (6) ______________ of learning, and to be a (7) ______________________________________, nurse, secretary, (8) ______________________________ supervisor, and coach or referee at (9) ________________. For (10) ________________, they received room and board with a (11) ______________________ who had children attending the school. Men teachers (12) ________________ $5.00 to $15.00 per (13) ________________, while women received far less. Part of their pay was also in (14) ________________ and produce such as chickens, eggs, (15) ________________, meat and grain.

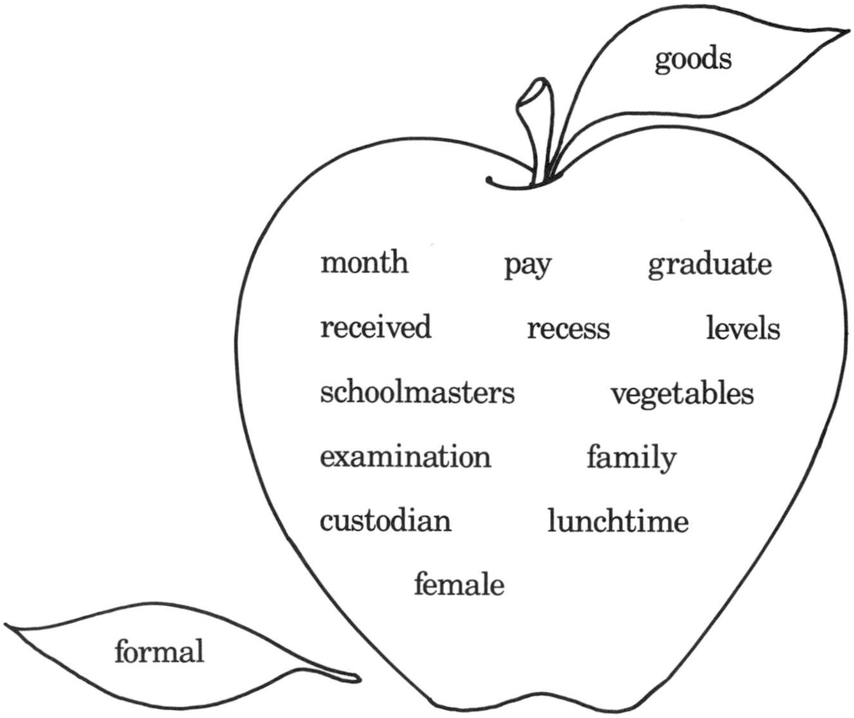

Name ______________________________

COUNTRY SCHOOLHOUSE

Directions: Fill in the blanks with words from the stove.

In the one-room (1) ______________________, one teacher taught all the (2) ______________________. The teacher was also responsible for doing (3) ______________ such as sweeping, cleaning the (4) ______________, carrying in the drinking (5) ______________________, and keeping a (6) ______________________ going in the potbellied stove that stood in the middle of the room.

Students who had a (7) ______________ near the stove (8) ______________, while others farther away (9) ______________. The stove used up the (10) ______________ in the room, so someone had to keep opening the outside door to let in (11) ______________ air. Students unlucky enough to have a desk near the (12) ______________ kept getting icy (13) __________ down their backs.

Since most children (14) ______________ school from October to March when there weren't as many (15) __________ chores, the (16) ______________ was a very important part of the school.

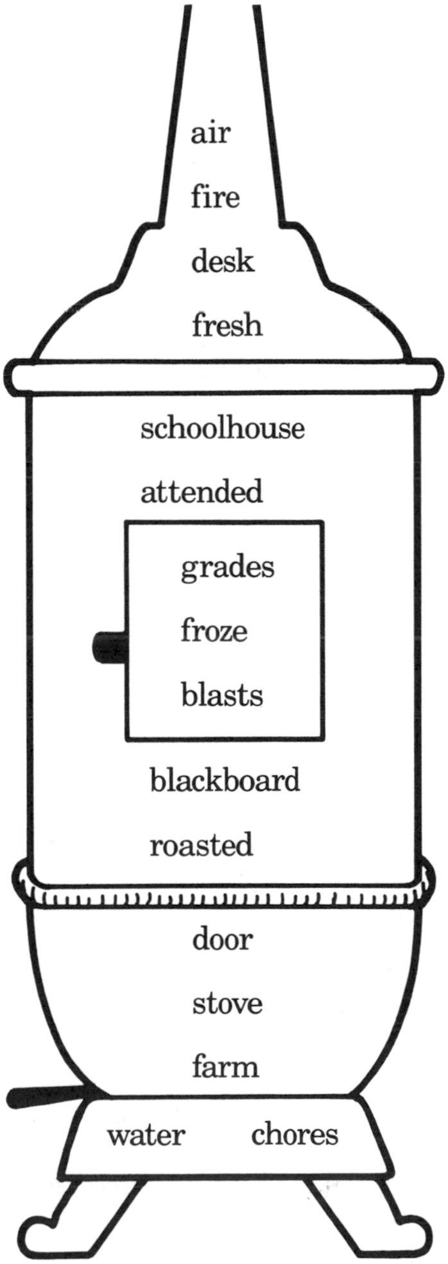

Name ______________________________

THE HICKORY STICK

Directions: Fill in the blanks with words from the box.

The schoolmarm who taught in a one-room schoolhouse tried to keep strict (1) ____________. Some students were expected to sit quietly and do their (2) ____________ lessons while the teacher was helping another group of students recite a (3) ____________.

In the spring and (4) ____________, the younger more (5) ____________ students attended school. During the fall and (6) ____________ terms, the (7) ____________ farm boys returned to school. They often tried the teacher's (8) ____________. One of their favorite (9) ____________ was to hide bugs, spiders, snakes, lizards, or frogs in the teacher's (10) ____________.

The teacher would (11) ____________ them by swatting them with a hickory (12) ____________, making them stand in a (13) ____________, or making them sit with the (14) ____________. Boys (15) ____________ getting thrashed with a hickory stick to having to sit with the girls.

written	discipline
tricks	desk
corner	lesson
summer	winter
preferred	girls
stick	docile
patience	punish
rambunctious	

Name ______________________________

SCHOOL TOOLS

Directions: Fill in the blanks with words from the quill.

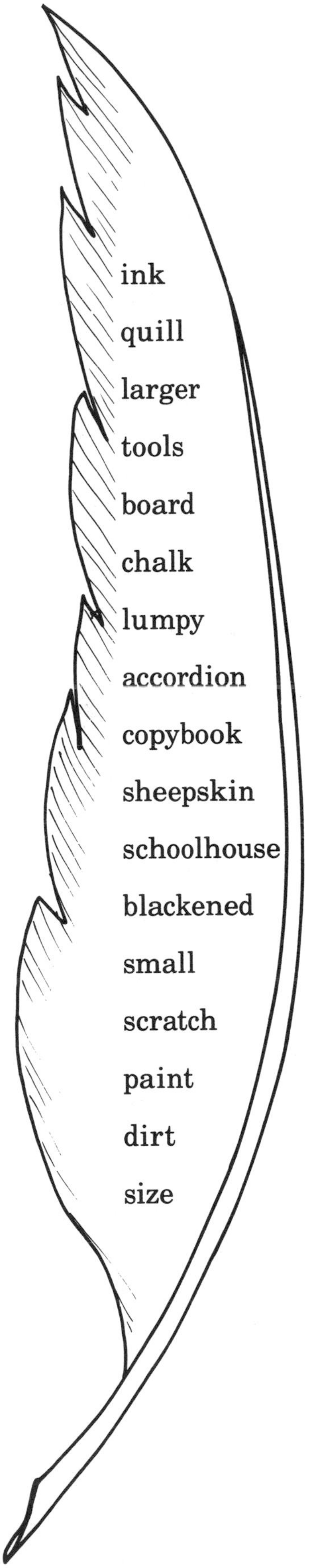

The equipment or tools of the country (1) ____________ were different from those of today. For instance, the blackboard was simply a (2) ________ that had been (3) ________ with carbon or (4) _________. The teacher didn't have a nice slim piece of (5) __________ to write with, but a (6) __________ piece of chalkstone. For an eraser, she had to wrap a rag or piece of (7) ________________ around a wooden block. Some teachers didn't even have these (8) ____________. They had to (9) ____________ lessons into the (10) ____________floor.

Students used a homemade (11) ________________ pen and homemade (12) __________ when they wanted to write. They wrote in a (13) ___________ made by sewing sheets of foolscap together by hand.

Desks were all one (14) __________. (15) ___________ students could barely see over the top, while (16) __________ students had to fold themselves up like an (17) ____________ in order to squeeze in.

Name ____________________________________

SCHOOLHOUSE WORD HUNT

Directions: Circle the hidden words. You may go across and down.

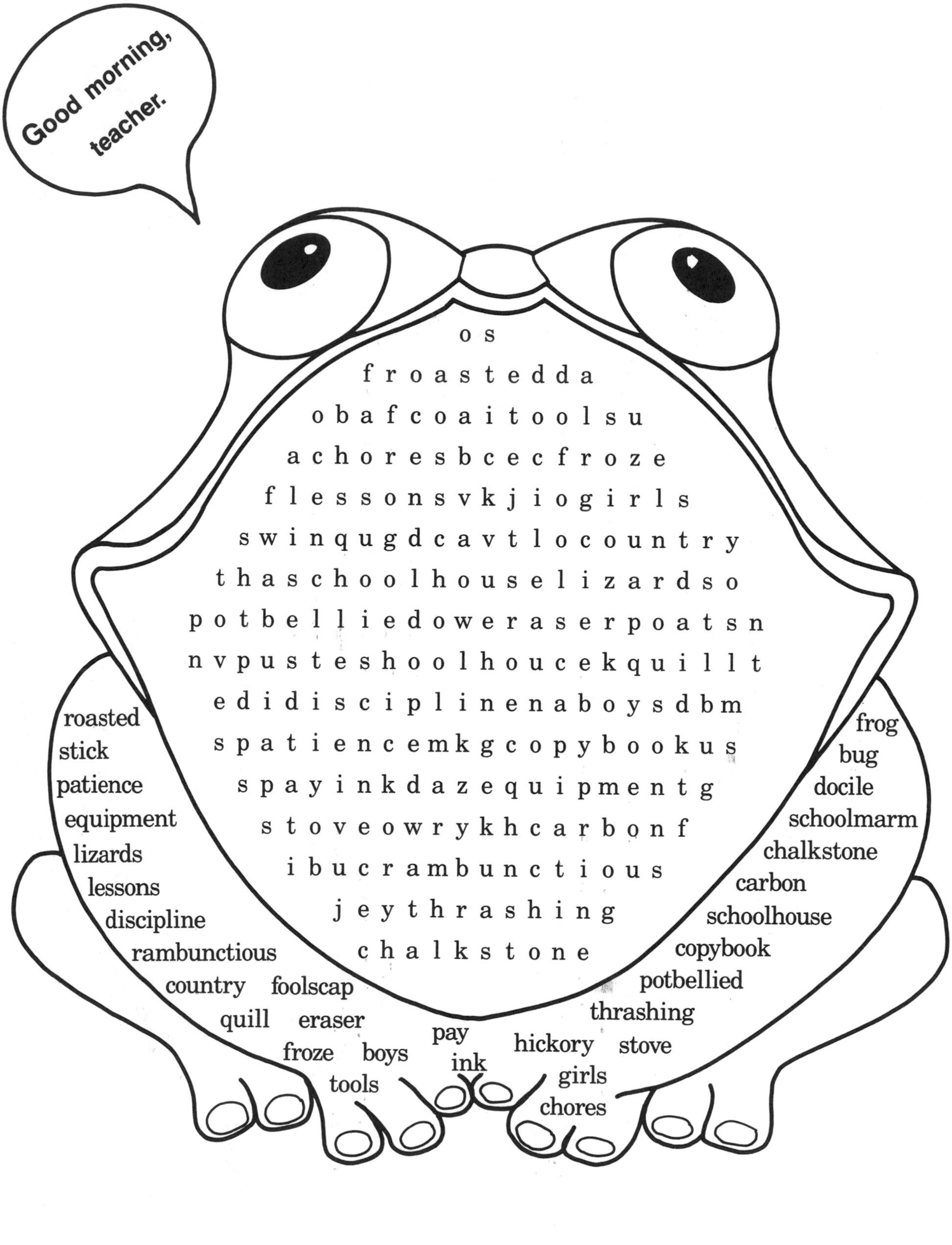

Name ______________________

SCHOOLHOUSE SCRAMBLE

Directions: Unscramble the words. Write the unscrambled words in the correct places.

1. r a m o l o m c h s
2. b d b k r o a c l a
3. e s r e r a
4. p a c o s f o l
5. t d a e n t d e
6. i i i e d l p c s n
7. s s s l n o e
8. y r o k c i h
9. d t e h h r s a
10. c k o o p o y b

OCTOBER

The Fun Box • 37

Grading Papers • 37

Vocabulary • 37

Game Boards • 38

Activity Number and Title		Special Day
2-1	Columbus Day	Columbus Day
2-2	Columbus Day Maze	Columbus Day
2-3	Columbus Day Word Hunt	Columbus Day
2-4	A Picture to Color	Halloween
2-5	Same or Different	Halloween
2-6	Alphabet Scramble	Halloween
2-7	Who Is It?	Halloween
2-8	The Lost Broomstick	Halloween
2-9	Halloween Maze	Halloween
2-10	Jack-o'-Lantern Puzzle	Halloween
2-11	Halloween Word Match	Halloween
2-12	Trick-or-Treat	Halloween
2-13	Halloween Word Hunt	Halloween
2-14	A Bloodchilling Story	Halloween
2-15	Sh! It's a Secret!	Halloween
2-16	Missing Consonant Puzzle	Halloween
2-17	Missing Vowel Puzzle	Halloween
2-18	Who Needs It?	Halloween
2-19	Make a Word	Halloween
2-20	The Unfinished Spell	Halloween
2-21	A Halloween Story	Halloween
2-22	Look Who's Cooking	Halloween
2-23	Halloween Word Scramble	Halloween
2-24	Halloween Divination	Halloween
2-25	Halloween Spirits	Halloween
2-26	Word Hunt	Halloween

The Fun Box

Take a cardboard box large enough to hold file folders, and label it "Fun Box." Fill this box with a variety of holiday games and stories. You can set aside a special time when each child is allowed to choose an activity from the Fun Box.

Activities for the Fun Box can include sequencing cards that you make by cutting cartoons out of the comics sections of newspapers. The cartoons should be laminated and cut into individual frames. These sequencing cards can be placed in a large envelope and filed in the Fun Box.

You can also cut holiday stories from magazines, laminate each page, staple the story in a file folder, draw an appropriate picture on the front of the folder, and write the title of the story on the tab. These stories can then be placed in the Fun Box.

You can make a concentration style game by cutting out various holiday pictures, making sure that you have pairs of pictures that begin with the same sound. Mount each picture on a card and laminate it. Each concentration game can be placed in a large envelope and filed in the Fun Box.

Grading Papers

As you are grading papers in October, you can begin adapting the happy faces for the holidays throughout the year. Here are some examples.

Vocabulary

The following three word lists will help develop your students' vocabularies in October.

Columbus Day Word List	**Halloween Word List 1**	**Halloween Word List 2**
founder	haunted	midnight
discoverer	jack-o'-lantern	divining
October	bat	foretell
celebrated	spook	terrifying
voyage	trick-or-treat	future

Columbus Day Word List	Halloween Word List 1	Halloween Word List 2
America	candy	demons
west	ghost	sweetheart
Spain	witch	hollowed
fleet	October	spirits
sailing	afraid	costumes
August	goblins	weapon
persuading	Halloween	turnips
history	broom	torches
events	screech	cross
westward	bloodchilling	windowsills
king	scared	candle
honors	dark	frighten
seaman	horror	horseshoes
finance	scream	initial
queen	pumpkin	evil

Game Boards

Here are four game board patterns for you to use in October. For the bingo style game board, don't forget to arrange the words on the other cards in a different order.

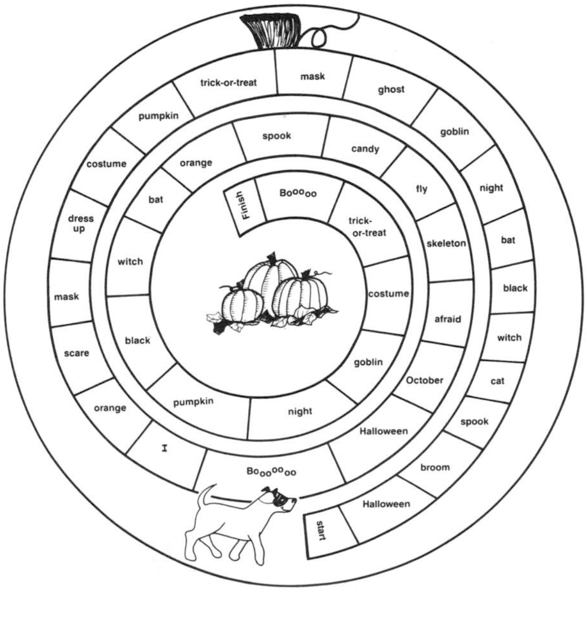

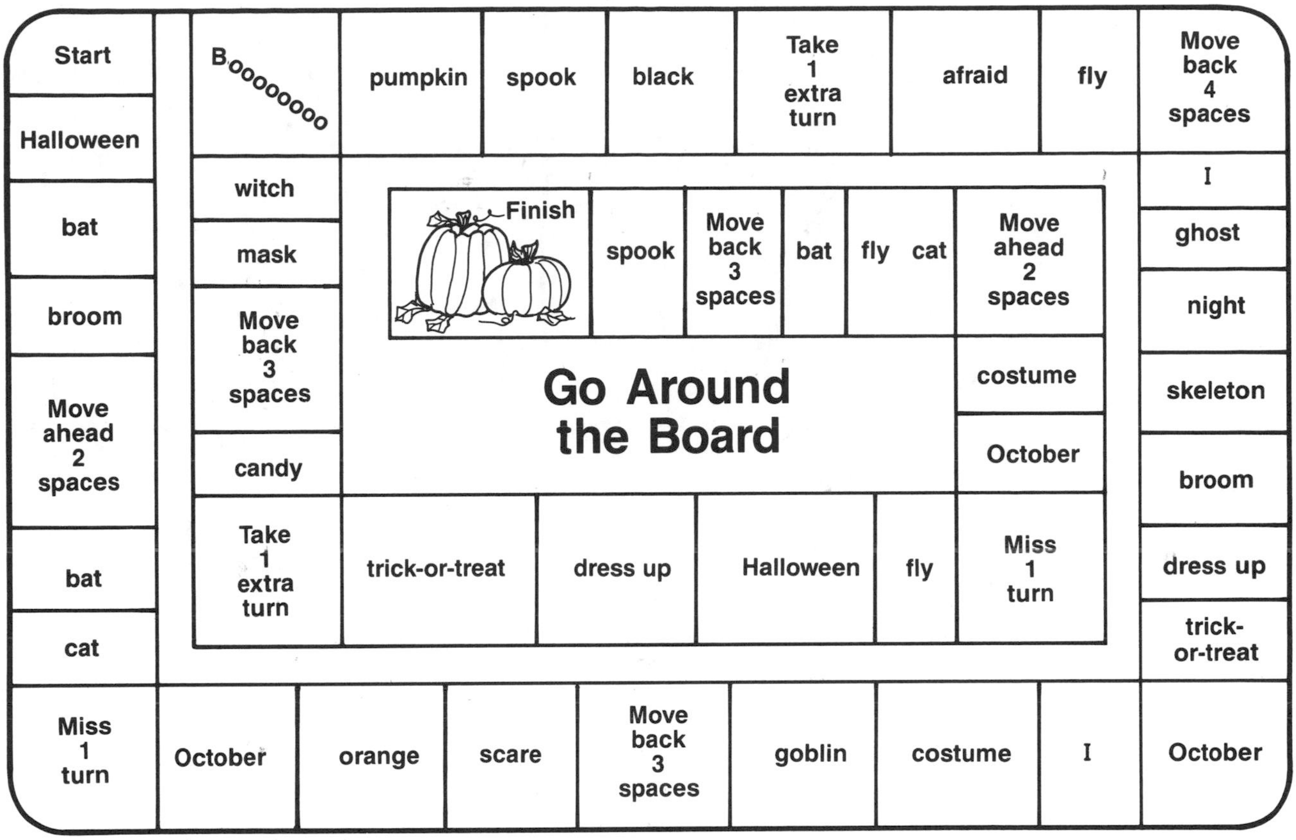

bat	fly	ghost	black	cat
broom	night	October	spook	screech
orange	trick-or-treat		Halloween	witch
scare	dress up	Booooo	pumpkin	mask
goblin	costume	skeleton	afraid	candy

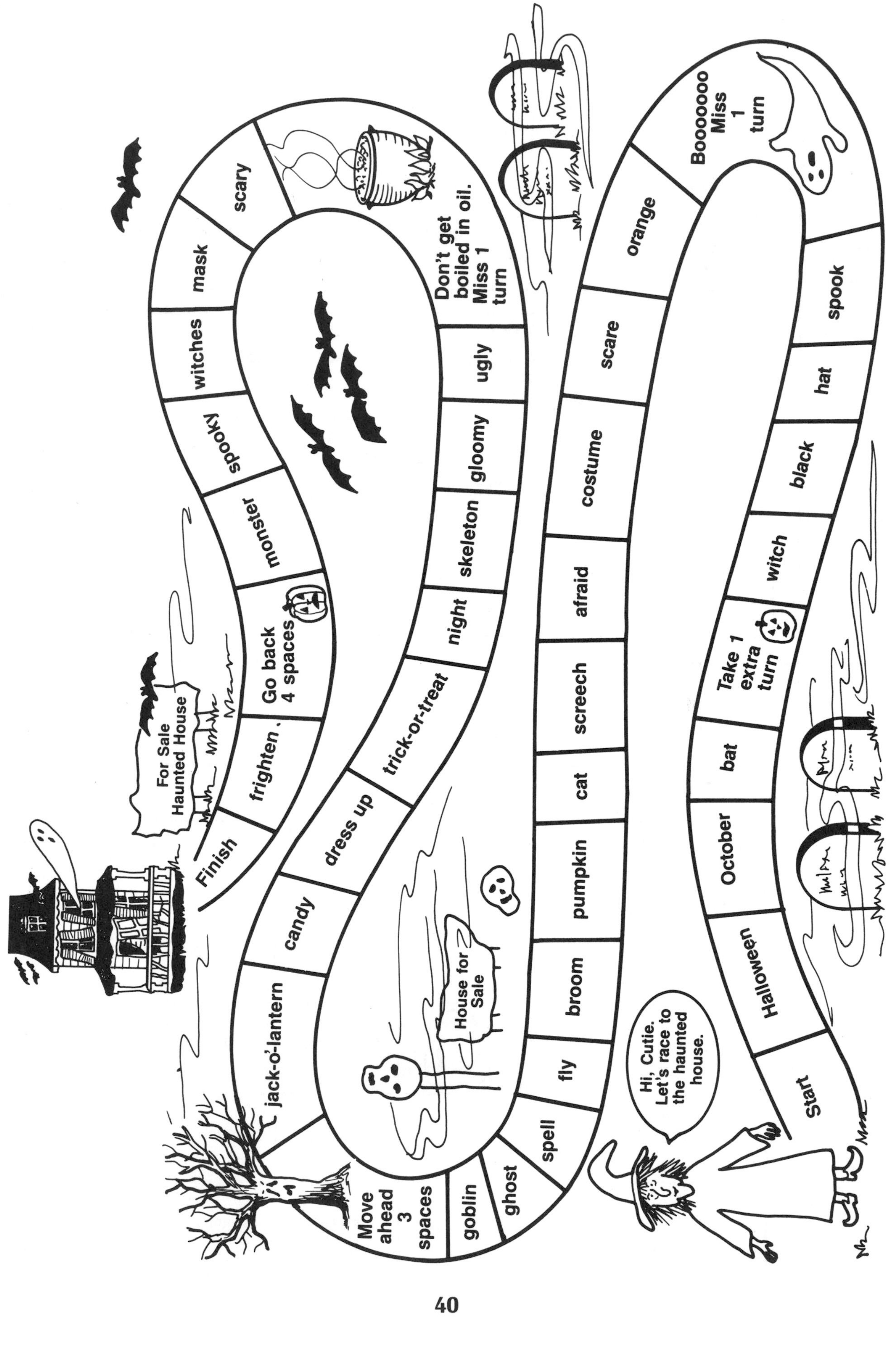
Hi, Cutie. Let's race to the haunted house.
Start
Halloween
October
bat
Take 1 extra turn
witch
black
hat
spook
Booooooo Miss 1 turn
orange
scare
costume
afraid
screech
cat
pumpkin
broom
fly
spell
ghost
goblin
Move ahead 3 spaces
jack-o'-lantern
candy
dress up
trick-or-treat
night
skeleton
gloomy
ugly
Don't get boiled in oil. Miss 1 turn
scary
mask
witches
spooky
monster
Go back 4 spaces
frighten
Finish
House for Sale
For Sale Haunted House

Name ______________________________

COLUMBUS DAY

Directions: Fill in the blanks with words from the ocean.

Christopher Columbus is called the (1) ________________ of America. King Ferdinand and (2) ________________ Isabella of Spain helped finance his first voyage to the (3) ________________ World. The three ships in his fleet were the Nina, the Pinta, and the Santa Maria. They set (4) __________ on August 3, 1492. After three weeks of sailing (5) ________________ without seeing land, Columbus had a (6) ______________________ time persuading his sailors to keep going. They (7) ______________ landed in the New World on October 12, 1492. This first (8) ________________ ranks among history's most important events.

Columbus Day, which is (9) ________________ on the second Monday in (10) ________________, honors this great seaman's first voyage to America.

old
New
October
honored
finally
founder
west
sail
princess
easy
Queen
discoverer
east
September
prince
suddenly
voyage
hard
celebrated

Name ______________________________

COLUMBUS DAY MAZE

Directions: Help Christopher Columbus find the Nina, Pinta, and Santa Maria by drawing a line from him through all of the Columbus Day words.

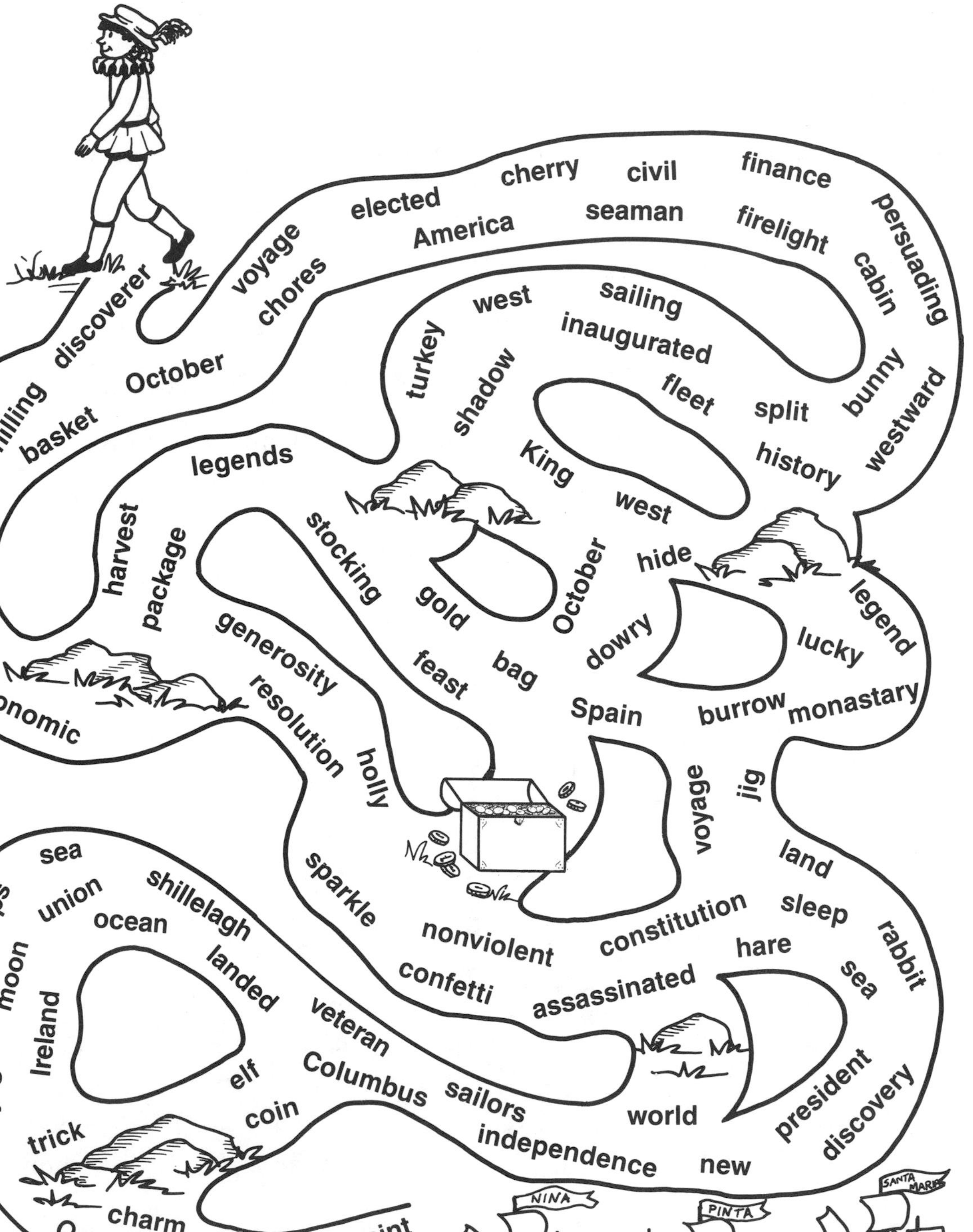

Name ______________________________

COLUMBUS DAY WORD HUNT

Directions: Circle the hidden words. You may go across and down.

c	i	b	k	i	n	g	c	q	c	e	t	o	c	v
o	c	t	o	b	e	p	o	u	o	b	j	c	e	o
l	a	n	d	e	d	e	l	e	l	p	s	t	l	y
u	c	d	i	s	c	o	v	e	r	y	h	o	e	a
m	o	w	u	o	c	e	a	n	b	a	i	b	b	g
b	l	e	e	c	o	c	e	a	u	z	p	e	r	e
u	o	s	o	t	o	b	u	r	v	s	s	e	a	o
s	m	t	h	o	n	o	r	e	d	p	u	s	t	u
d	b	w	l	b	e	w	s	h	s	a	i	l	e	d
a	s	a	t	e	a	u	p	e	p	i	a	q	d	s
w	u	r	o	r	s	s	a	e	t	n	e	m	t	o
y	e	d	q	s	l	t	i	y	a	u	g	u	s	t

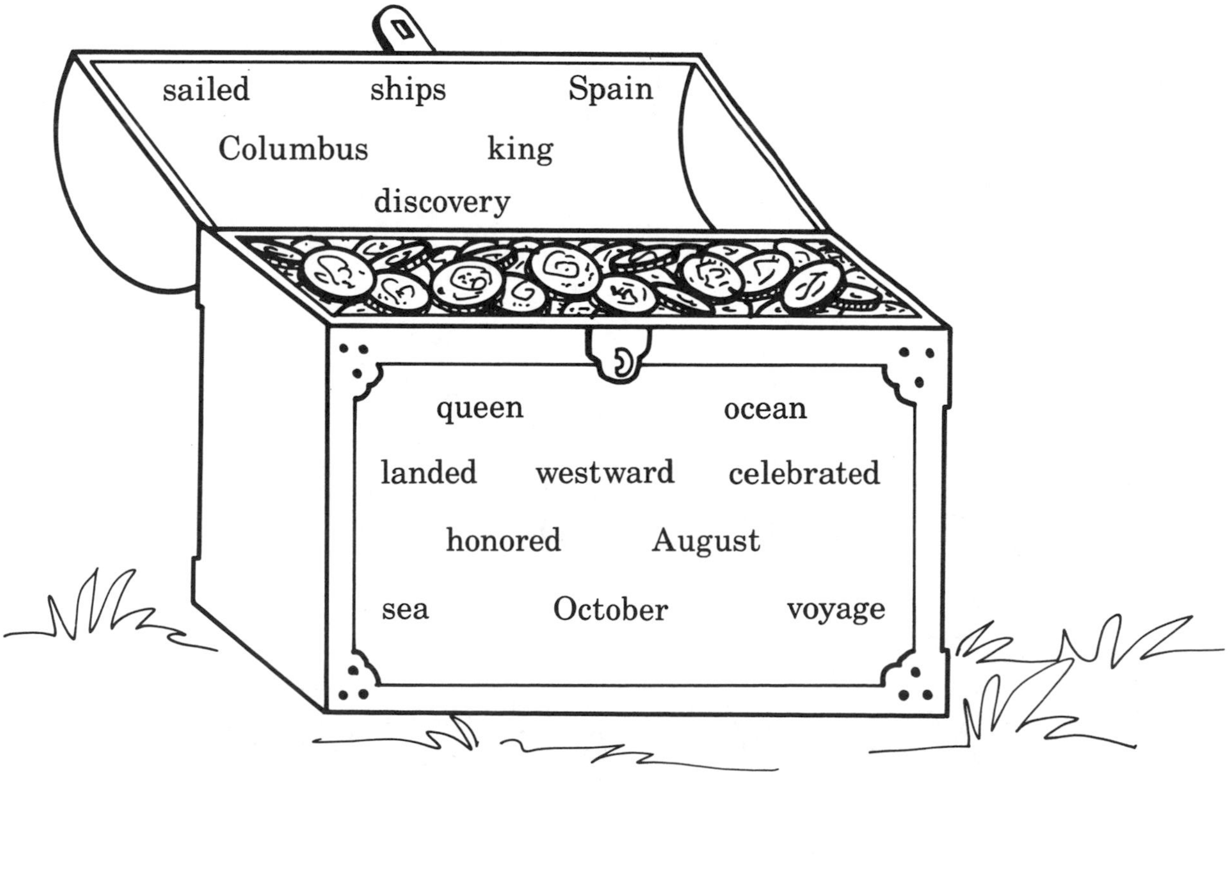

Name ______________________________ 2-4

A PICTURE TO COLOR

Directions: Color the picture.

Name ________________________________

SAME OR DIFFERENT

Directions: Look at the word on the left. Circle the word on the right that is like the one on the left.

witch	watch	witch	wich	with
pumpkin	pumpkin	pumpken	pumpkun	pumkin
ghost	gost	ghust	ghosts	ghost
bat	cat	bat	hat	rat
treats	traets	treets	treats	treat
haunted	hounted	huanted	hanted	haunted
goblins	goblins	gobluns	goblens	godlins
house	mouse	huose	house	hous
candy	handy	candy	dandy	canby
tricks	trickes	tricks	trecks	triks

ALPHABET SCRAMBLE

Directions: Write the letters of the alphabet in the correct order. Some of the letters have already been filled in for you.

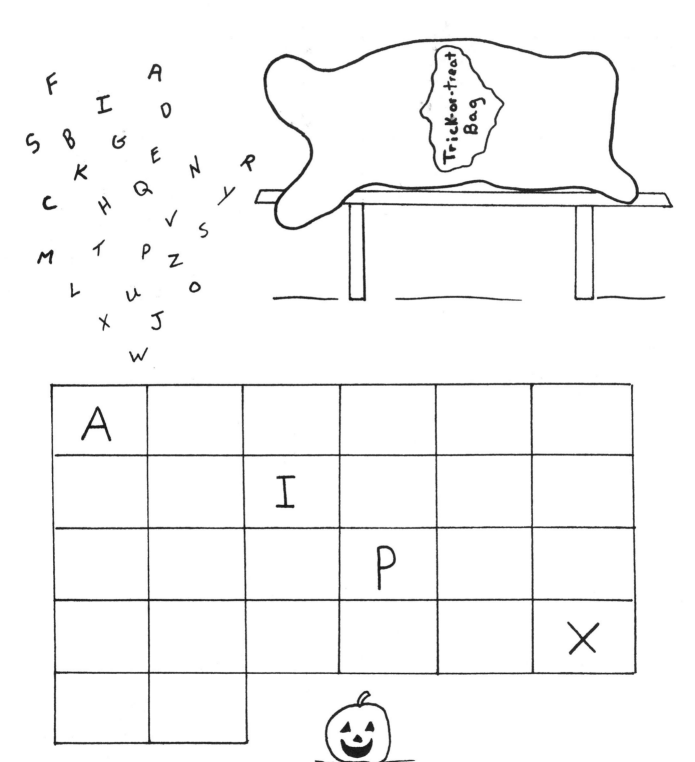

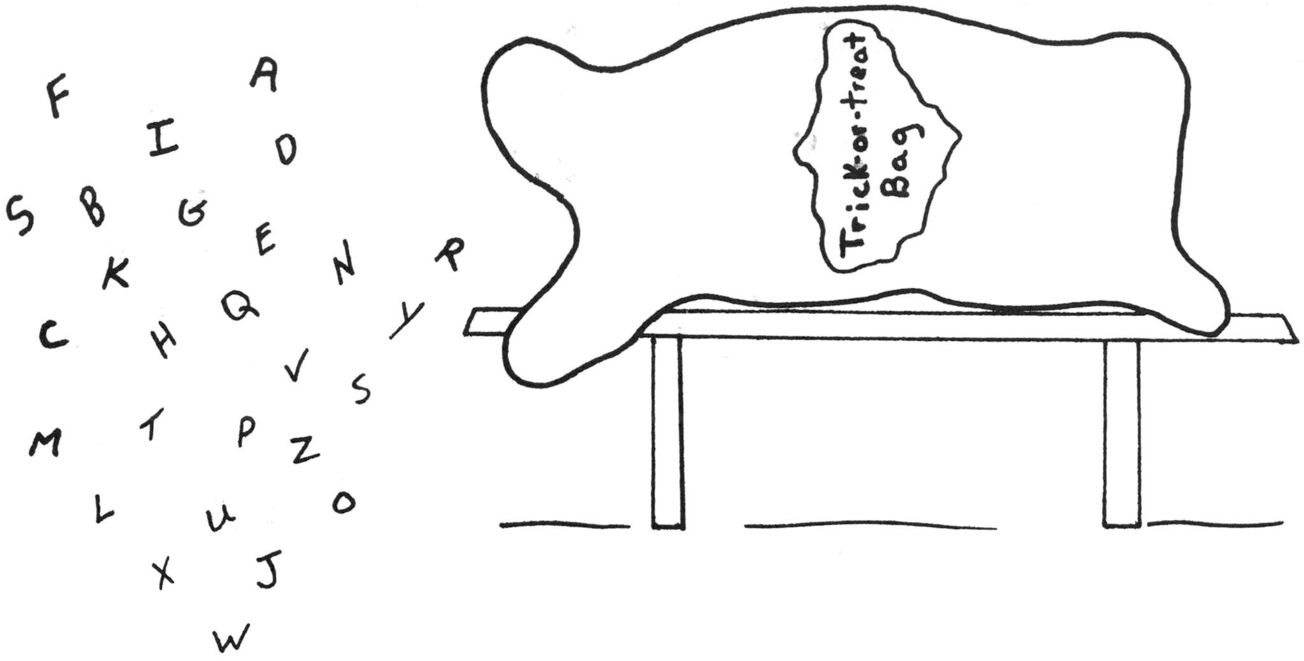

A					
		I			
			P		
					X

Name ______________________________

WHO IS IT?

Directions: Connect the dots to find out who is in this picture. Start with the first letter of the alphabet. First, connect the lower case letters. Then, connect the capital letters.

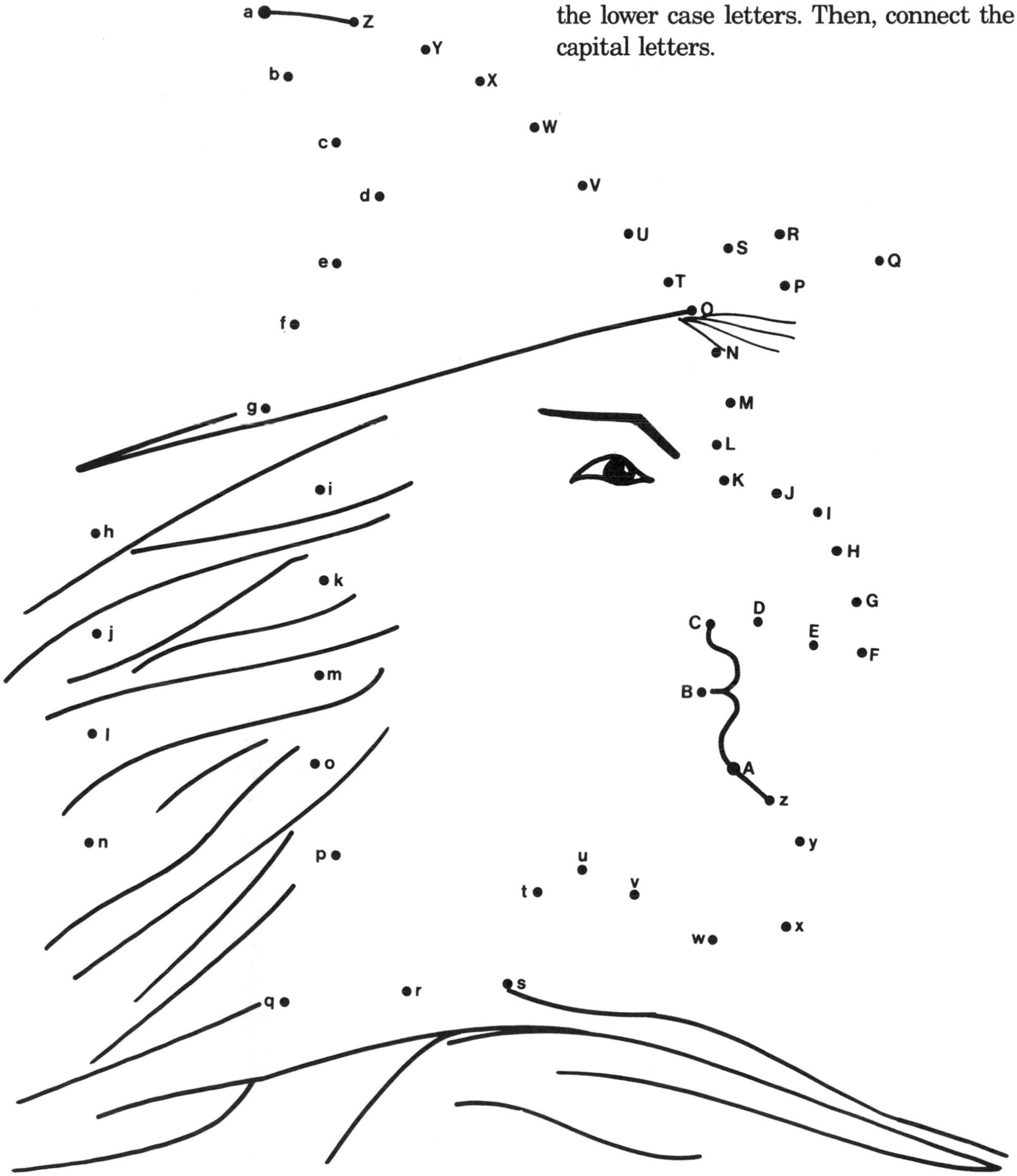

THE LOST BROOMSTICK

Directions: Help the witch get to her broom by drawing a line from her through the Halloween words.

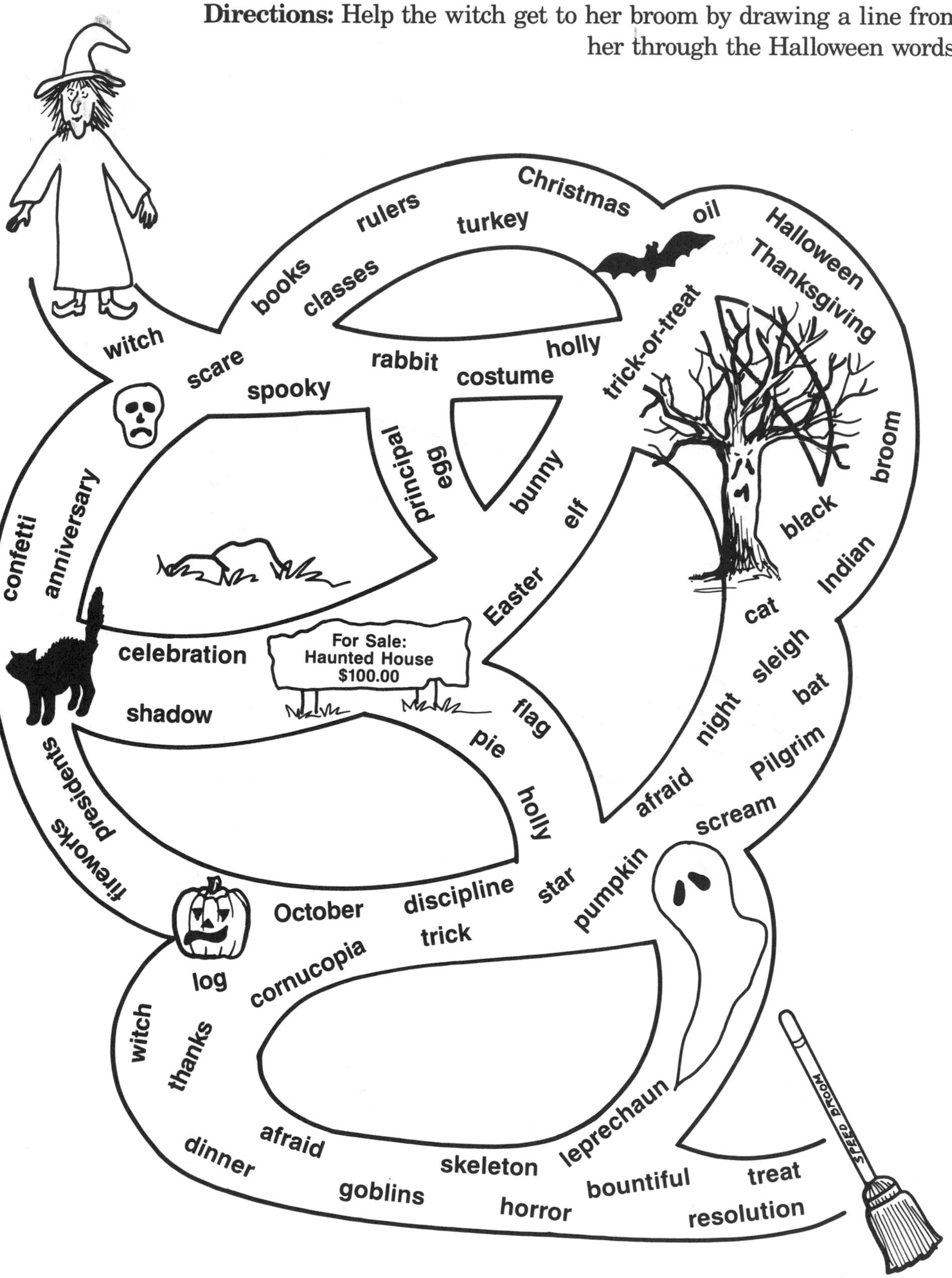

HALLOWEEN MAZE

Directions: The witch has lost her cauldron. Help her find it by drawing a line from her through the Halloween words.

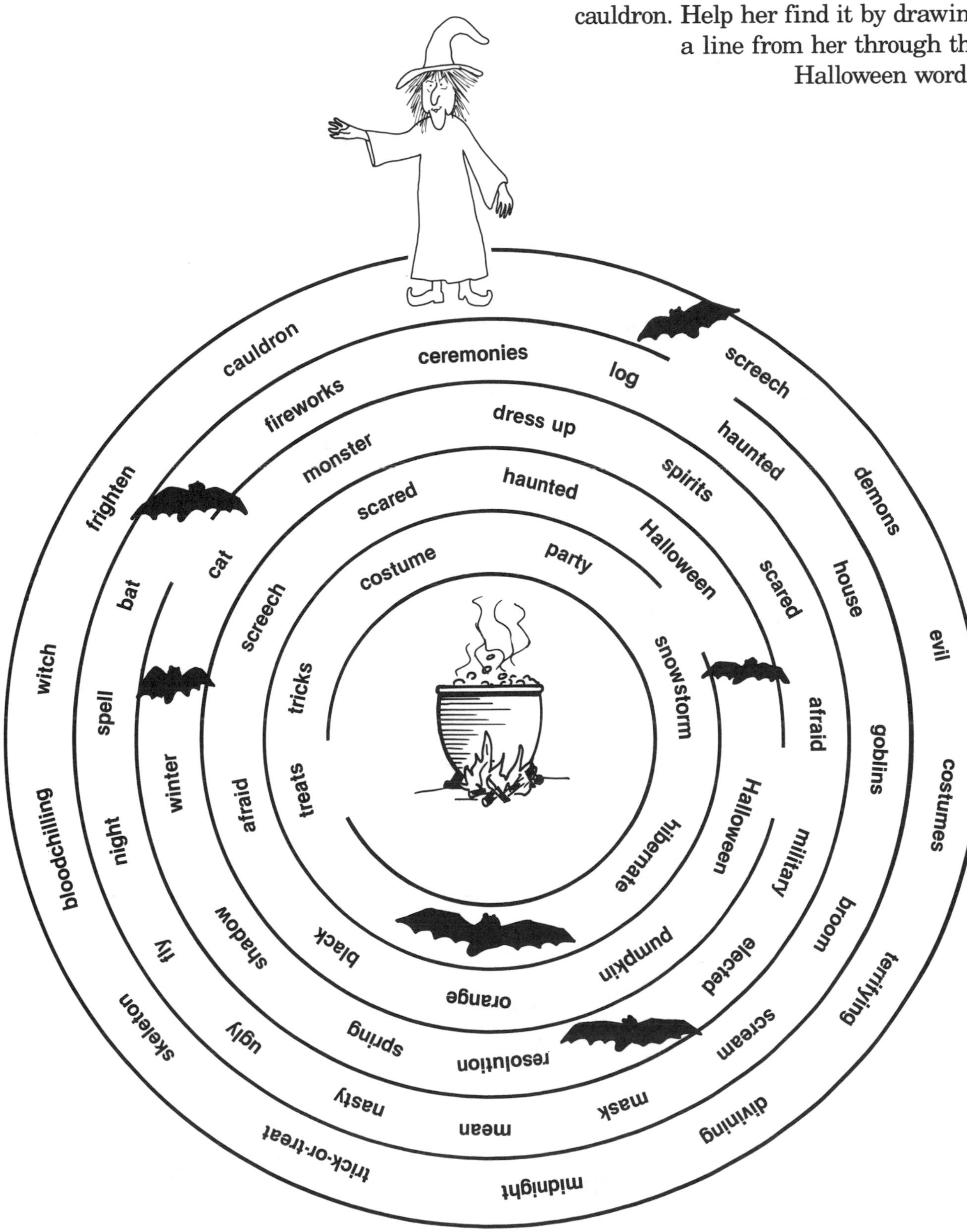

JACK-O'-LANTERN PUZZLE

Directions: Color the vowels orange. Color the consonants yellow.

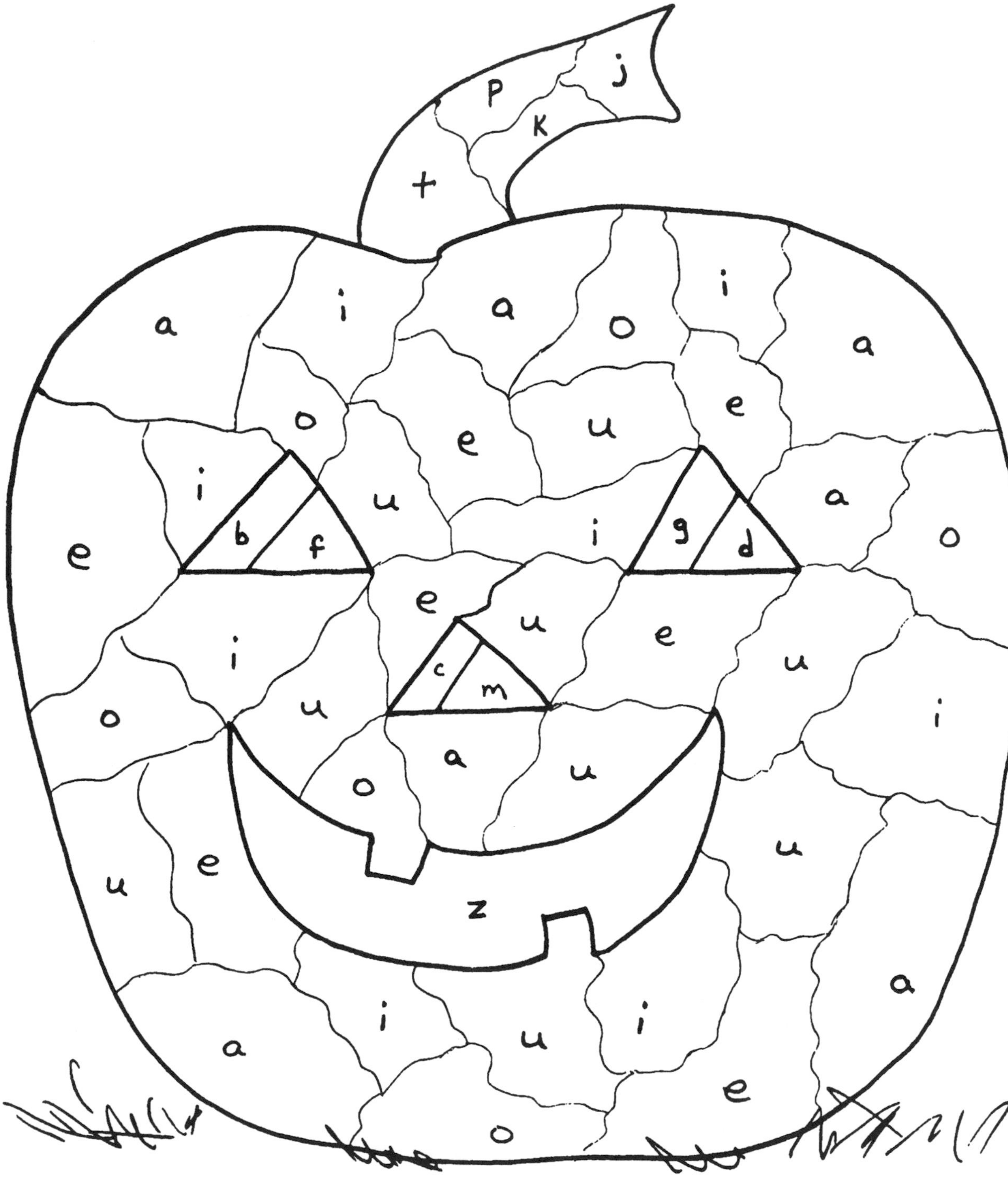

Name ______________________________

HALLOWEEN WORD MATCH

Directions: Draw a line to match the pictures to the correct words.

jack-o'-lantern

cat

witch

bat

ghost

Name ______________________________ 2-12

TRICK-OR-TREAT

Directions: Draw a picture of five things you would like to get in your trick-or-treat bag. Label and color them.

Name ______________________________

HALLOWEEN WORD HUNT

Directions: Find the Halloween words and circle them. You may go across and down.

a	h	a	l	l	o	w	e	e	n	m	d
b	a	t	s	z	d	b	r	s	m	o	a
c	u	g	h	o	c	t	o	b	e	r	r
i	n	l	p	u	m	d	s	r	e	u	k
s	t	r	e	a	t	s	z	o	f	e	b
u	e	k	b	j	a	g	h	o	s	t	s
j	d	w	i	t	c	h	g	m	y	x	n
l	m	j	w	e	g	o	b	l	i	n	s

Name ____________________

A BLOODCHILLING STORY

Directions: Read each sentence. Write a word on each blank to complete each sentence. Illustrate part of this story in the space below.

1. Susie was walking all alone past a haunted ____________________.

2. Suddenly a ____________________ ran in front of her.

3. She heard a bloodchilling screech that sounded like it was made by a __________ .

4. Susie was running as fast as she could, when she tripped over a __________ .

5. When she got home, Susie hid in the ____________________ .

Name ______________________________

SH! IT'S A SECRET!

Directions: Use the following code to learn the secret. Write the letters on the correct lines.

A	B	C	D	E	F	G	H	I	J	K	L	M
1	2	3	4	5	6	7	8	9	10	11	12	13
N	O	P	Q	R	S	T	U	V	W	X	Y	Z
14	15	16	17	18	19	20	21	22	23	24	25	26

12 15 15 11   15 21 20

___ ___ ___ ___   ___ ___ ___!

8 5 18 5   3 15 13 5 19   1

___ ___ ___ ___   ___ ___ ___ ___ ___   ___

23 9 3 11 5 4   23 9 20 3 8

___ ___ ___ ___ ___ ___   ___ ___ ___ ___ ___!

18 21 14   18 21 14   18 21 14

___ ___ ___!   ___ ___ ___!   ___ ___ ___!

MISSING CONSONANT PUZZLE

Directions: Fill in the missing consonants.

1. hau ___ ted ___ ou ___ e
2. ___ ack-o'-la ___ te ___ ___
3. ___ ___ ick-or-t ___ ea ___
4. ___ itch
5. ___ a ___ ___ o ___ ee ___
6. ___ ___ ess u ___

Name ______________________________

MISSING VOWEL PUZZLE

Directions: Fill in the missing vowels.

1. H ___ ll ___ w ___ ___ n
2. ___ ct ___ b ___ r
3. j ___ ck-o'-l ___ nt ___ rn
4. dr ___ ss up
5. w ___ tch
6. gh ___ st
7. h ___ ___ nt ___ d
8. d ___ rk
9. g ___ bl ___ ns
10. sc ___ ry
11. h ___ ___ s ___
12. c ___ ndy
13. tr ___ ck-or-tr ___ ___ t
14. gl ___ ___ my
15. m ___ nst ___ r
16. c ___ ___ ldr ___ n

I scared some
of the vowels away.
Can you fill them in?
Boooooooooooooooooo!

Name ______________________________

WHO NEEDS IT?

Directions: Circle the word in each sentence that isn't needed. Write the words that you circled in the correct boxes below. Does a special message appear?

1. Happy Halloween is the last night of October.
2. Boys and girls Halloween dress up in costumes.
3. They boys go out trick-or-treating.
4. A favorite trick is to and put soap on windows.
5. One of everyone's favorite Halloween treats is candy girls.

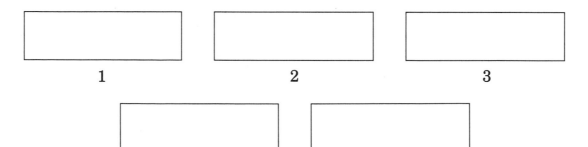

[ ]	[ ]	[ ]
1	2	3

[ ]	[ ]
4	5

Name ______________________________

MAKE A WORD

Directions: Use the letters in the word "Halloween" to make as many different words as you can.

HALLOWEEN

______	______	______
______	______	______
______	______	______
______	______	______
______	______	______
______	______	______
______	______	______
______	______	______
______	______	______
______	______	______
______	______	______
______	______	______
______	______	______
______	______	______
______	______	______
______	______	______
______	______	______

Name ____________________

THE UNFINISHED SPELL

Directions: Draw a picture and write a story.

I tried to change you into an animal, but my spell only **half** worked. Draw a picture of yourself under this unfinished spell.
Heeeee! Heeeeeee! Heeeeeee!

How can you break this spell? ____________________

____

____

____

____

____

____

Name ____________________

A HALLOWEEN STORY

Directions: Complete the story.

One dark and stormy Halloween night, Susie, Freddy, and Ricky were out trick-or-treating, when suddenly ____________________

Name ______________________________

LOOK WHO'S COOKING

Directions: Write a recipe using at least six of the following ingredients. What's the name of your recipe? How do you fix it? How do you cook it?

toadstool	snail head
spider web	prussic acid
frog leg	sheep eye
bat wing	pig tail
scorpion	snake venom
chicken claw	Tabasco sauce
persimmon juice	arsenic

Recipe Title: ______________________________

Ingredients: ______________________________

____

____

How to fix: ______________________________

____

____

____

____

How to cook: ______________________________

____

Name ____________________

HALLOWEEN WORD SCRAMBLE

Directions: Unscramble the words. Write them in the correct places.

1.
2.
3.
4.
5.
6.
7.
8.
9.
10.

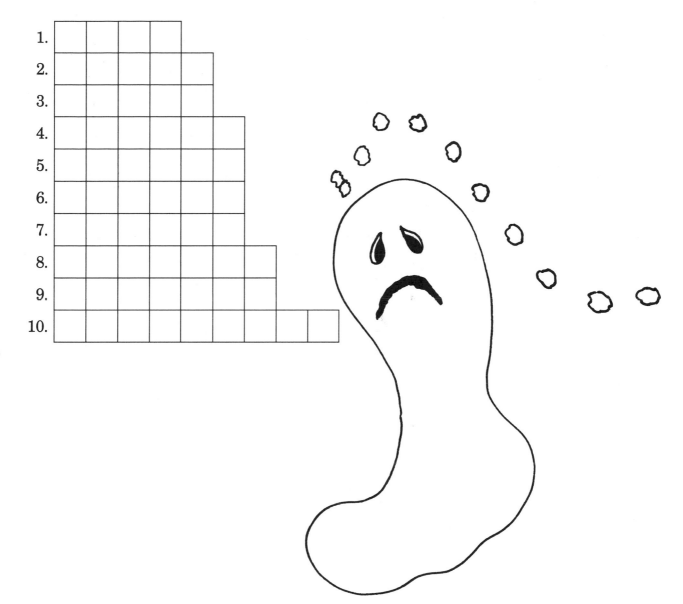

1. radk
2. lpsel
3. ctiwh
4. orhror
5. msacer
6. sogths
7. ysopok
8. emutsoc
9. kpinpum
10. olewnleHa

Name ______________________________

HALLOWEEN DIVINATION

Directions: Fill in the blanks with words from the apple.

Divination is the practice of trying to foretell the (1) ________________ from signs and omens. On (2) ________________, girls have used various methods of (3) ________________ the future.

A girl would go into her bedroom at (4) ____________________ and cut an (5) ______________ into nine (6) ________________. She would hold each slice on the tip of the (7) __________________ before eating it. She thought she could look in the (8) ______________ and see the face of her future (9) ______________ behind her shoulder. He would then ask to eat the last (10) ____________ of apple.

Sometimes a girl would peel an apple being careful to keep the (11) ____________ in one piece. Then she would swing it around her head three times and drop it over her left (12) ______________. It was supposed to fall to the (13) ______________ in the shape of her future sweetheart's (14) ______________.

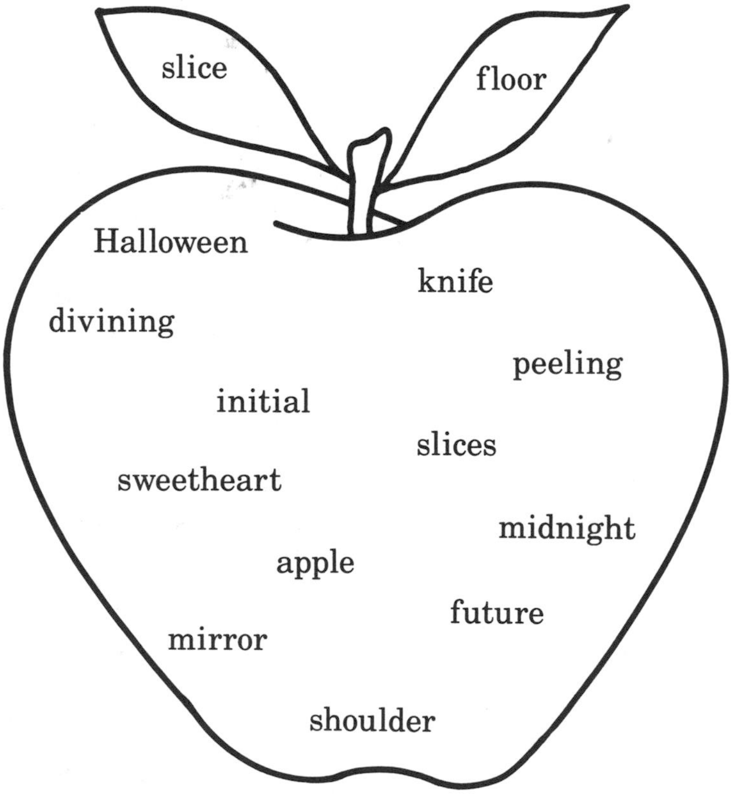

Name ______________________________

HALLOWEEN SPIRITS

Directions: Fill in the blanks with words from the witch.

In ancient times, people thought that ghosts, demons, and witches (1) ________ the earth on Halloween night. People began dressing in terrifying (2) ________ to try to (3) ________ these evil spirits away.

Fire was believed to be a good (4) ________ against witches, so some people carried lighted (5) ________ on Halloween (6) ________. Others hollowed out a turnip or (7) ________, carved a scary face on it, placed a lighted (8) ________ inside and carried this jack-o'-lantern around to scare away the witches and all other evil spirits. Some people placed these jack-o'-lanterns on (9) ________ or windowsills to frighten the spirits away from the (10) ________.

Although fire was considered to be the most trustworthy weapon against witches, (11) ________ was also supposed to be good. Iron (12) ________ were carried or hung above doors.

Other people relied on making the sign of the (13) ________ to keep the evil spirits from harming them.

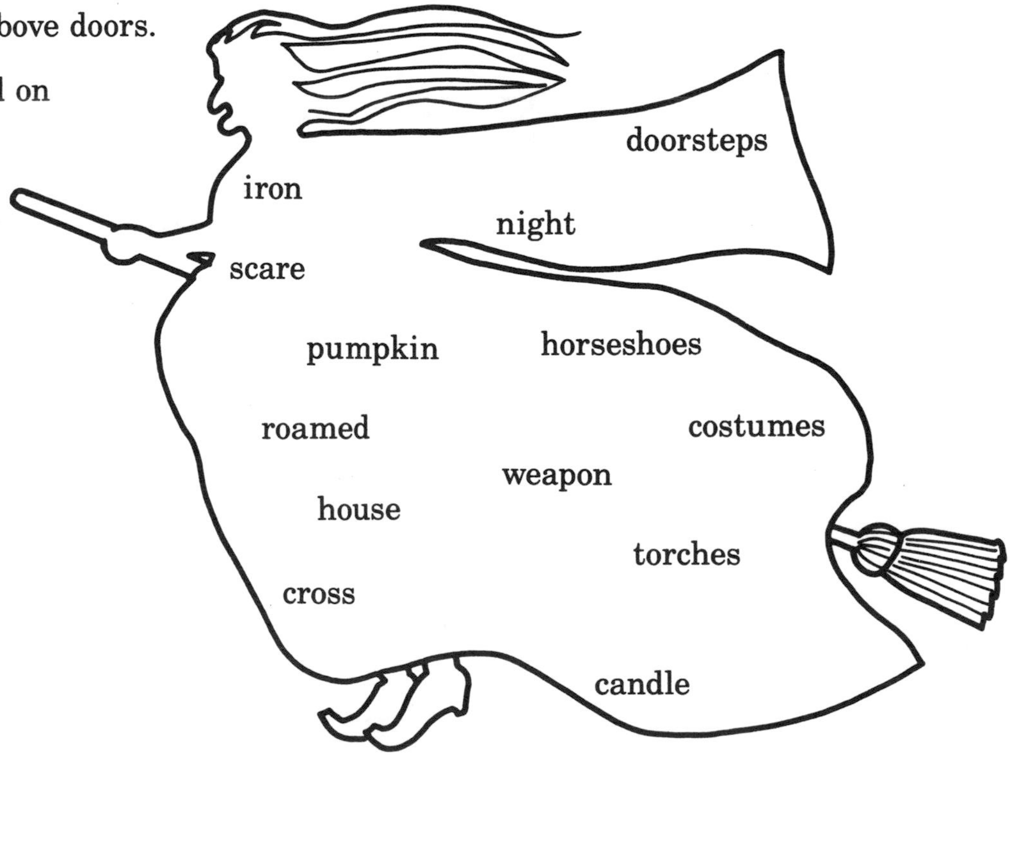

Name ______________________________

WORD HUNT

Directions: Circle the hidden words. You may go across and down.

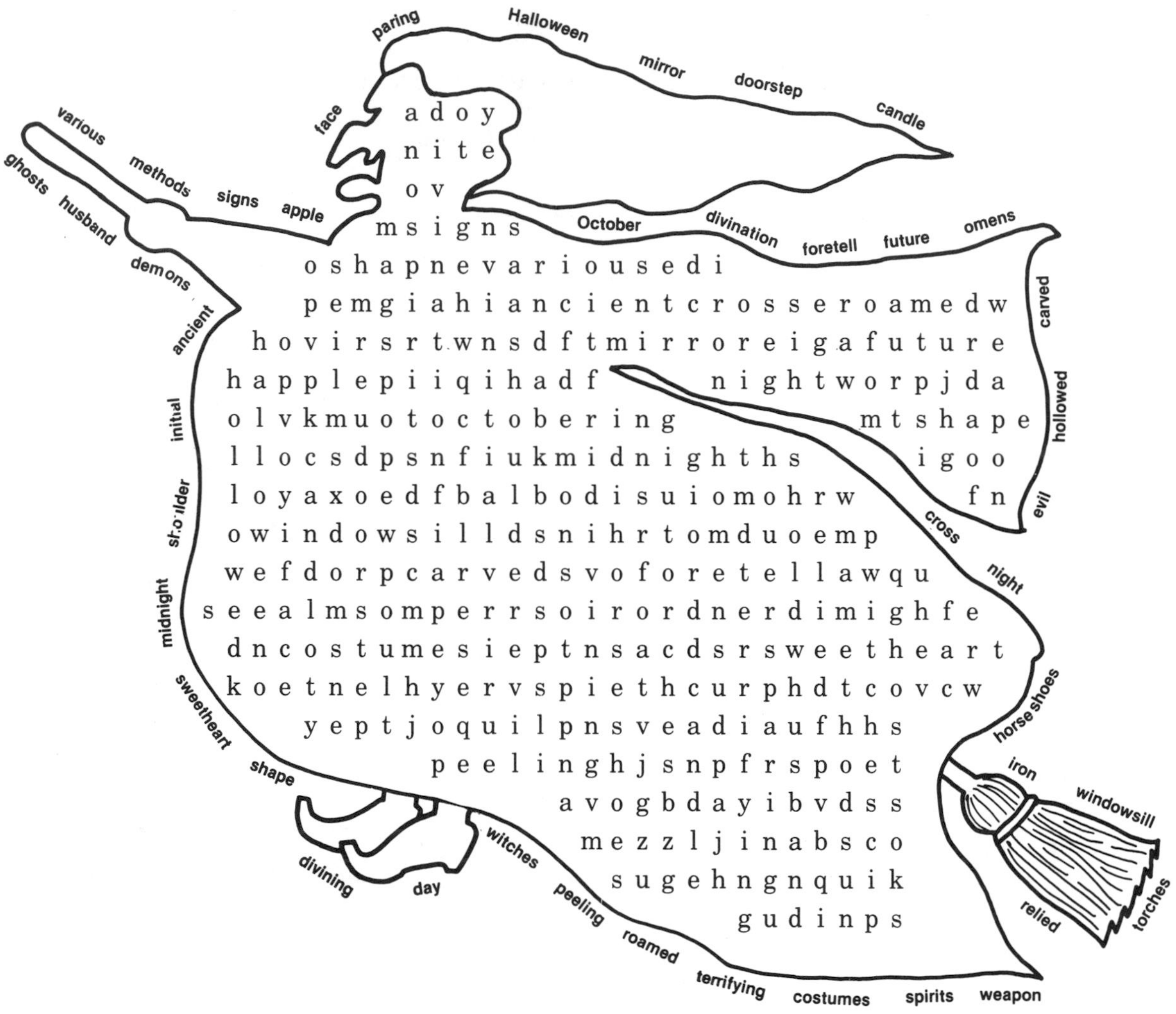
paring
Halloween
mirror
doorstep
candle
face
various
methods
signs
apple
ghosts
husband
demons
ancient
October
divination
foretell
future
omens
carved
hollowed
evil
initial
shoulder
cross
night
midnight
sweetheart
horseshoes
shape
iron
windowsill
divining
day
witches
peeling
roamed
terrifying
costumes
spirits
weapon
relied
torches
a d o y
n i t e
o v
m s i g n s
o s h a p n e v a r i o u s e d i
p e m g i a h i a n c i e n t c r o s s e r o a m e d w
h o v i r s r t w n s d f t m i r r o r e i g a f u t u r e
h a p p l e p i i q i h a d f n i g h t w o r p j d a
o l v k m u o t o c t o b e r i n g m t s h a p e
l l o c s d p s n f i u k m i d n i g h t h s i g o o
l o y a x o e d f b a l b o d i s u i o m o h r w f n
o w i n d o w s i l l d s n i h r t o m d u o e m p
w e f d o r p c a r v e d s v o f o r e t e l l a w q u
s e e a l m s o m p e r r s o i r o r d n e r d i m i g h f e
d n c o s t u m e s i e p t n s a c d s r s w e e t h e a r t
k o e t n e l h y e r v s p i e t h c u r p h d t c o v c w
y e p t j o q u i l p n s v e a d i a u f h h s
p e e l i n g h j s n p f r s p o e t
a v o g b d a y i b v d s s
m e z z l j i n a b s c o
s u g e h n g n q u i k
g u d i n p s

NOVEMBER

Visitor's Day • 69

Vocabulary • 69

Game Boards • 70

Activity Number and Title		**Special Day**
3-1	Veterans Day	Veterans Day
3-2	Turkey Time	Thanksgiving
3-3	Same or Different	Thanksgiving
3-4	Alphabet Scramble	Thanksgiving
3-5	Who Is It?	Thanksgiving
3-6	The Lost Feast	Thanksgiving
3-7	Thanksgiving Maze	Thanksgiving
3-8	Thanksgiving Puzzle	Thanksgiving
3-9	Thanksgiving Word Match	Thanksgiving
3-10	Give Thanks	Thanksgiving
3-11	Thanksgiving Feast	Thanksgiving
3-12	Thanksgiving Word Hunt	Thanksgiving
3-13	The First Thanksgiving Day	Thanksgiving
3-14	Sh! It's a Secret!	Thanksgiving
3-15	Missing Consonant Puzzle	Thanksgiving
3-16	Missing Vowel Puzzle	Thanksgiving
3-17	Thanksgiving Word Scramble	Thanksgiving
3-18	Who Needs It?	Thanksgiving
3-19	Make a Word	Thanksgiving
3-20	My Thanksgiving Day	Thanksgiving
3-21	Thanksgiving Story	Thanksgiving
3-22	Thanksgiving	Thanksgiving
3-23	Thanksgiving Customs	Thanksgiving
3-24	Word Hunt	Thanksgiving

Visitor's Day

Some classes tend to have a stigma attached to them. If you are a remedial reading teacher or special education teacher, November is a good time to initiate Visitor's Day. If your students have been working on the story wall and other projects from this book, word has spread that the special class can be an interesting and desirable place to be. Set aside a day when each of your students is allowed to bring a guest to class to work on a holiday project; you'll find that the stigma soon disappears.

Vocabulary

The following two word lists will help develop your students' vocabularies in November.

Word List	Word List
ceremonies	cornucopia
ringing	cornstalk
proclaimed	Pilgrims
honors	Mayflower
women	pumpkin
remembrance	pie
country	Indians
world	feast
weeping	turkey
following	November
flashed	Thanksgiving
services	cranberry
ended	corn
November	holiday
veterans	Thursday
known	dinner
dead	thankful
celebrations	parade
armistice	customs
tape	celebrate

Game Boards

Here are three game boards for you to use in November. For the bingo style game board, don't forget to arrange the words on the other cards in a different order.

corn	day	bountiful	dinner	today
thanks	turkey	holiday	ship	Mayflower
ago	long		country	Thanksgiving
thankful	harvest	cornucopia	Pilgrim	Indian
pumpkin	November	church	first	log

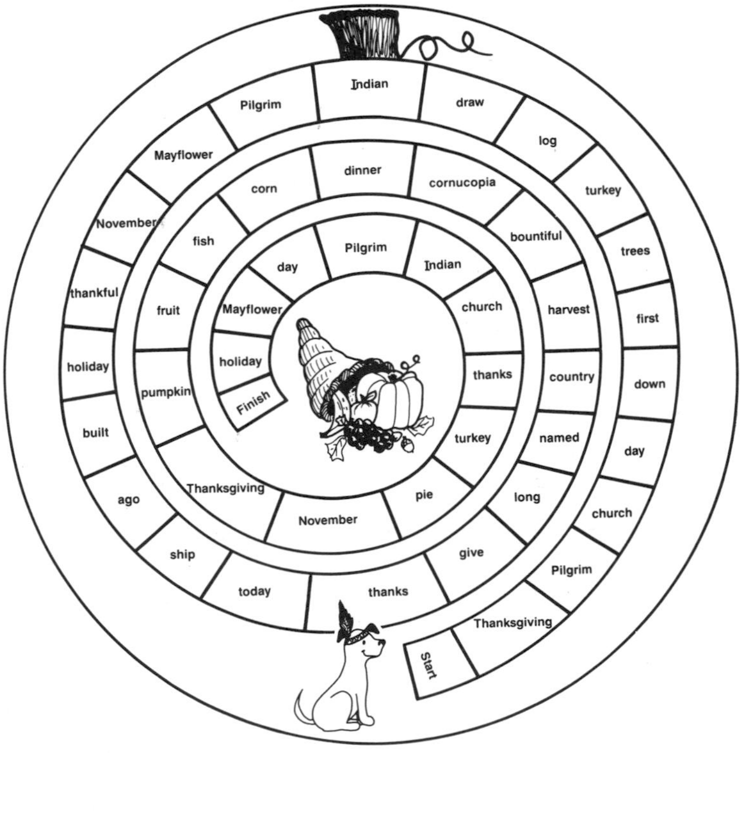

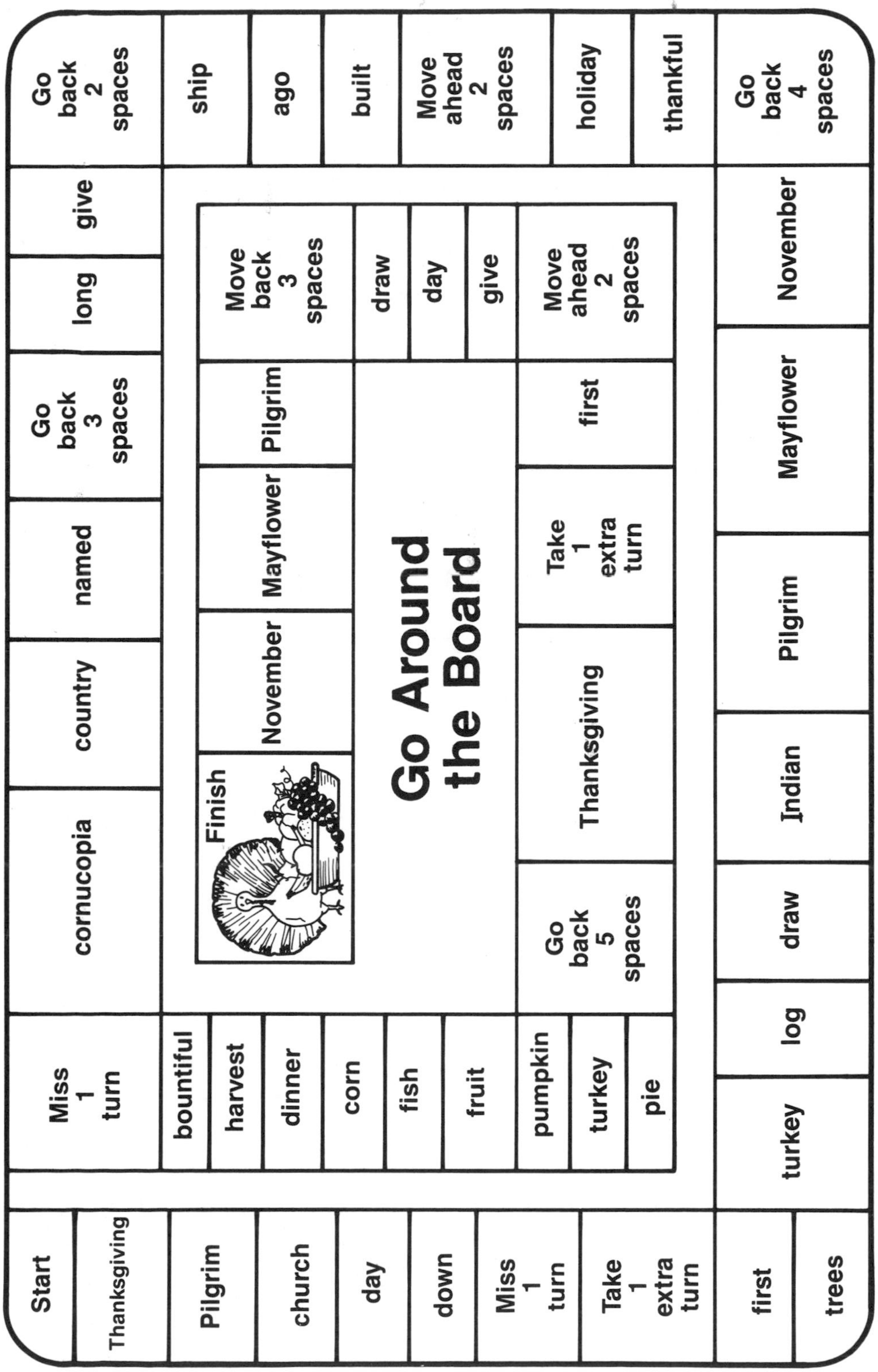
Go Around the Board
Start
Thanksgiving
Pilgrim
church
day
down
Miss 1 turn
Take 1 extra turn
first
trees
turkey
log
draw
Indian
Pilgrim
Mayflower
November
Go back 4 spaces
thankful
holiday
Move ahead 2 spaces
built
ago
ship
Go back 2 spaces
give
long
Go back 3 spaces
named
country
cornucopia
Miss 1 turn
bountiful
harvest
dinner
corn
fish
fruit
pumpkin
turkey
pie
Go back 5 spaces
Thanksgiving
Take 1 extra turn
first
Move ahead 2 spaces
give
day
draw
Move back 3 spaces
Pilgrim
Mayflower
November
Finish

VETERANS DAY

Directions: Fill in the blanks with words from the ticker tape.

At one time, Veterans Day was (1) ______________ as Armistice Day. On November 11, 1918, an (2) ______________________ was signed which (3) ______________ World War I. When this news was (4) ______________ around the world, it triggered spontaneous (5) ______________. In this country, church bells started (6) ______________, people were (7) ______________ and dancing in the (8) ______________, and ticker (9) ______________ was thrown out of office windows in the cities.

The following year, President Woodrow Wilson (10) ______________ November 11 as Armistice Day in (11) ______________________ of the war (12) ______________ of World War I. After World War II, the name was changed to Veterans Day. Veterans Day (13) ______________________ the men and (14) ______________ who have served in the armed (15) ______________.

Observances include parades, speeches, (16) ______________ services, and special (17) ______________ at Arlington National Cemetery.

Name ______________________________

TURKEY TIME

Directions: Color the turkey using the colors shown.

Name ______________________________

SAME OR DIFFERENT

Directions: Look at the word on the left. Circle the word on the right that is like the one on the left.

thanks	thinks	thanks	thank	tanks
November	Novimber	Novembur	Novumber	November
turkey	turkey	turkay	turky	turkee
feast	faest	feest	feast	feost
Pilgrim	Pilgrum	Pilgrem	Pillgrim	Pilgrim
pies	pies	peis	pie	pises
dinner	binner	dinner	diner	dinnur
Mayflower	Mayflowur	Mayflour	Mayflower	Moyflower
corn	corns	corne	corn	curn
Indians	Indian	Indians	Inbians	Indains

Name ______________________________

ALPHABET SCRAMBLE

Directions: Write the letters of the alphabet in the correct order. Some of the letters have been filled in for you.

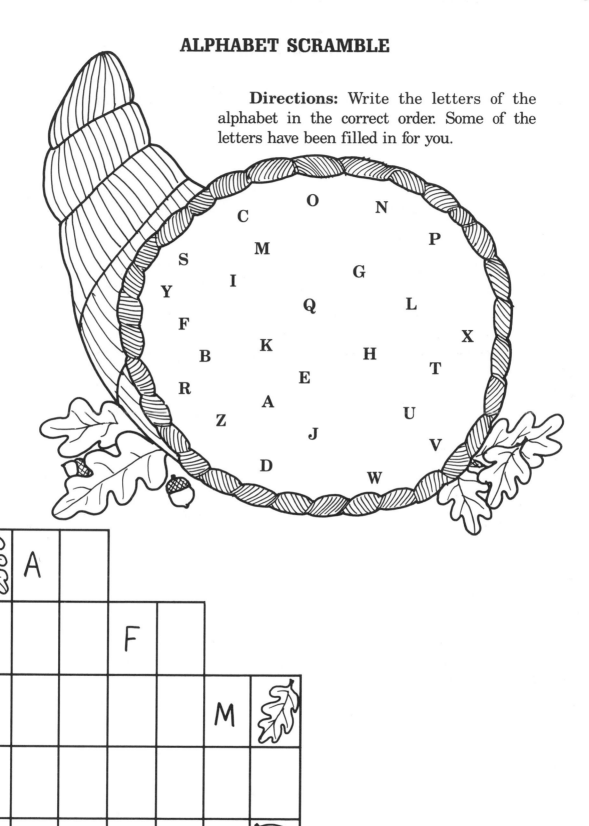

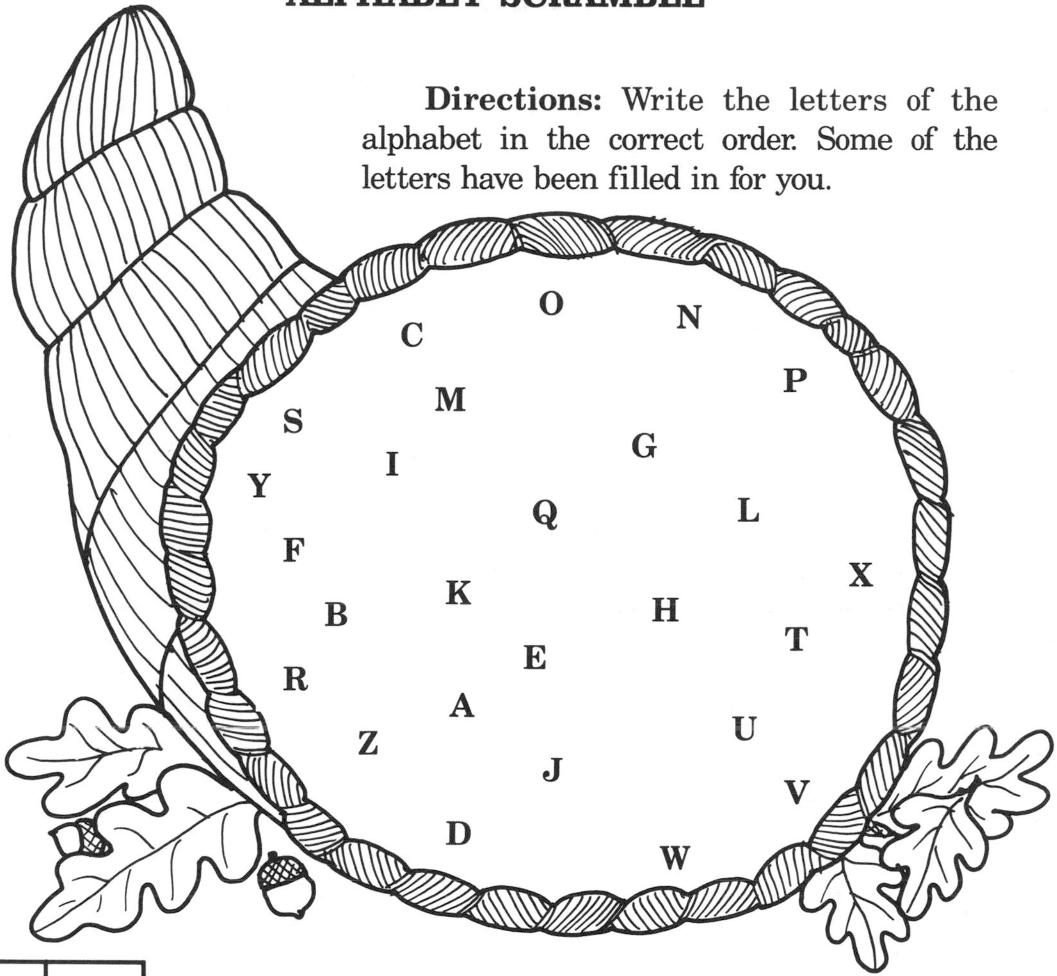

	A					
			F			
					M	
			X			

Name ________________________________

WHO IS IT?

Directions: Connect the dots to find out who is in this picture. Start with the first letter of the alphabet.

THE LOST FEAST

Directions: Help the Pilgrim find the Thanksgiving feast by drawing a line from him through the Thanksgiving words.

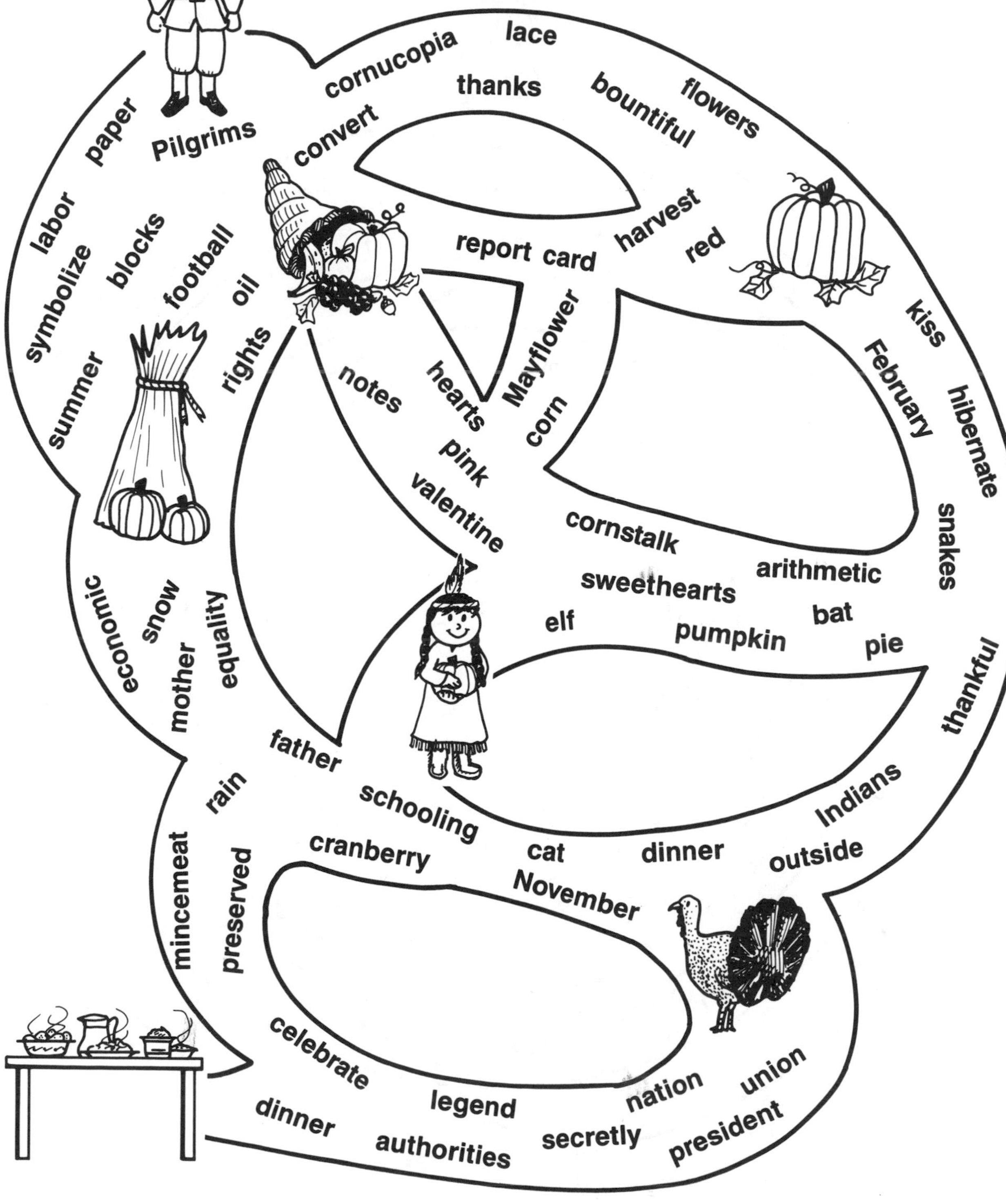

Name ________________________________

THANKSGIVING MAZE

Directions: Someone has hidden the pumpkin pie. Help find it by drawing a line from the Pilgrim through the Thanksgiving words.

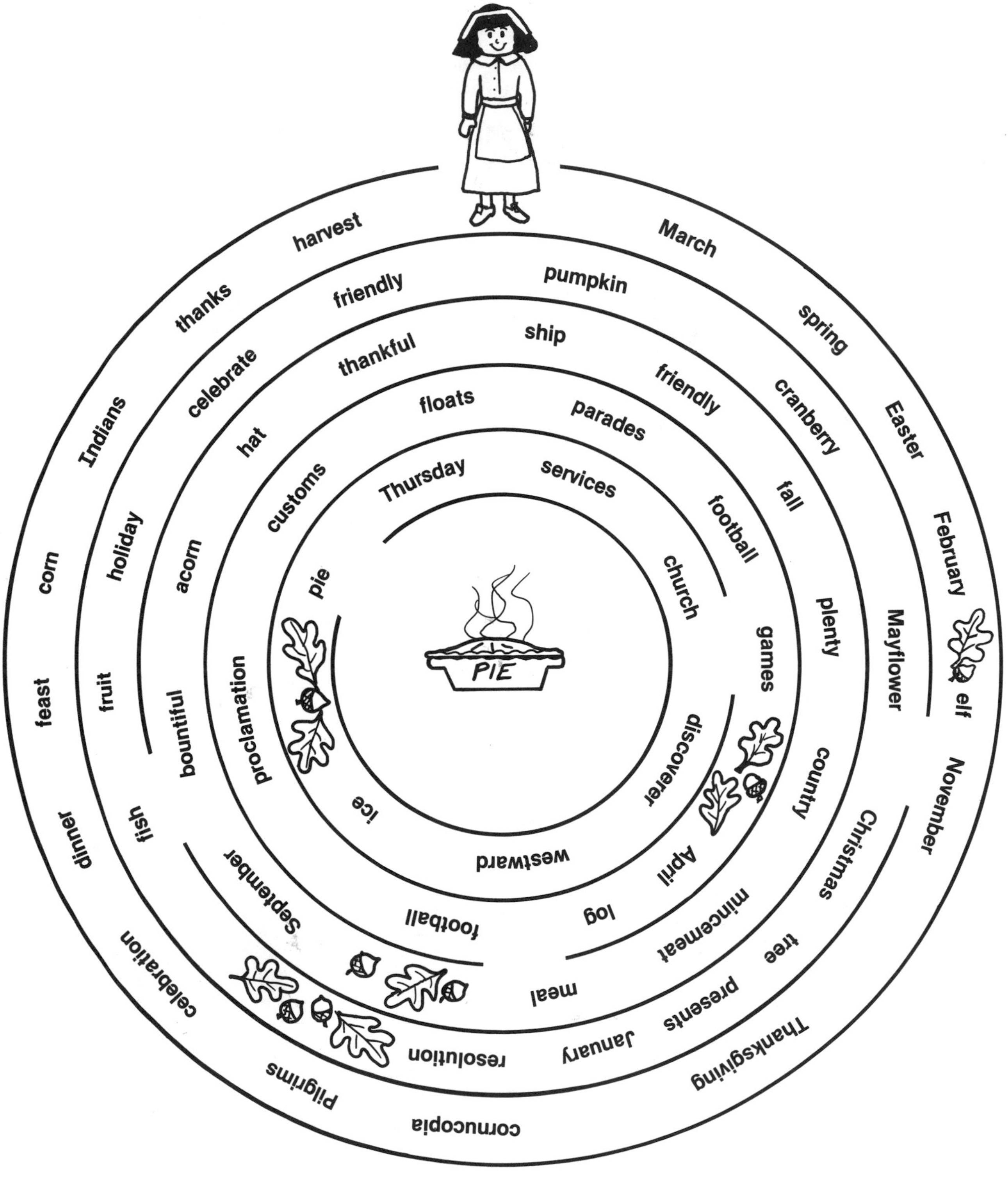

Name ________________________________

THANKSGIVING PUZZLE

Directions: Color the vowels green. Color the consonants brown.

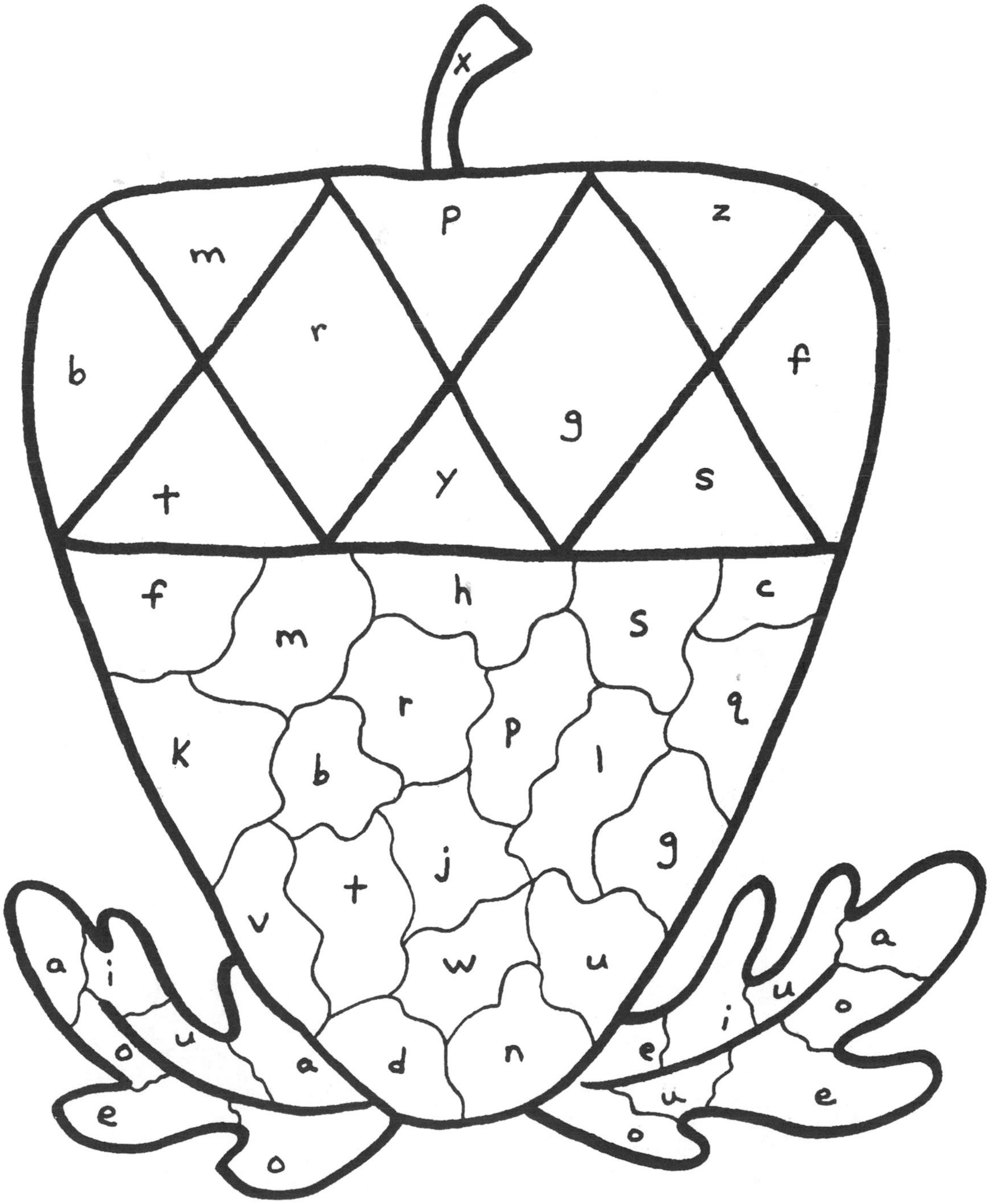

Name ______________________________

THANKSGIVING WORD MATCH

Directions: Draw a line to match the pictures to the correct words.

cornstalk

cornucopia

Pilgrim

hat

turkey

feast

Indian

Mayflower

pumpkin

pie

acorn

Name ________________________________

GIVE THANKS

Directions: Draw a picture of five things you are thankful for. Label and color them.

THANKSGIVING FEAST

Directions: Draw five things you would like to eat for Thanksgiving dinner. Label and color them.

Name ______________________________

THANKSGIVING WORD HUNT

Directions: Find the Thanksgiving words and circle them. You may go across and down.

t	h	a	n	k	s	g	i	v	i	n	g
h	o	l	i	d	a	y	c	x	z	o	f
u	z	p	n	c	o	r	n	g	i	v	e
r	t	u	d	q	r	o	v	d	w	e	a
s	u	m	i	s	h	i	p	i	e	m	s
d	r	p	a	n	p	m	b	n	x	b	t
a	k	k	n	z	l	o	l	n	p	e	z
y	e	i	c	r	a	n	b	e	r	r	y
h	y	n	i	q	s	t	m	r	n	x	s
g	j	m	e	k	t	h	a	n	k	s	a
p	i	l	g	r	i	m	s	t	f	d	i
u	m	a	y	f	l	o	w	e	r	a	l

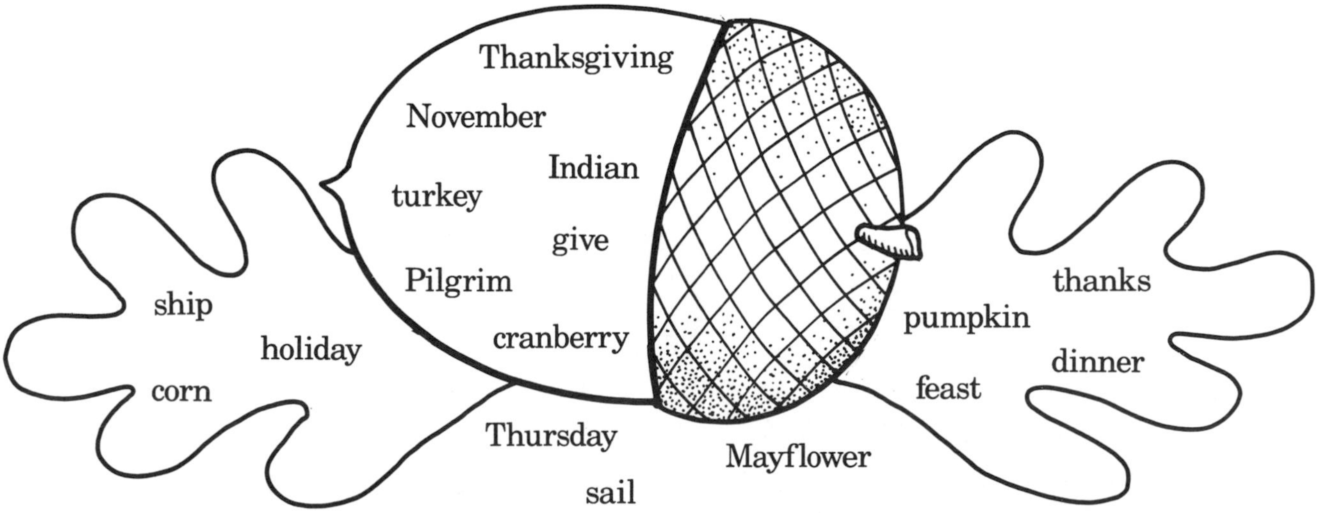

Name ______________________________

THE FIRST THANKSGIVING DAY

Directions: Read each sentence. Write a word on each blank to complete each sentence. Illustrate part of this story in the space below.

1. The Indians and the Pilgrims went hunting in the woods for a ____________.
2. The Indians taught the Pilgrims how to grow ______________________.
3. They prepared a big feast of ______________________________.
4. They were thankful for ______________________________________

   ____.

Name ______________________________

SH! IT'S A SECRET!

Directions: Use the following code to learn the secret. Write the letters on the correct line.

A	B	C	D	E	F	G	H	I	J	K	L	M
1	2	3	4	5	6	7	8	9	10	11	12	13
N	O	P	Q	R	S	T	U	V	W	X	Y	Z
14	15	16	17	18	19	20	21	22	23	24	25	26

20 8 5   9 14 4 9 1 14 19

___ ___ ___   ___ ___ ___ ___ ___ ___ ___

1 14 4   16 9 12 7 18 9 13 19

___ ___ ___   ___ ___ ___ ___ ___ ___ ___ ___

3 5 12 5 2 18 1 20 5 4   20 8 5

___ ___ ___ ___ ___ ___ ___ ___ ___ ___   ___ ___ ___

6 9 18 19 20

___ ___ ___ ___ ___

20 8 1 14 11 19 7 9 22 9 14 7

___ ___ ___ ___ ___ ___ ___ ___ ___ ___ ___ ___

20 15 7 5 20 8 5 18

___ ___ ___ ___ ___ ___ ___ ___

Name ______________________________

MISSING CONSONANT PUZZLE

Directions: Fill in the missing consonants.

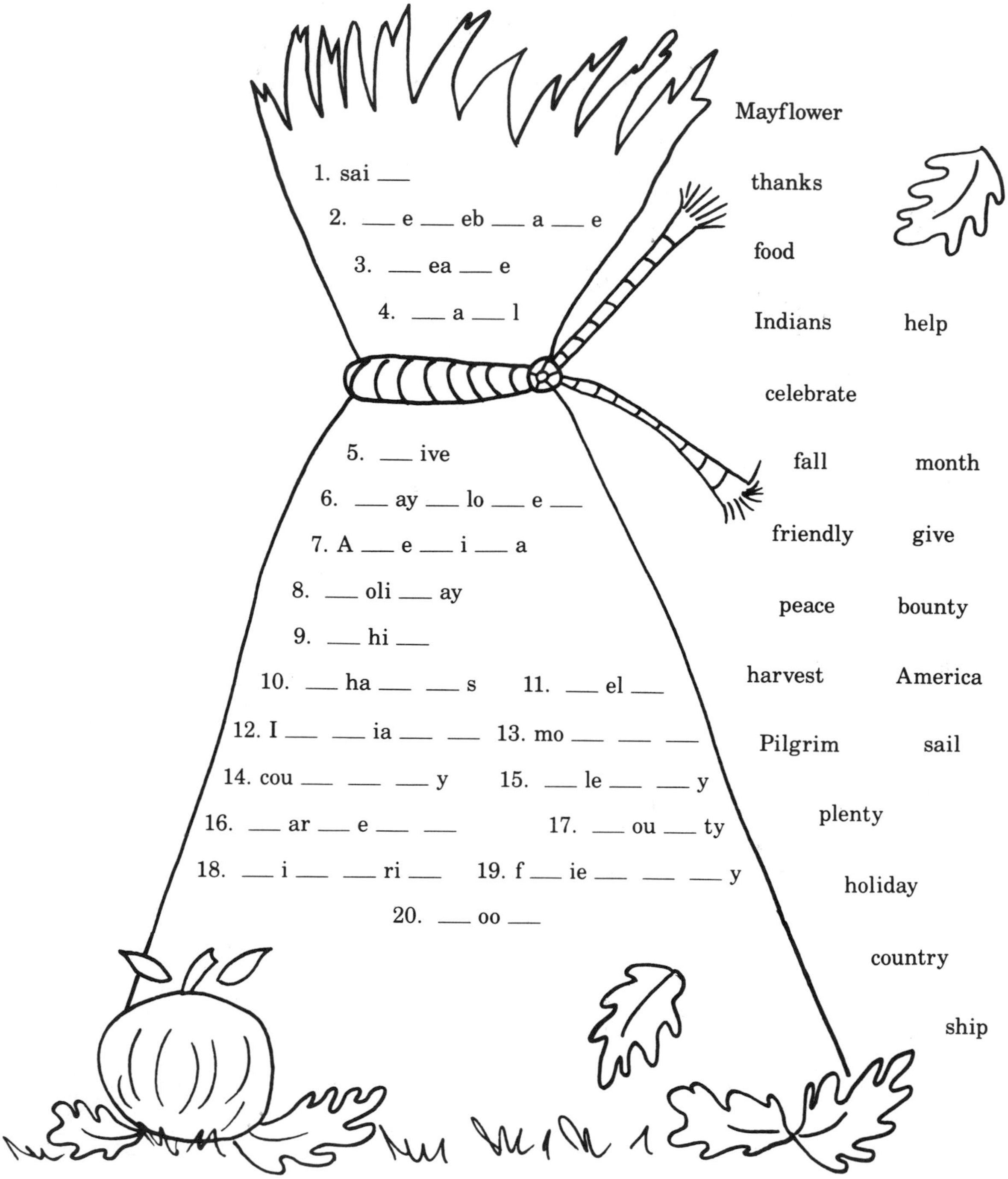

1. sai ___
2. ___ e ___ eb ___ a ___ e
3. ___ ea ___ e
4. ___ a ___ l
5. ___ ive
6. ___ ay ___ lo ___ e ___
7. A ___ e ___ i ___ a
8. ___ oli ___ ay
9. ___ hi ___
10. ___ ha ___ ___ s
11. ___ el ___
12. I ___ ___ ia ___ ___
13. mo ___ ___ ___
14. cou ___ ___ ___ y
15. ___ le ___ ___ y
16. ___ ar ___ e ___ ___
17. ___ ou ___ ty
18. ___ i ___ ___ ri ___
19. f ___ ie ___ ___ ___ y
20. ___ oo ___

Mayflower
thanks
food
Indians help
celebrate
fall month
friendly give
peace bounty
harvest America
Pilgrim sail
plenty
holiday
country
ship

Name ______________________________

MISSING VOWEL PUZZLE

Directions: Fill in the missing vowels.

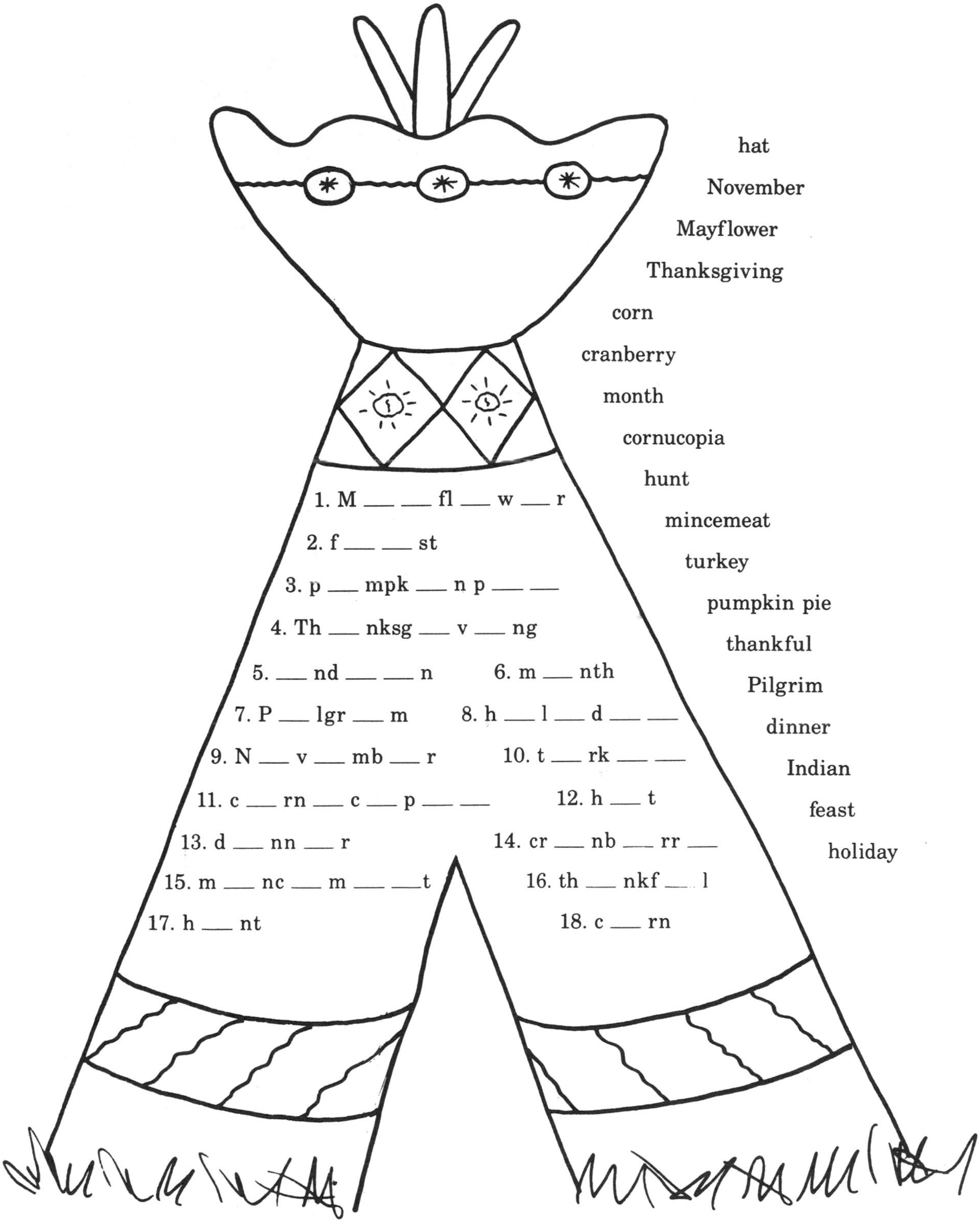

1. M ___ ___ fl ___ w ___ r
2. f ___ ___ st
3. p ___ mpk ___ n p ___ ___
4. Th ___ nksg ___ v ___ ng
5. ___ nd ___ ___ n
6. m ___ nth
7. P ___ lgr ___ m
8. h ___ l ___ d ___ ___
9. N ___ v ___ mb ___ r
10. t ___ rk ___ ___
11. c ___ rn ___ c ___ p ___ ___
12. h ___ t
13. d ___ nn ___ r
14. cr ___ nb ___ rr ___
15. m ___ nc ___ m ___ ___ t
16. th ___ nkf ___ l
17. h ___ nt
18. c ___ rn

hat
November
Mayflower
Thanksgiving
corn
cranberry
month
cornucopia
hunt
mincemeat
turkey
pumpkin pie
thankful
Pilgrim
dinner
Indian
feast
holiday

Name ______________________________

THANKSGIVING WORD SCRAMBLE

Directions: Unscramble each word and write it in the correct place.

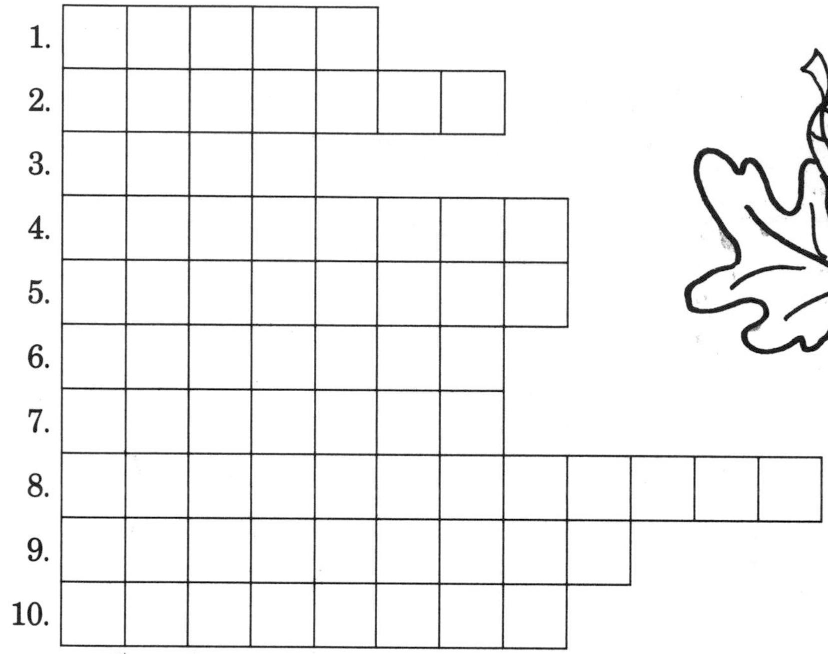

1. tsaef
2. ladioyh
3. iphs
4. srduyTah
5. lmigPrsi
6. yteukrs
7. nnisdIa
8. gsikvnianhgT
9. yaMrewlof
10. eoevrNmb

Name ________________________________

WHO NEEDS IT?

Directions: Circle the word in each sentence that isn't needed. Write the words that you circled in the correct boxes below. Does a message appear?

1. Thanksgiving Happy Day is the last Thursday in November.

2. It is a day to pause and Thanksgiving give thanks for all the good things in our lives.

3. Many people celebrate this holiday by preparing a boys big meal including turkey, dressing, and pumpkin pie.

4. It's a happy day because we spend it with our family and and friends.

5. After Thanksgiving, we start looking forward to Christmas girls.

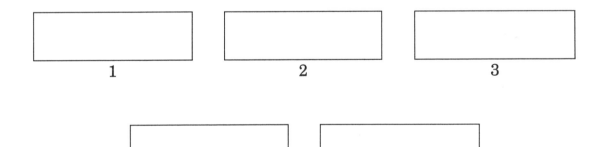

[ ]	[ ]	[ ]
1	2	3

[ ]	[ ]
4	5

Name ______________________

MAKE A WORD

Directions: Use the letters in the word "Thanksgiving" to make as many different words as you can.

THANKSGIVING

Name ______________________________

MY THANKSGIVING DAY

Directions: Complete the story. Illustrate your story in the space below.

On Thanksgiving Day, I am going to ______________________________

THANKSGIVING STORY

Directions: Complete the story. Illustrate your story in the space below.

The Pilgrims had no meat to eat because hunting had been poor. Running Bear, an Indian boy, decided to help his family and friends by ____

____

____

____

____

____

____

____

____

____

____

____

____

Name ________________________________

THANKSGIVING

Directions: Fill in the blanks with words from the scroll.

The Pilgrims (1) ________________ the first Thanksgiving in 1621. For over two (2) ________________, days of Thanksgiving were held at various times in different (3) ________________ of the (4) ________________.

In 1827, Sara Josepha Hale, (5) ________________ of a popular ladies' (6) ________________, began a (7) ________________ to have Thanksgiving Day celebrated as a national (8) ________________. For many years, she wrote (9) ________________ for the magazine and sent letters to the President, (10) ________________, and other important people.

She finally won the (11) ________________ of President Abraham Lincoln. In 1863, he (12) ________________ that the last (13) ________________ in November should be observed as a (14) ________________ day of Thanksgiving.

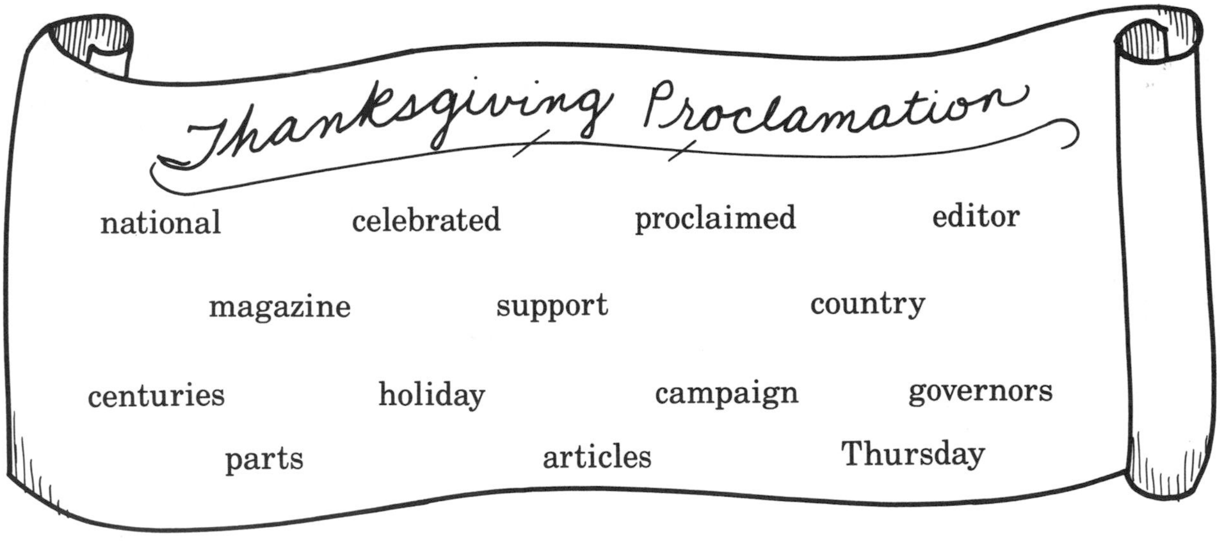
Thanksgiving Proclamation
national
celebrated
proclaimed
editor
magazine
support
country
centuries
holiday
campaign
governors
parts
articles
Thursday

Name ______________________

THANKSGIVING CUSTOMS

Directions: Fill in the blanks with words from the cornucopia.

Many (1) ______________ have been associated with Thanksgiving Day. Some customs, such as poor children dressing in (2) ______________ and begging for food or (3) ______________, have died out. Other customs, such as (4) ______________ and shooting matches, have been popular for over a century.

Some of today's most cherished customs are the big family (5) ______________, special church (6) ______________, football games, and parades. The mere thought of Thanksgiving Day can make our mouths (7) ______________ for turkey, cranberry (8) ______________, and pumpkin pie. While dinner is being prepared, many children watch the (9) ______________ Macy's Thanksgiving Day Parade on television. This parade is the kickoff of the Christmas (10) ______________. Santa Claus has a special float in the parade. Speaking of kickoffs, many people, after stuffing themselves at the dinner table, like to (11) ______________ by watching football on TV all afternoon.

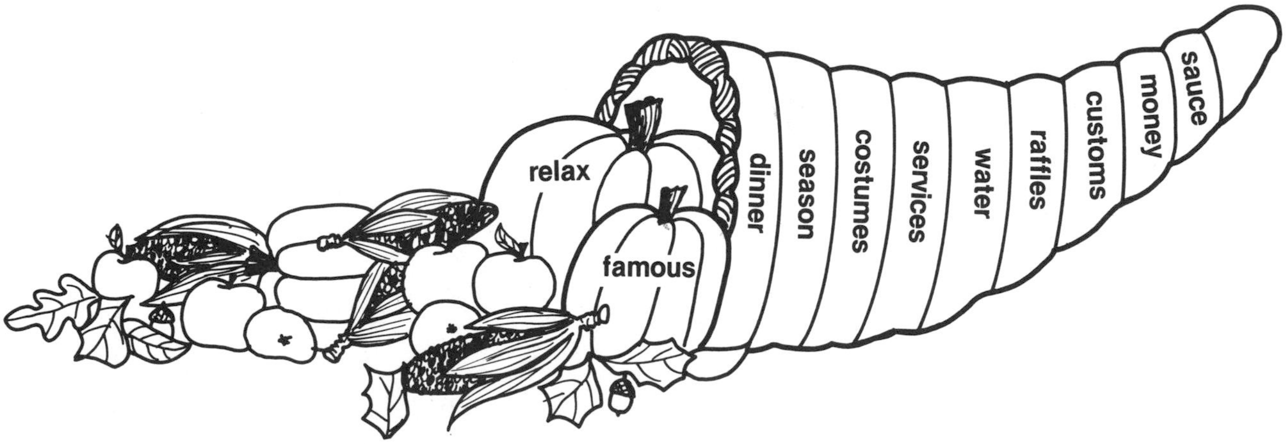

WORD HUNT

Directions: Circle the hidden words. You may go across and down.

p e i s d a t i m e n r t h k a g
r a s t t h u r s d a y o x p i c
m a d a y p   e s k e h n c f o k t u f a m t o
s p u m p k i n   d s s o l a m e o e d i t o r c u s t o m
s c k a y e c a c n i g i o t e n d l o c n o i v t p e c h s x
a o f p o s n d c m v k i e t p u n q u i r k e s u a
n s a a k g c e i n i s r b b s m a t n c o u n t r y
f o t m r i r o n a p s g u r a f f l e s l c i t e f h
b l v u o a s c m t t n i i m a l p l h d u e l m u b e r
u k o e m u d w h o d e k o v l t l i o o q p s a r r y t m r
w g a m e s e r u p s d h n i j e g l a l u p x i d i n n e r
a m b s o s e r v i c e s n u d a g t i v o w m s e f o z
t e l e v l c a m p a i g n j m r s d i r c e t s d
r e l a x h m a g a z i n e f i c a e t o d s g u
k p q i c k s g u a s m d y t

DECEMBER

A Library Center • 99
Vocabulary • 100
Game Boards • 100

Activity Number and Title		Special Day
4-1	A Picture to Color	Christmas
4-2	Same or Different	Christmas
4-3	Alphabet Scramble	Christmas
4-4	Who Is It?	Christmas
4-5	What Is It?	Christmas
4-6	Christmas Eve Maze	Christmas
4-7	Christmas Maze	Christmas
4-8	Christmas Puzzle	Christmas
4-9	Christmas Match	Christmas
4-10	A Christmas Wish	Christmas
4-11	Christmas Word Hunt	Christmas
4-12	Sh! It's a Secret!	Christmas
4-13	Christmas Consonant Puzzle	Christmas
4-14	Christmas Vowel Puzzle	Christmas
4-15	Christmas Word Scramble	Christmas
4-16	Who Needs It?	Christmas
4-17	Make a Word	Christmas
4-18	A Letter to Santa	Christmas
4-19	A Christmas Story	Christmas
4-20	What's Cooking?	Christmas
4-21	Saint Nicholas	Christmas
4-22	Christmas	Christmas
4-23	Word Hunt	Christmas
4-24	Hanukkah	Hanukkah

A Library Center

If you haven't already set up a library center, December is a good time to do it. Fill the center with library books, student made books, and stories from magazines that you have filed in the Fun Box.

After the library center is ready, schedule Read-In time. During Read-In, all of the students (and yourself) read with no interruptions for a specified number of minutes.

To encourage students to curl up with a good book, you can make Reading Caves for the library center. Use the large boxes that washing machines and dryers are packed in. Paint the outside with tempera paint and place a carpet remnant inside. Allow only one student at a time to use a Reading Cave.

One resource not to be overlooked is the variety of old radio shows that are available on cassettes. One favorite is "The Burns and Allen Christmas Show—1940s" with Edna Mae Oliver and Paul Whiteman. You can make a worksheet to accompany the program. Either ditto the worksheet and give it to the students to fill in as they listen, or go over the main points before the show, allow students to take notes during the show, then give the questions orally after the show, allowing students to refer to their notes as they answer the questions in writing.

Here are some sample questions.

1. What is the name of the sponsor? (Swan Soap)
2. What is the name of George and Gracie's pet duck? (Herman)
3. What is the sponsor's product supposed to do that is unusual? (float)
4. How did Gracie and her pet duck get to the North Pole? (by a magic carpet)
5. Who stole all of Santa's toys? (the wicked witch)
6. Who sang for his supper?(Little Tommy Tucker)
7. What song did he sing? ("Beautiful Dreamer")
8. What happened to Herman? (he was ducknapped)
9. What did Herman leave behind as a trail for George and Gracie to follow? (his tail feathers)
10. Who helped George and Gracie hunt for the witch? (Humpty Dumpty and his eggs)
11. What type of house did the witch live in? (a castle)
12. Why did Herman fly to the North Pole? (to get Santa)
13. Why did the witch's butler become a skeleton? (he was a heavy loser in a strip poker game)
14. What was the witch's first name? (Gwendolyn)
15. Who was the witch's long lost love? (Kriss Kringle)

Vocabulary

The following four word lists will help develop your students' vocabularies in December.

Christmas Word List 1	Christmas Word List 2	Christmas Word List 3	Hanukkah Word List
toys	parties	patron	feast
delivering	chestnuts	saint	dedication
pudding	decorations	century	lights
Christmas	holiday	gold	month
green	elf	bag	festival
red	ball	legends	miraculously
stocking	gingerbread	holiday	consecrated
tree	horn	shoes	oil
cookies	wreath	horse	temple
candle	dinner	goodies	evening
snowman	mittens	dowry	eight
reindeer	drum	generosity	December
bells	star	Europe	Hanukkah
holly	package	bishop	Jewish
candy cane	sleigh	wrap	traditions
fudge	milk	happiest	burning
Santa	awakened	traditions	exchanged
noel	bake	services	commemorates
carol	merry	symbolizes	candelabrum
presents	ornaments	share	holy

Game Boards

Here are three game board patterns for you to use in December. For the bingo style game board, don't forget to arrange the words on the other cards in a different order.

happy	star	card	merry	December
bell	angel	decorate	holiday	candy cane
sock	carols	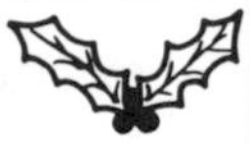	Santa Claus	presents
Christmas	toy	candle	reindeer	elves
tree	sled	holly	sing	snow

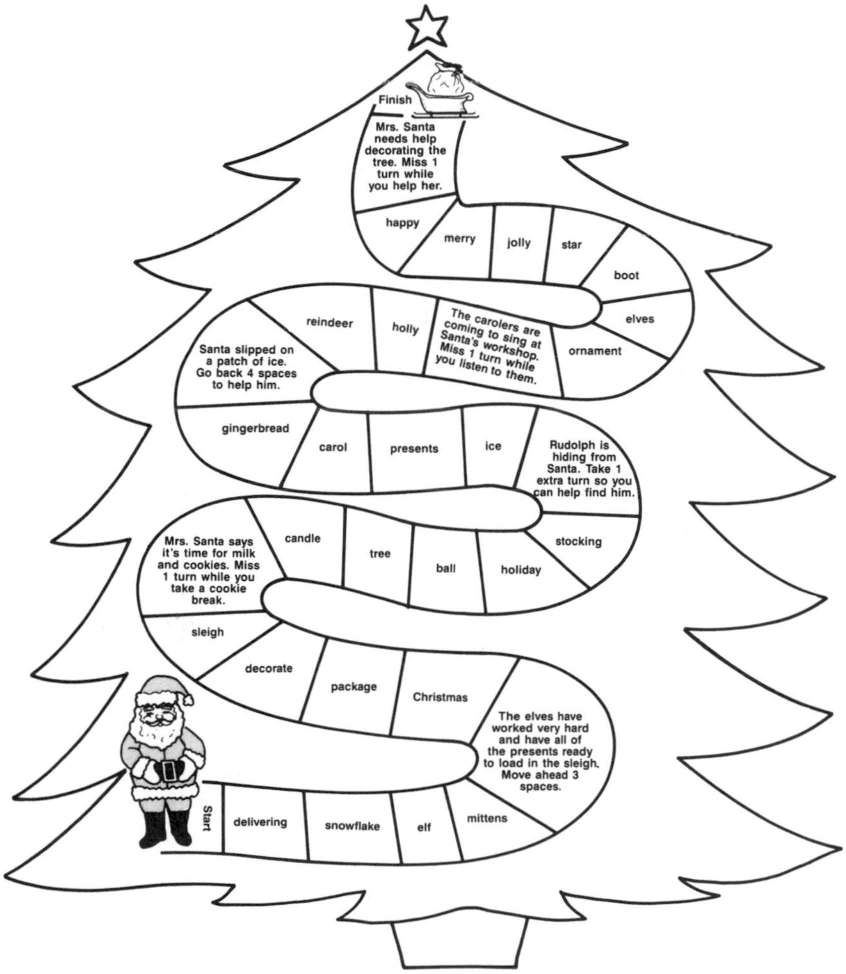

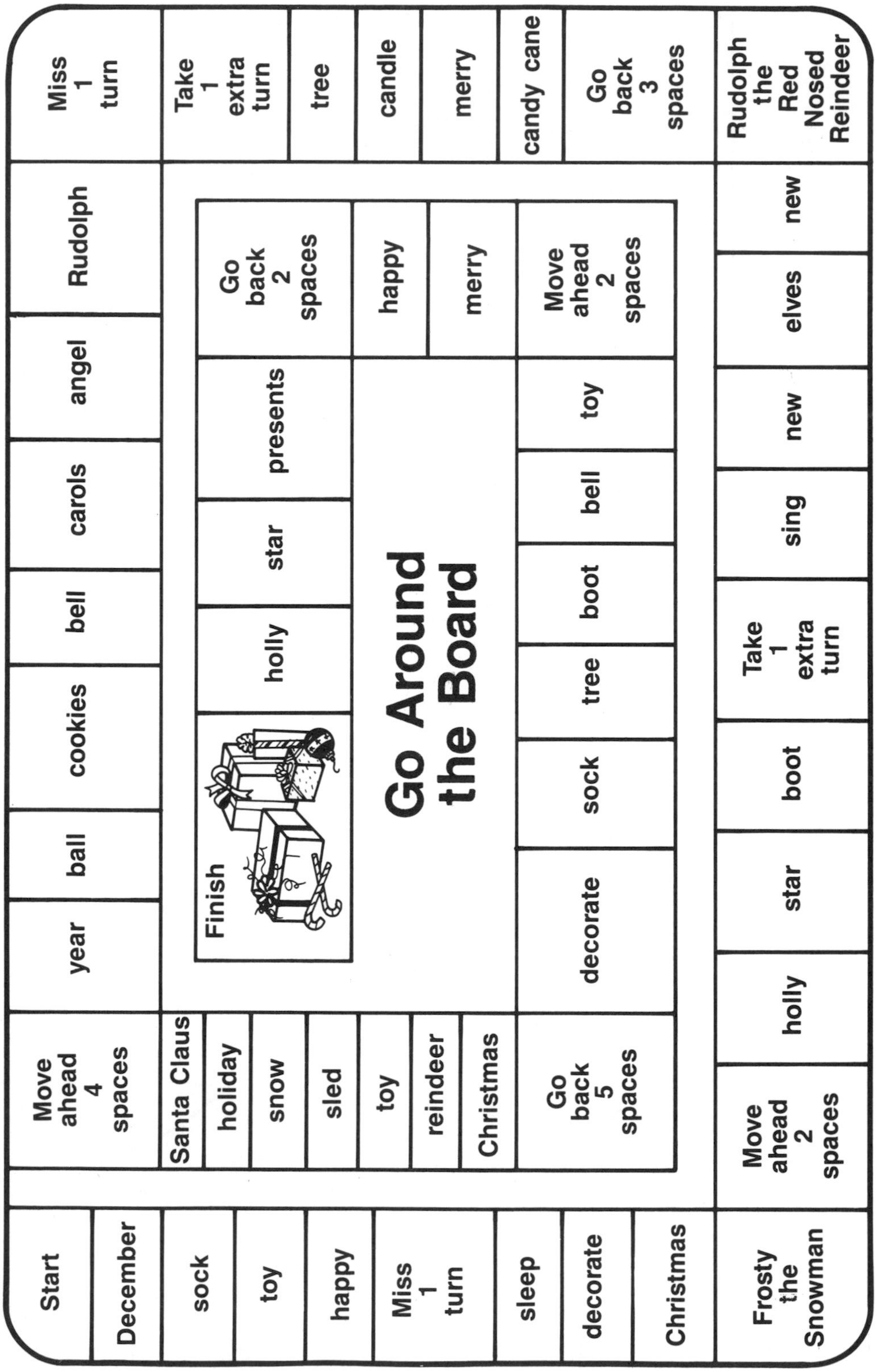
Go Around the Board
Start
December
sock
toy
happy
Miss 1 turn
sleep
decorate
Christmas
Frosty the Snowman
Move ahead 2 spaces
holly
star
boot
Take 1 extra turn
sing
new
elves
new
Rudolph the Red Nosed Reindeer
Go back 3 spaces
candy cane
merry
candle
tree
Take 1 extra turn
Miss 1 turn
Rudolph
angel
carols
bell
cookies
ball
year
Move ahead 4 spaces
Santa Claus
holiday
snow
sled
toy
reindeer
Christmas
Go back 5 spaces
decorate
sock
tree
boot
bell
toy
Move ahead 2 spaces
merry
happy
Go back 2 spaces
presents
star
holly
Finish

Name ________________________________

A PICTURE TO COLOR

Directions: Color the picture.

Name ______________________________

SAME OR DIFFERENT

Directions: Look at the word on the left. Circle the word on the right that is like the one on the left.

stockings	stocking	stokings	stockins	stockings
cookies	cookies	cookie	cooky	codkies
candle	canble	candles	candle	condle
reindeer	raindeer	reindeer	reindear	rainbeer
gifts	gifts	gift	giffs	gefts
tree	three	tree	tee	treeh
decorations	dicorations	decurations	decorashuns	decorations
sleigh	slay	sliegh	sleigh	slaigh
carol	carrol	carol	carul	caroll
holiday	holuday	holeday	holiday	holibay

ALPHABET SCRAMBLE

Name ______________________________

WHO IS IT!

Directions: Connect the dots to find out who is in this picture. Start with the first letter of the alphabet. First, connect the lower case letters. Then, connect the capital letters.

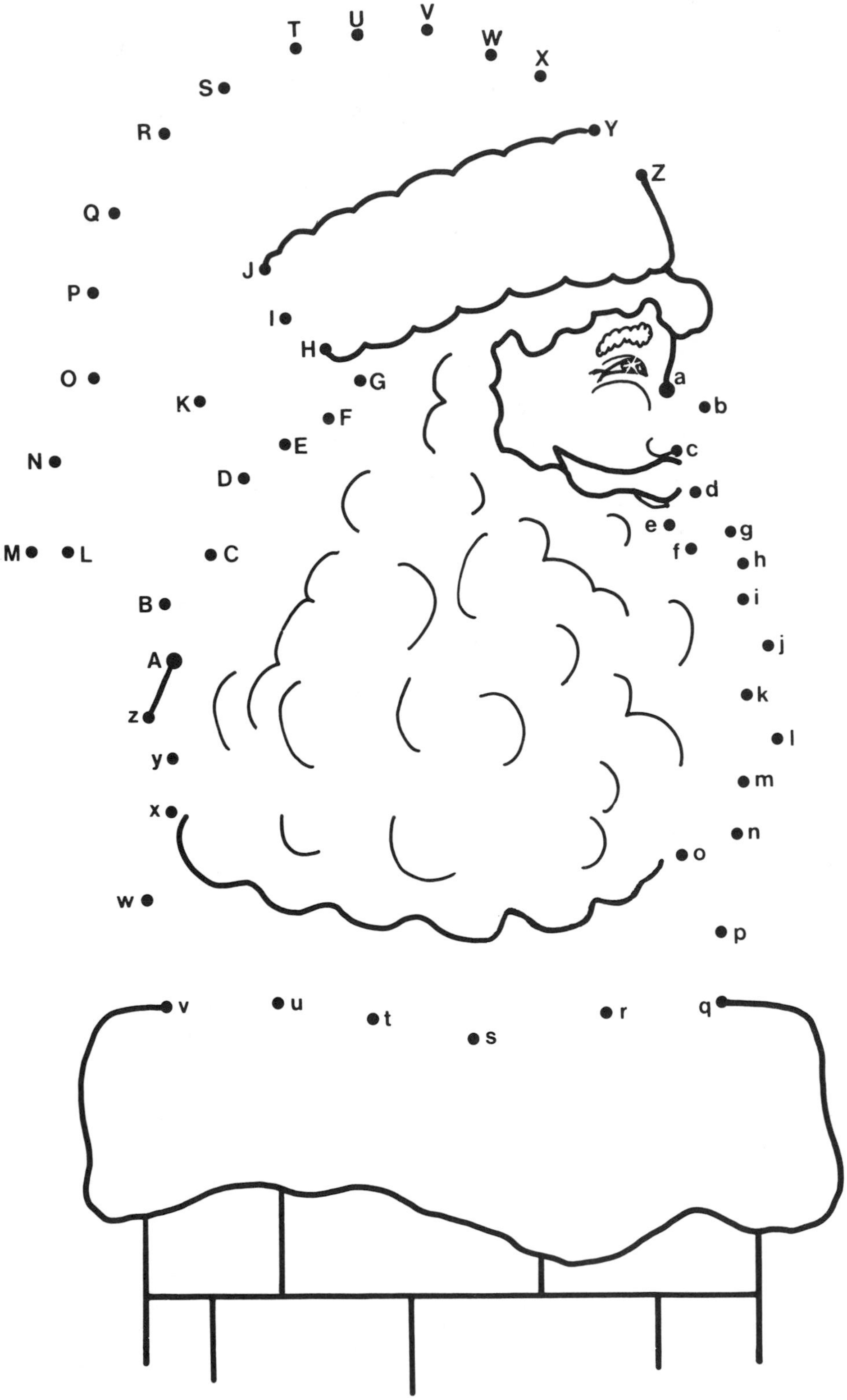

Name ______________________________

WHAT IS IT?

Directions: Connect the dots to find out what is in this picture. Start with the first letter of the alphabet.

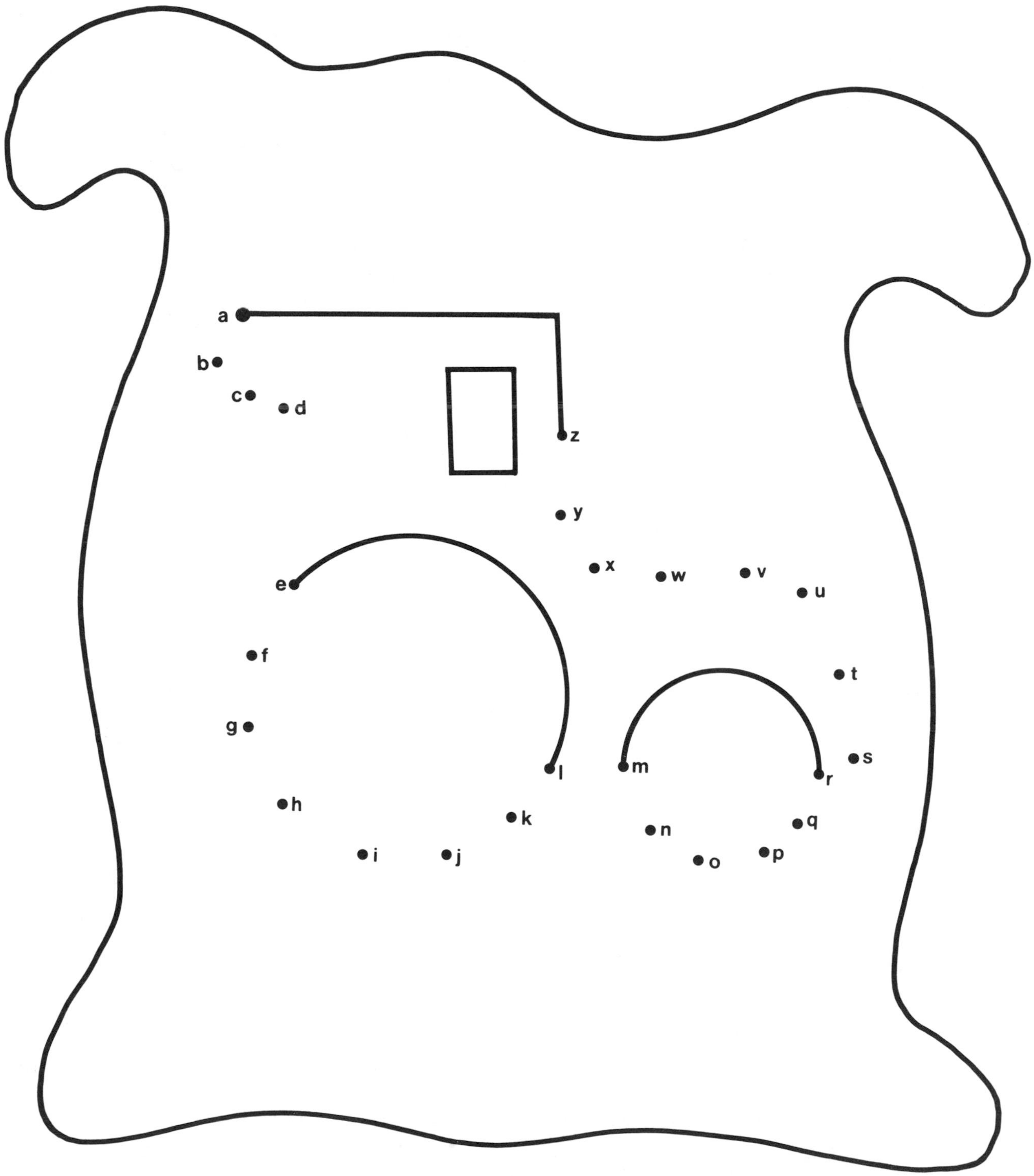

Name ______________________________ 4-6

CHRISTMAS EVE MAZE

Directions: Rudolph is hiding from Santa. Help Santa find him so they can begin delivering toys. Draw a line from Santa through the Christmas words.

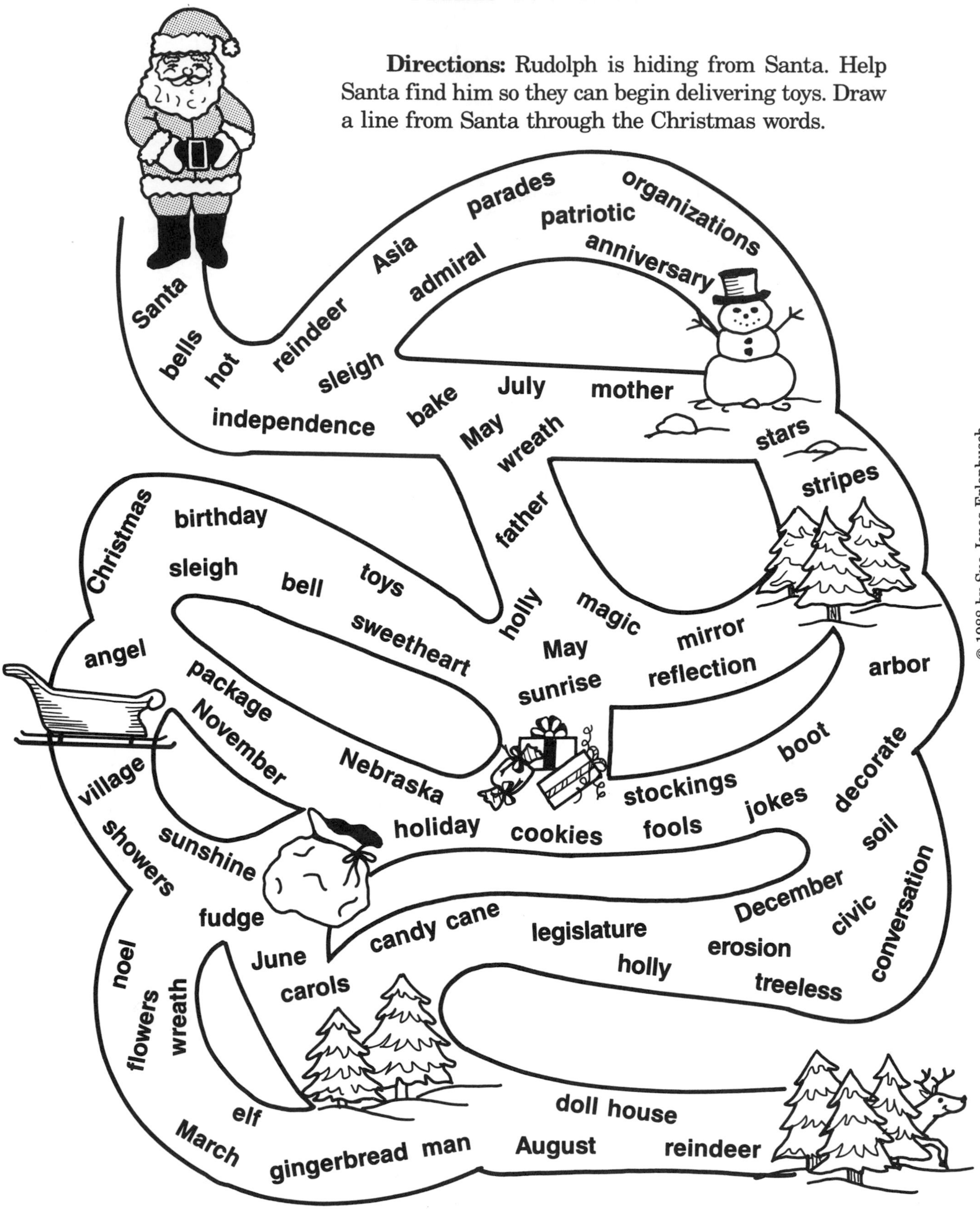

Name ______________________________

CHRISTMAS MAZE

Directions: Mrs. Santa has lost her Christmas pudding. Help her find it by drawing a line from her through the Christmas words.

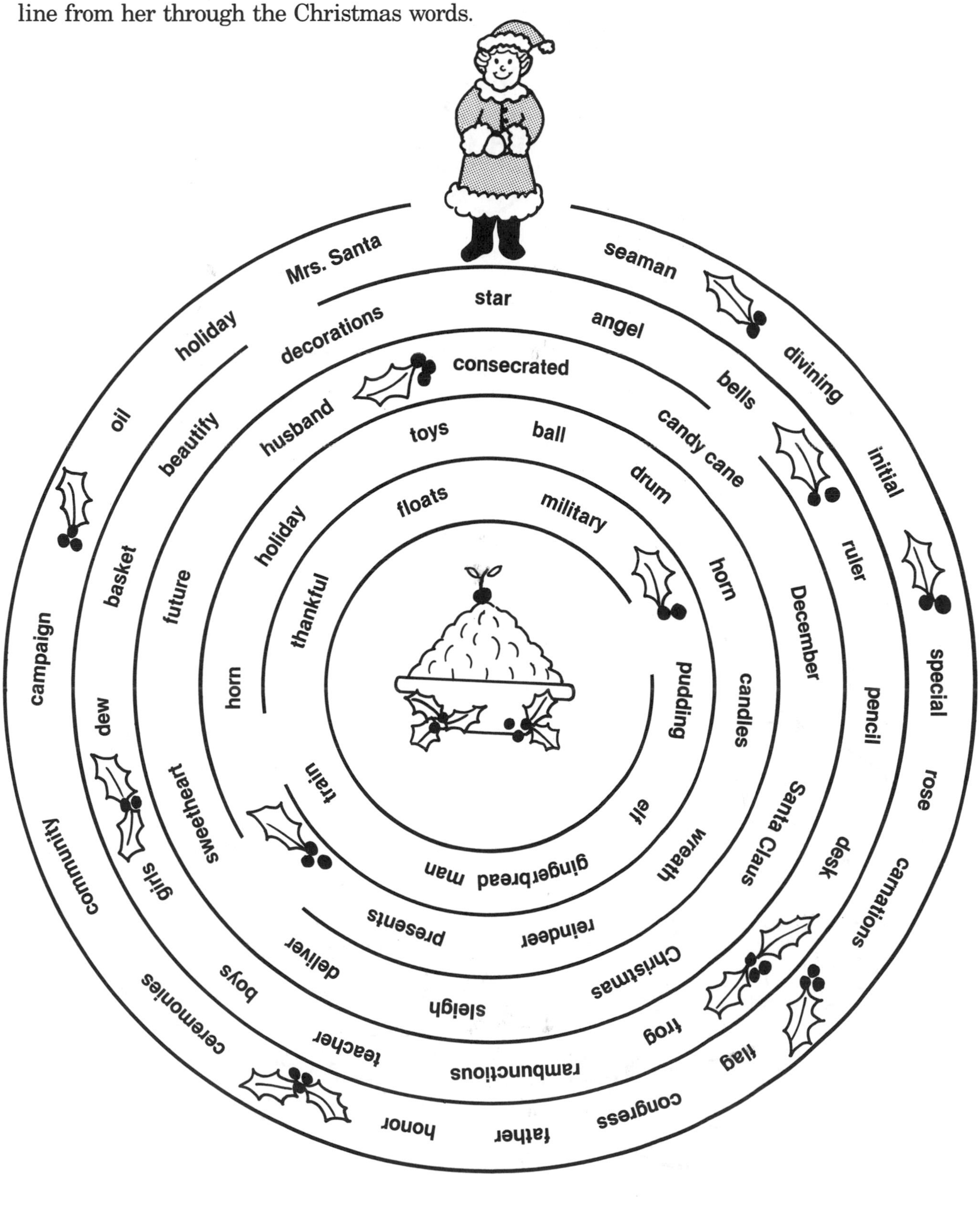

CHRISTMAS PUZZLE

Directions: Color all food words blue. Color all the toy words green. Color all the animal words red.

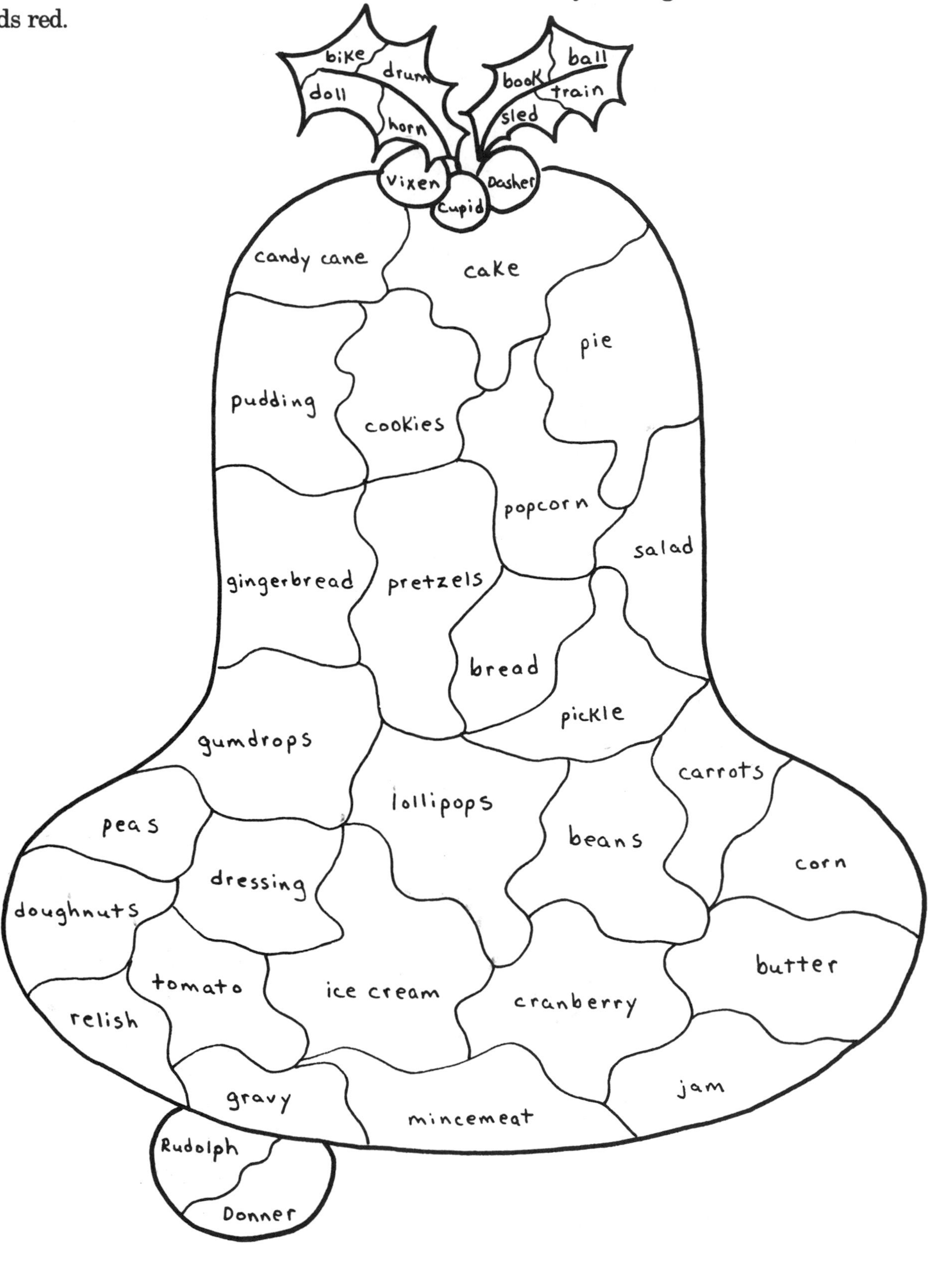

Name ______________________________

CHRISTMAS MATCH

Directions: Draw a line to match the pictures to the correct words.

Santa Claus

sleigh

Christmas stocking

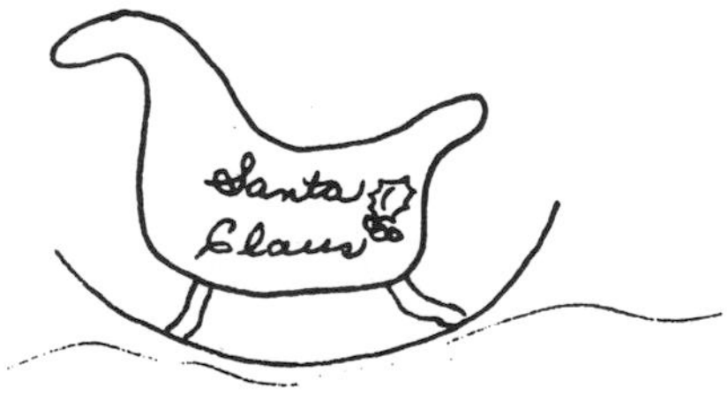

Christmas tree

candle

Name ______________________________

A CHRISTMAS WISH

Directions: Draw five things that you want for Christmas. Label and color each picture.

Name ______________________________

CHRISTMAS WORD HUNT

Directions: Circle the hidden words. You may go across and down.

c	a	r	o	l	k	m	o	z	b	p
h	o	l	l	y	u	s	t	j	e	r
r	e	d	k	q	c	a	n	d	l	e
i	x	r	s	t	a	r	u	w	k	s
s	a	c	a	n	d	y	c	a	n	e
t	d	b	n	o	c	s	n	o	w	n
m	e	f	t	e	h	i	g	i	f	t
a	g	m	a	l	t	b	e	l	l	s
s	t	o	c	k	i	n	g	k	l	o
j	n	p	c	o	o	k	i	e	s	q
t	r	e	e	r	s	f	u	d	g	e

SH! IT'S A SECRET!

Directions: Use the following code to learn the secret. Write the letters on the correct lines.

A	B	C	D	E	F	G	H	I	J	K	L	M
1	2	3	4	5	6	7	8	9	10	11	12	13
N	O	P	Q	R	S	T	U	V	W	X	Y	Z
14	15	16	17	18	19	20	21	22	23	24	25	26

4 15 14 ' 20   6 15 18 7 5 20   20 15

___ ___ ___'___   ___ ___ ___ ___ ___ ___   ___ ___

12 5 1 22 5   1   16 12 1 20 5

___ ___ ___ ___ ___   ___   ___ ___ ___ ___ ___

15 6   3 15 15 11 9 5 19   6 15 18

___ ___   ___ ___ ___ ___ ___ ___ ___   ___ ___ ___

19 1 14 20 1

___ ___ ___ ___ ___!

Name ______________________________

CHRISTMAS CONSONANT PUZZLE

Directions: Fill in the missing consonants.

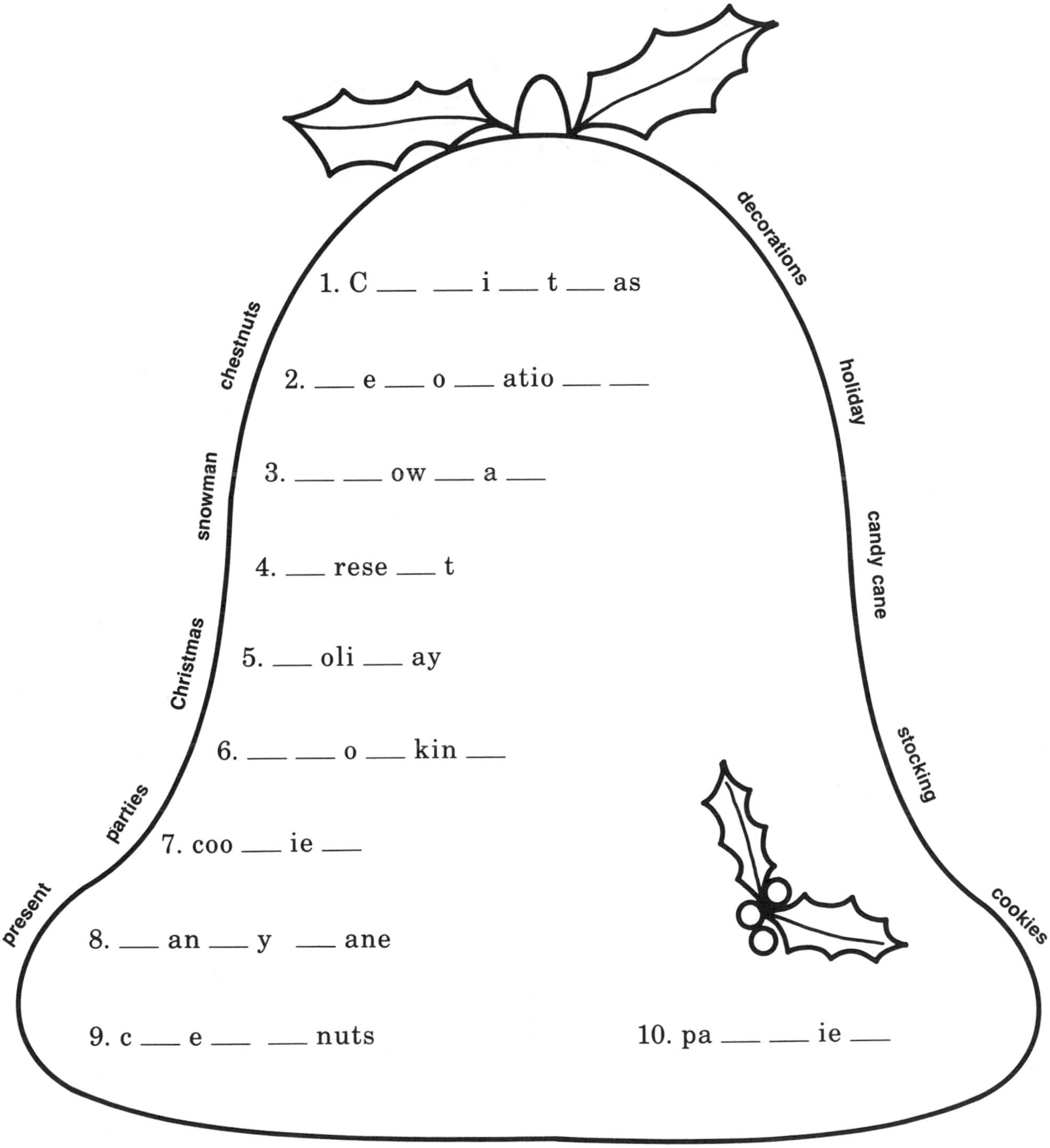

1. C ___ ___ i ___ t ___ as
2. ___ e ___ o ___ atio ___ ___
3. ___ ___ ow ___ a ___
4. ___ rese ___ t
5. ___ oli ___ ay
6. ___ ___ o ___ kin ___
7. coo ___ ie ___
8. ___ an ___ y ___ ane
9. c ___ e ___ ___ nuts
10. pa ___ ___ ie ___

Name ______________________

CHRISTMAS VOWEL PUZZLE

Directions: Fill in the missing vowels.

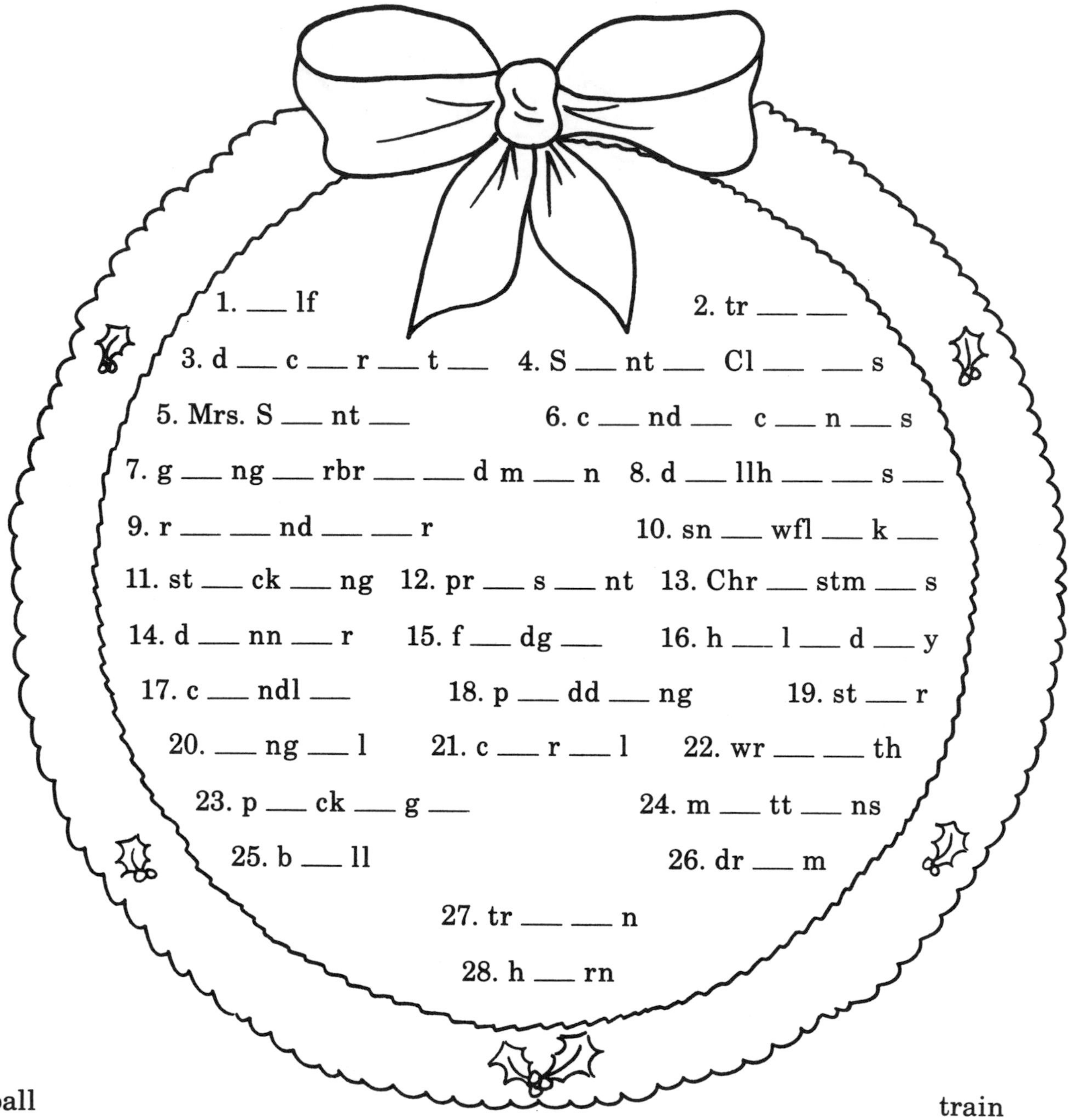

1. ___ lf
2. tr ___ ___
3. d ___ c ___ r ___ t ___
4. S ___ nt ___ Cl ___ ___ s
5. Mrs. S ___ nt ___
6. c ___ nd ___ c ___ n ___ s
7. g ___ ng ___ rbr ___ ___ d m ___ n
8. d ___ llh ___ ___ s ___
9. r ___ ___ nd ___ ___ r
10. sn ___ wfl ___ k ___
11. st ___ ck ___ ng
12. pr ___ s ___ nt
13. Chr ___ stm ___ s
14. d ___ nn ___ r
15. f ___ dg ___
16. h ___ l ___ d ___ y
17. c ___ ndl ___
18. p ___ dd ___ ng
19. st ___ r
20. ___ ng ___ l
21. c ___ r ___ l
22. wr ___ ___ th
23. p ___ ck ___ g ___
24. m ___ tt ___ ns
25. b ___ ll
26. dr ___ m
27. tr ___ ___ n
28. h ___ rn

ball
tree
gingerbread man
decorate
horn
stocking
Christmas

snowflake
carol
Santa Claus
doll house
reindeer

mittens
angel
candle
candy canes

elf
pudding
dinner
holiday
package

train
fudge
Mrs. Santa
present
wreath
drum
star

Name ______________________________

CHRISTMAS WORD SCRAMBLE

Directions: Unscramble the words. Write the unscrambled words in the correct place.

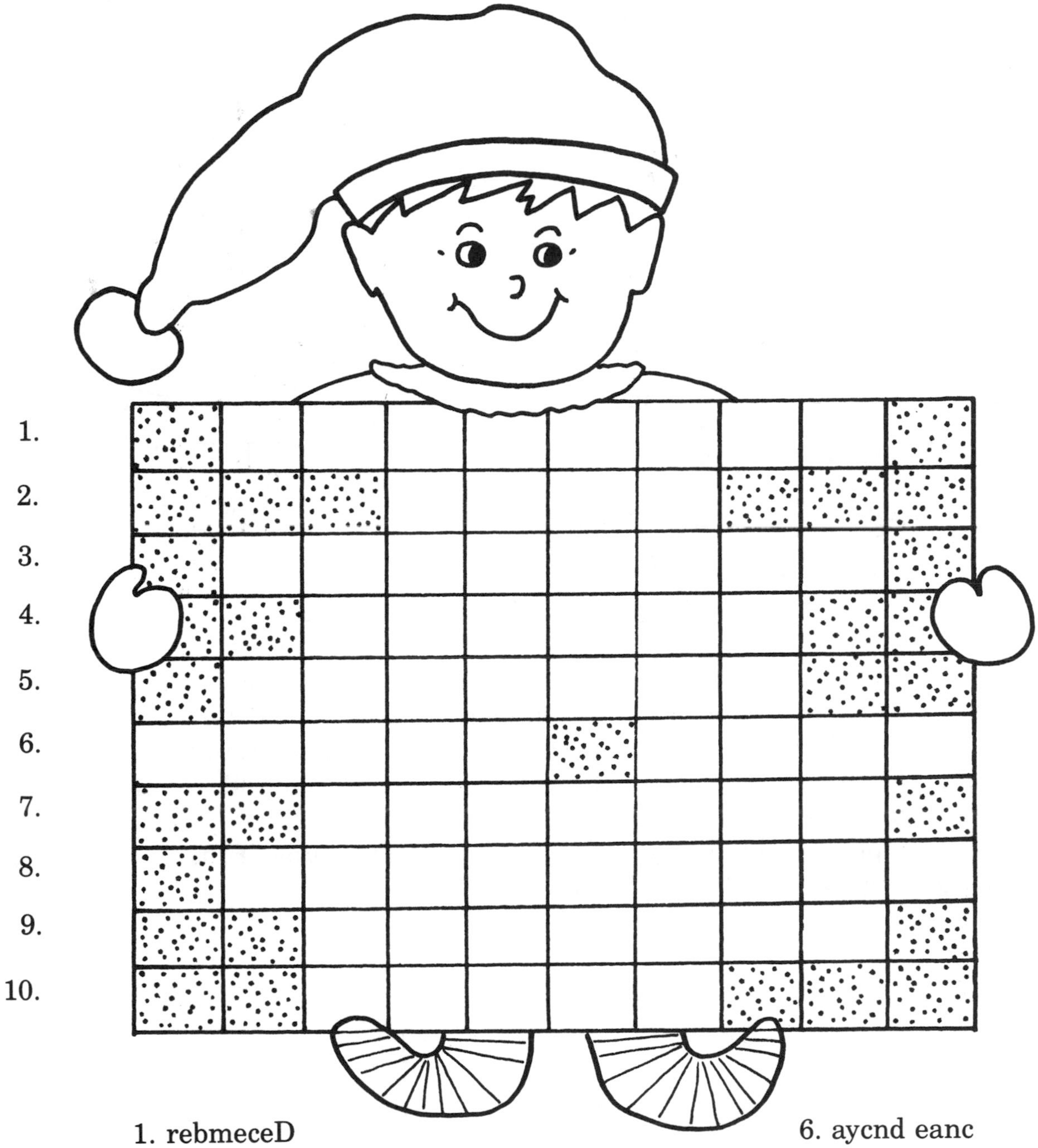

1. rebmeceD
2. erte
3. eoaedcrt
4. ehlgsi
5. namwosn
6. aycnd eanc
7. yoialhd
8. ssatihCrm
9. ateprsi
10. atSna

Name ________________________________

WHO NEEDS IT?

Directions: Circle the word in each sentence that isn't needed. Write the words that you circled in the correct boxes below. Does a message appear?

1. Mr. and Mrs. Merry Santa Claus live at the North Pole.
2. Little Christmas elves help them make toys for good little girls and boys.
3. Mrs. Santa Claus loves to bake cookies and boys decorate the Christmas tree.
4. On Christmas Eve, Mr. and Mrs. Santa Claus and and all the elves fill the sleigh.
5. Rudolph's bright, shiny, red nose helps girls guide Blitzen, Comet, Cupid, Dancer, Dasher, Donner, Prancer, and Vixen.

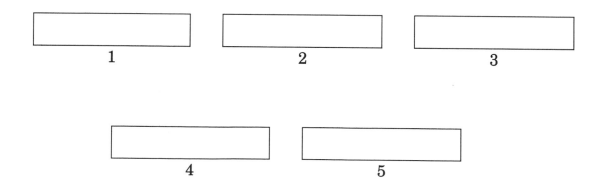

1	2	3
4	5	

Name ______________________________

MAKE A WORD

Directions: Use the letters in the word "Christmas" to make as many different words as possible.

CHRISTMAS

______	______	______
______	______	______
______	______	______
______	______	______
______	______	______
______	______	______
______	______	______
______	______	______
______	______	______
______	______	______
______	______	______
______	______	______

Name ______________________________

A LETTER TO SANTA

Directions: Complete the letter.

Dear Santa:

I have tried to be very good this year. Would you please bring me ________

____

____

____

____

____

____

____

____

____

____

I will leave some milk and cookies for you. Thanks, Santa

Your friend,

____

Name ________________________________

A CHRISTMAS STORY

Directions: Complete the story. Illustrate your story in the space below.

On Christmas Eve, Susie, Freddy, and Ricky, were upstairs sleeping, when suddenly they were awakened by ____

____

____

____

____

____

____

____

____

____

____

____

____

Name ________________________

WHAT'S COOKING?

Oh! Someone has erased the name of the recipe and scrambled the ingredients. Can you help me?

Directions: First, unscramble the ingredients. Then, write the name of the recipe on the line.

Recipe: ________________________

1½	cups	guras	________
3¼	cups	loruf	________
⅔	cup	trebut	________
2		gesg	________
2½	teaspoons	kanbgi woprde	________
2	tablespoons	lkim	________
1	teaspoon	laivlan	________
½	teaspoon	lats	________

Place ingredients in a large bowl and beat until well mixed. Roll out and cut with Christmas cookie cutters. Bake at 400 degrees for 8 minutes. Makes 4 dozen.

Name ______________________________

SAINT NICHOLAS

Directions: Fill in the blanks with words from the wooden shoes.

Saint Nicholas was a (1) ____________________ who lived in Asia Minor in the fourth century. He is the patron (2) ____________________ of children.

Many legends tell of his (3) ____________________. One story tells how he gave a bag of gold as a (4) ____________________ to each of three poor sisters so they could be married. The (5) ____________________ in Saint Nicholas as a giver of gifts was developed from such legends.

Many countries in (6) ____________________ observe December 6, the date of his death, as a special holiday. On December 5, Saint Nicholas Eve, many European children fill their (7) ____________________ with straw for Saint Nicholas' (8) ____________________ and leave the shoes by the (9) ____________________. They believe that after the horse eats the (10) ____________________, Saint Nicholas will fill their shoes with (11) ____________________ and goodies.

The name Santa Claus comes from the (12) ____________________ Sinterklaas, which is Dutch for Saint Nicholas.

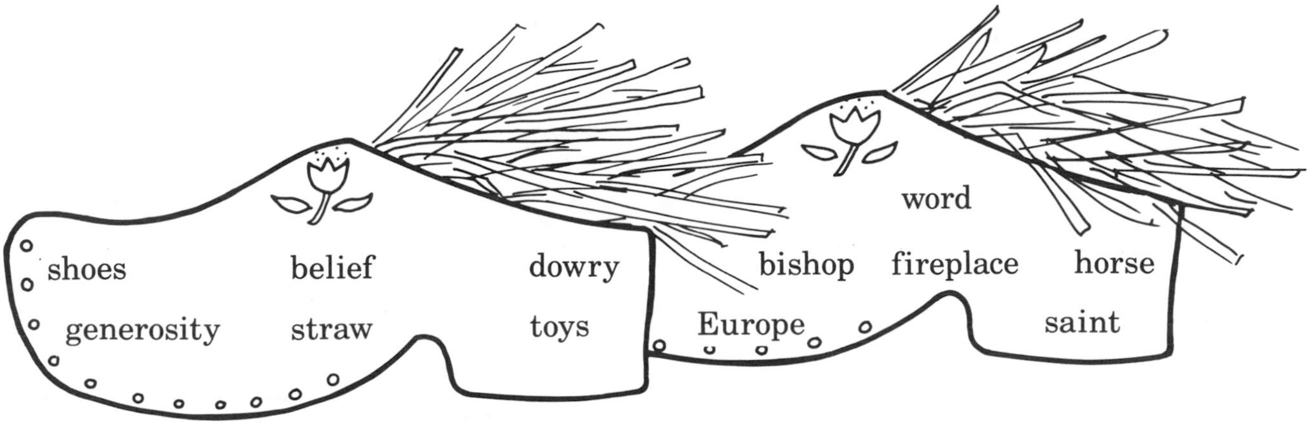

Name ______________________________

CHRISTMAS

Directions: Fill in the blanks with words from the stocking.

For Christians, Christmas is the most important (1) ________________ of the year. It is the (2) __________________ of the birth of Jesus Christ. Churches hold special (3) ________________ for this joyful occasion.

Many churches display a nativity (4) __________________ and decorate with evergreen branches and red poinsettias. Green and red are the (5) ______________ colors used for Christmas decorations. Green symbolizes eternal life through Christ and red the blood shed by Jesus when he was crucified.

At home, people (6) ____________________ using a nativity scene, greenery, poinsettias, mistletoe, wreaths, candles, and special (7) _________________ for the Christmas tree. In addition to decorating their homes, people buy and (8) _________ gifts, bake cookies and (9) ____________________, go caroling, send Christmas (10) ______________, hang (11) ______________ for Santa to fill, give or attend (12) ________________, and prepare a large Christmas (13) _________________ to share with (14) ________________ and friends. It's no wonder that Christmas is the busiest and (15) _______________________ time of the year for both children and (16) _______________.

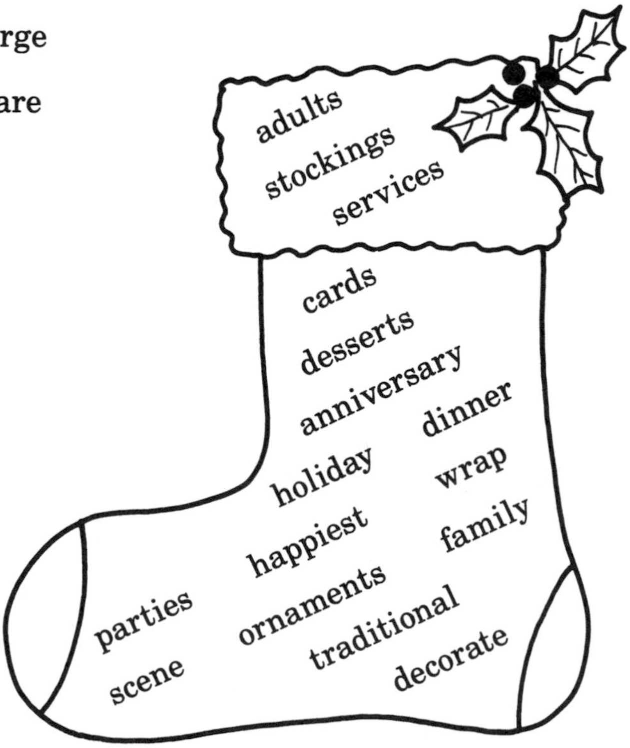

Name ______________________________

WORD HUNT

Directions: Circle the hidden words. You may go across and down.

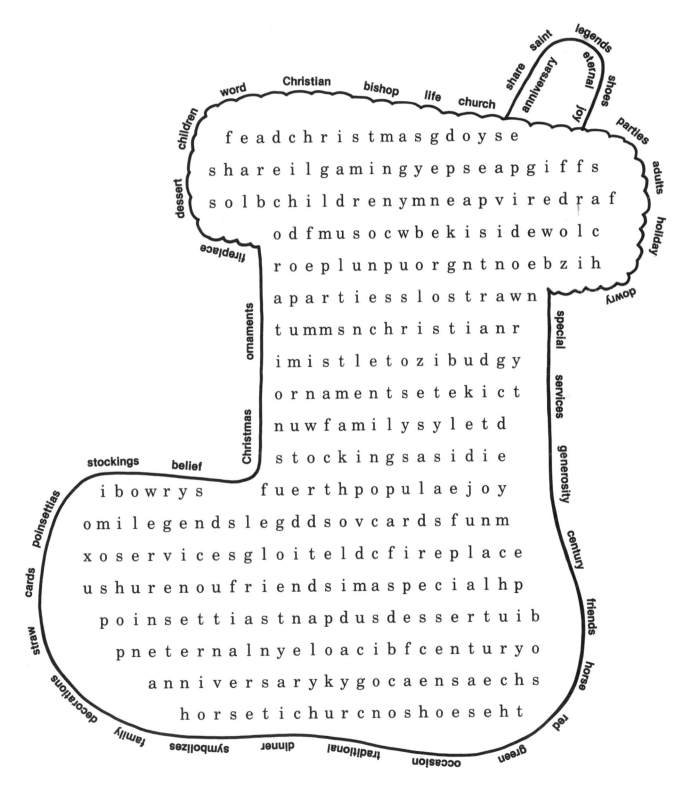

f e a d c h r i s t m a s g d o y s e
s h a r e i l g a m i n g y e p s e a p g i f f s
s o l b c h i l d r e n y m n e a p v i r e d r a f
o d f m u s o c w b e k i s i d e w o l c
r o e p l u n p u o r g n t n o e b z i h
a p a r t i e s s l o s t r a w n
t u m m s n c h r i s t i a n r
i m i s t l e t o z i b u d g y
o r n a m e n t s e t e k i c t
n u w f a m i l y s y l e t d
s t o c k i n g s a s i d i e
i b o w r y s f u e r t h p o p u l a e j o y
o m i l e g e n d s l e g d d s o v c a r d s f u n m
x o s e r v i c e s g l o i t e l d c f i r e p l a c e
u s h u r e n o u f r i e n d s i m a s p e c i a l h p
p o i n s e t t i a s t n a p d u s d e s s e r t u i b
p n e t e r n a l n y e l o a c i b f c e n t u r y o
a n n i v e r s a r y k y g o c a e n s a e c h s
h o r s e t i c h u r c n o s h o e s e h t

children
word
Christian
bishop
life
church
share
saint
anniversary
legends
eternal
joy
shoes
parties
adults
holiday
dowry
special
services
generosity
century
friends
horse
red
green
occasion
traditional
dinner
symbolizes
family
decorations
straw
cards
poinsettias
stockings
belief
Christmas
ornaments
fireplace
dessert

HANUKKAH

Directions: Fill in the blanks with words from the menorah.

The (1) ________________ word "Hanukkah" means "dedication." Hanukkah is the Jewish Feast of Dedication or Feast of Lights. Hanukkah (2) ________________ on the twenty-fifth day of the Hebrew (3) ________________ of Kislev, which usually (4) ________________ in December. The festival lasts for (5) ________________ days.

Each evening during Hanukkah, one (6) ________________ candle is lighted on a special (7) ________________ called a "menorah." The ninth candle, called a "shammash," is used to light the others. This practice (8) ________________ the rededication of the Jewish temple. When the temple was being rededicated, only a small amount of (9) ________________ oil was found. Miraculously, this oil kept the (10) ________________________ lamps burning for eight days until new (11) ________________ could be consecrated.

Today, Hanukkah has taken on some of the popular Christmas (12) ____________. Homes are decorated, (13) ________________ meals are prepared, and gifts are (14) ________________.

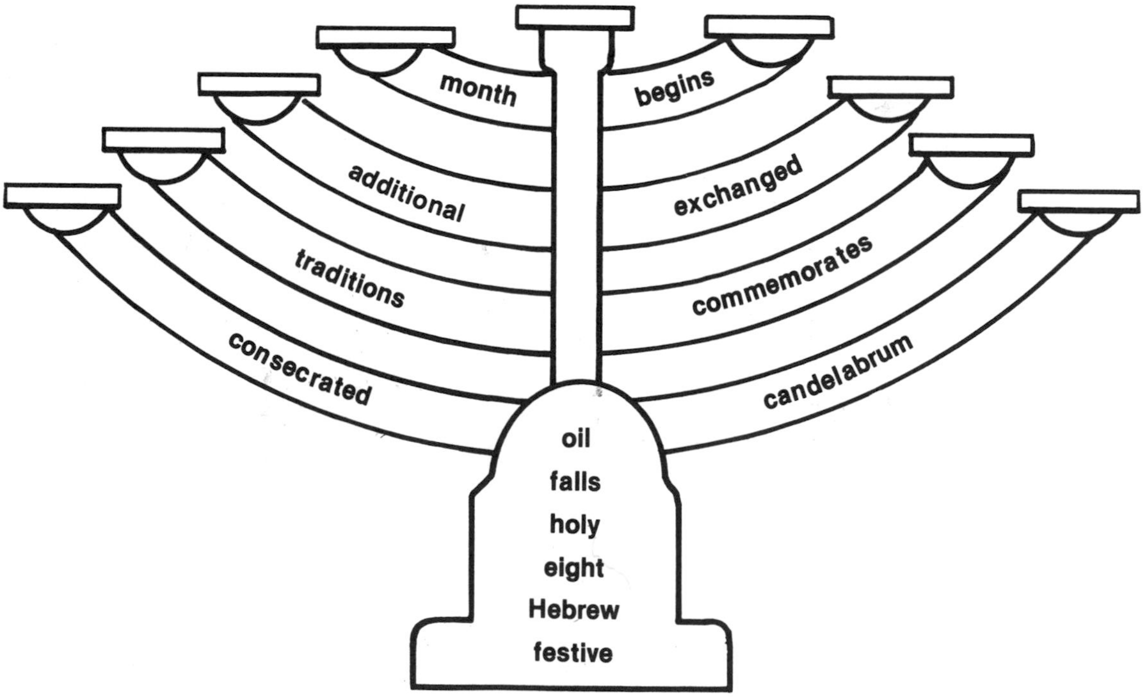

JANUARY

Superstars Bulletin Board • 129
Vocabulary • 129
Game Boards • 129

Activity Number and Title		Special Day
5-1	A Picture to Color	New Year's Day
5-2	Find the Hidden Mitten	New Year's Day
5-3	Same or Different	New Year's Day
5-4	Alphabet Scramble	New Year's Day
5-5	What Is It?	New Year's Day
5-6	The Hidden Sled	New Year's Day
5-7	Guess What	New Year's Day
5-8	New Year's Eve Puzzle	New Year's Day
5-9	Word Match	New Year's Day
5-10	Winter Fun	New Year's Day
5-11	Word Hunt	New Year's Day
5-12	Sh! It's a Secret!	New Year's Day
5-13	Missing Consonant Puzzle	New Year's Day
5-14	Missing Vowel Puzzle	New Year's Day
5-15	Make a Word	New Year's Eve
5-16	Make a Word	New Year's Day
5-17	Order! Order!	New Year's Day
5-18	The Snowball Fight	New Year's Day
5-19	Snow	New Year's Day
5-20	Ice	New Year's Day
5-21	Martin Luther King, Jr. Day	Martin Luther King, Jr. Day
5-22	Martin Luther King, Jr. Word Hunt	Martin Luther King, Jr. Day

Superstars Bulletin Board

A good way to fight the January "blahs" is to make a Superstars bulletin board. Cover a large bulletin board with stars of various shapes and sizes. Make some of the stars large enough to act as a background for a story starter activity sheet and a photograph of the student who did the sheet. Your Superstars bulletin board might look like the one shown here.

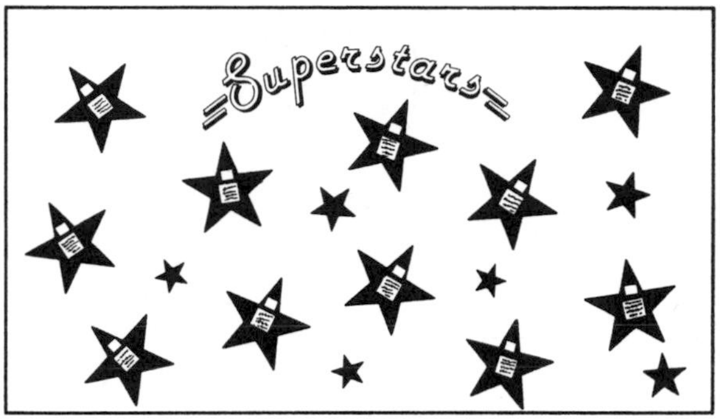

Vocabulary

The following two word lists will help develop your students' vocabularies in January.

New Year's Day Word List

party	happy
snowman	month
mitten	ice
snowballs	sparkle
January	warmest
holiday	confetti
season	slipped
new	sled
glove	fall
resolution	year

Martin Luther King, Jr. Day Word List

social	methods
born	equality
political	assassinated
prize	nonviolent
peace	civil
leader	efforts
national	great
birthday	honor
holiday	black
economic	believed

Game Boards

Here are two game board patterns for you to use in January. For the bingo style game board, don't forget to arrange the words on the other cards in a different order.

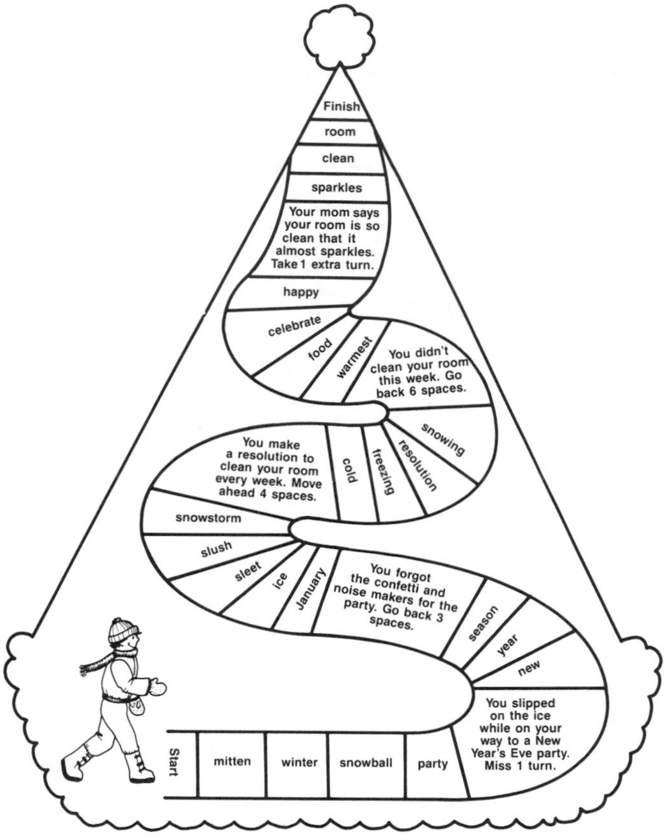

party	new	ice	month	social
glove	civil	mitten	black	sparkle
peace	snowballs		leader	confetti
sled	happy	glove	honor	prize
year	efforts	great	holiday	January

Name ______________________________

A PICTURE TO COLOR

Directions: Use the color chart below to help you color the picture.

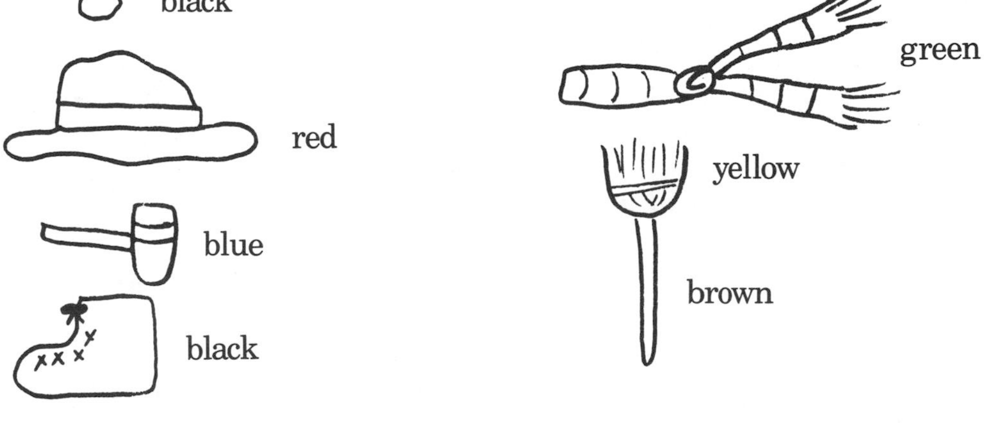

Name ______________________________

FIND THE HIDDEN MITTEN

Directions: Find the hidden mitten and circle it. Color the picture.

Name ________________________________

SAME OR DIFFERENT

Directions: Look at the word on the left. Circle the word on the right that is like the one on the left.

winter	wintur	winter	wintre	wintor
mittens	mitten	mittuns	mittons	mittens
snowman	snowman	snowmen	snuwman	snowmon
sled	sleb	sled	slede	seld
gloves	gluves	glove	gloves	glovs
first	first	frost	frist	flirst
month	munth	monch	minth	month
January	Janary	January	Junuary	Januree
season	seeson	seasun	season	seasons
snowballs	snowball	snowbals	snuwballs	snowballs

ALPHABET SCRAMBLE

Directions: Write the letters of the alphabet in the correct order. Some of the letters have already been filled in for you.

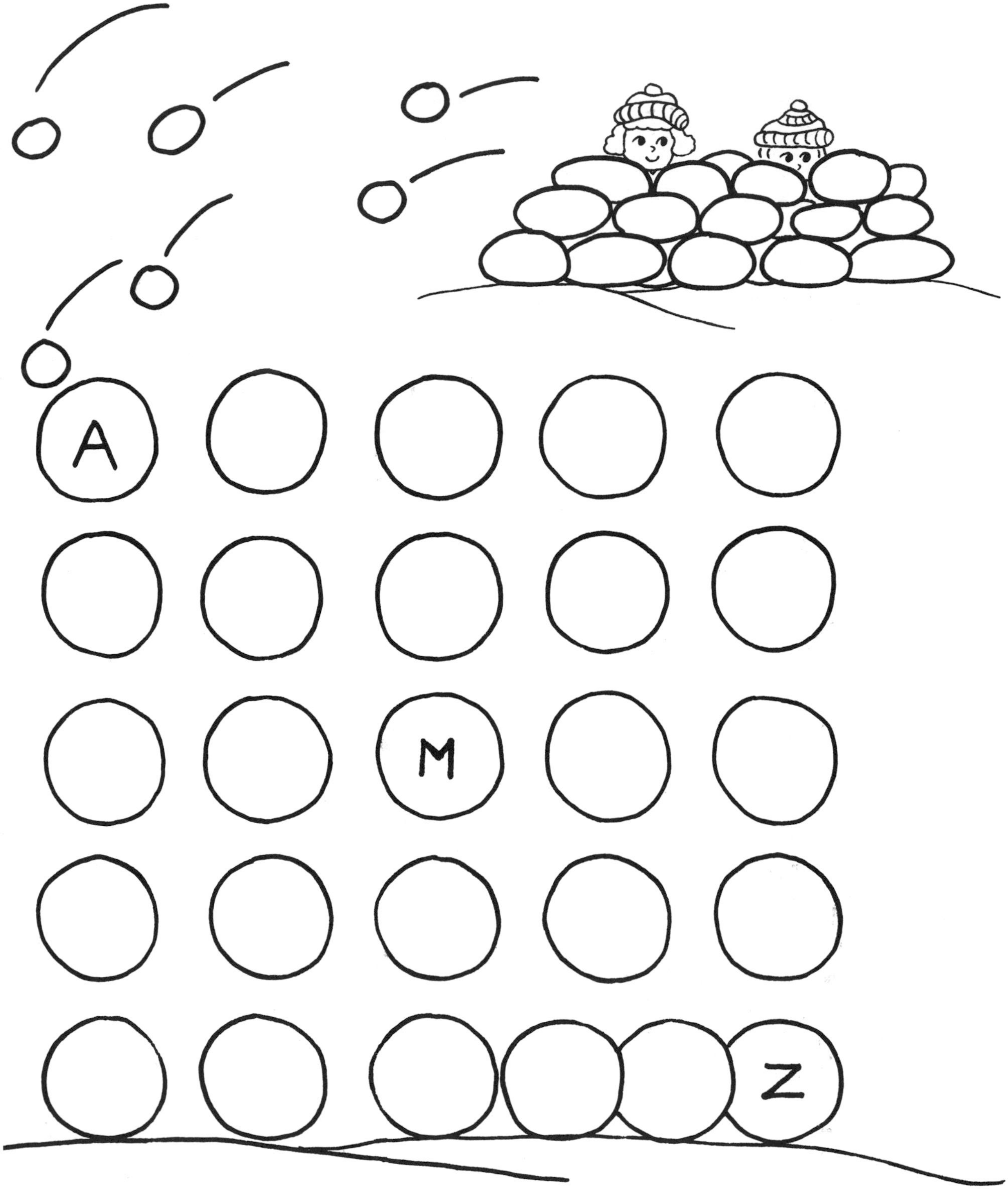

Name ______________________________

WHAT IS IT?

Directions: Connect the dots to find out what is in the picture. Start with the first letter of the alphabet.

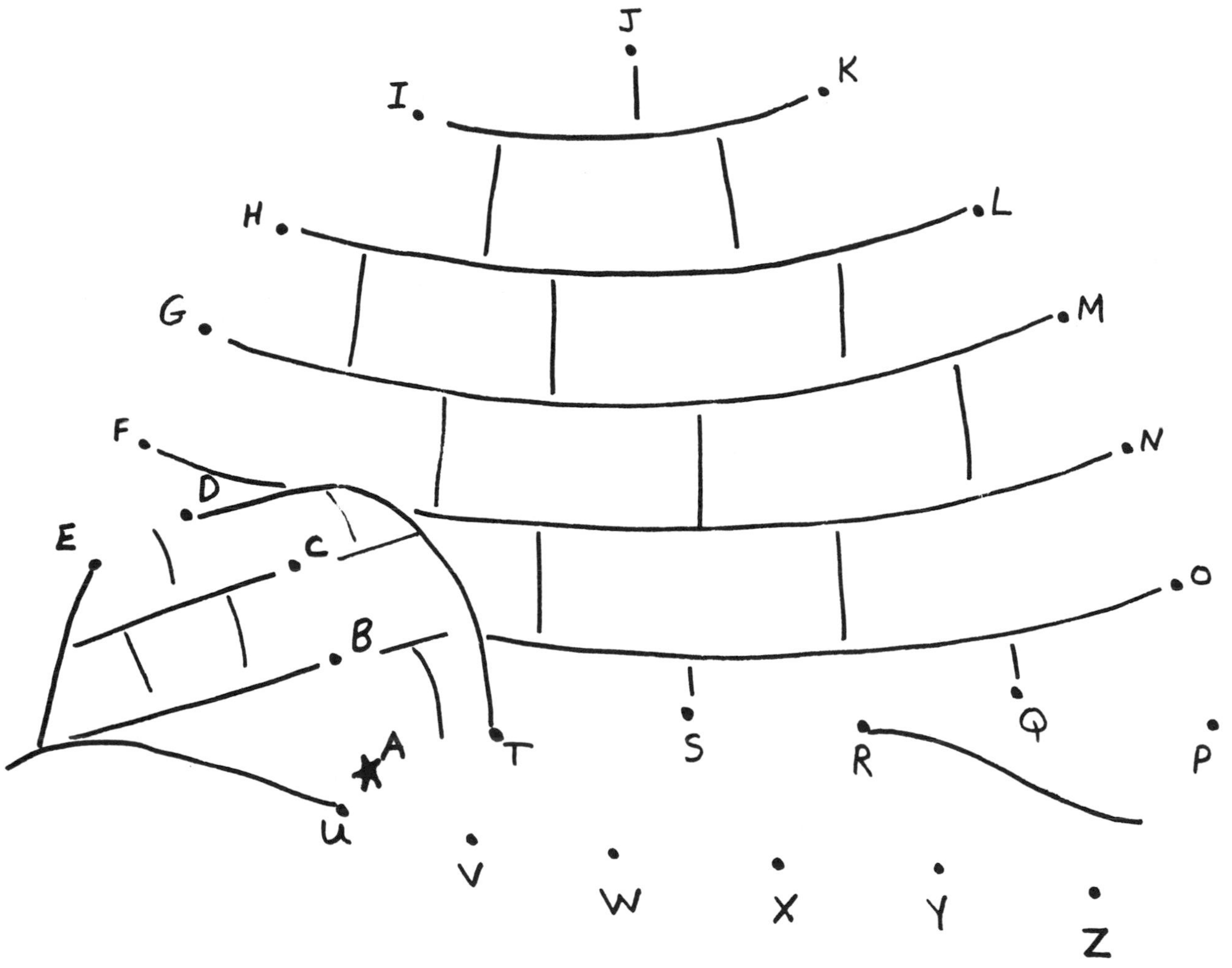

THE HIDDEN SLED

Directions: Help Freddy find his sled by drawing a line from him through the January words.

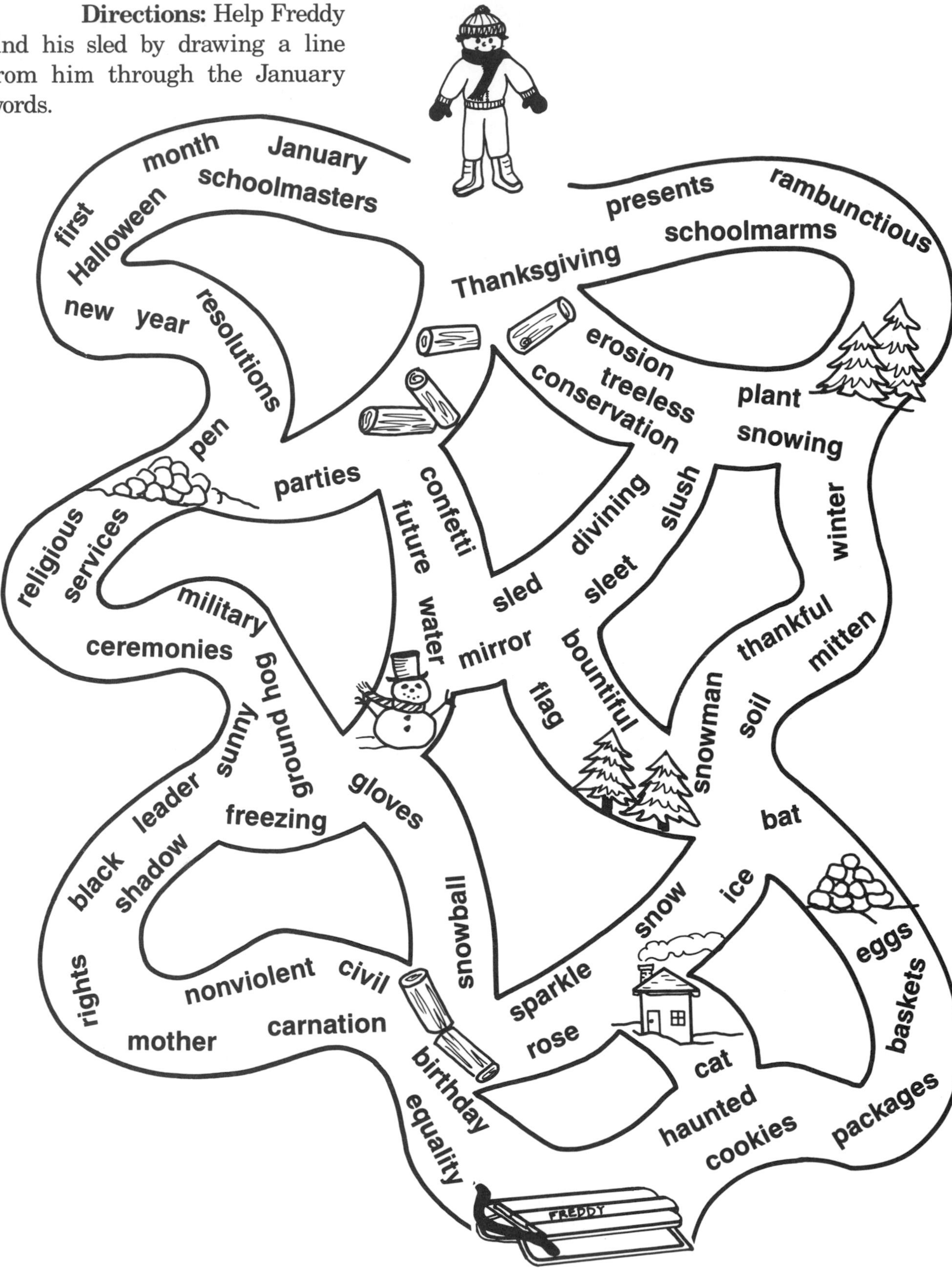

GUESS WHAT

Directions: Susie lost something. Help her find this item by following the maze to the first letter of the alphabet. Then connect the letters in order. Now you have a picture of what Susie lost.

Name ____________________

NEW YEAR'S EVE PUZZLE

Directions: Color the vowels yellow. Color the consonants blue.

Name ______________________________

WORD MATCH

Directions: Draw a line to match the pictures to the correct words.

party hat

mitten

snowballs

snowman

sled

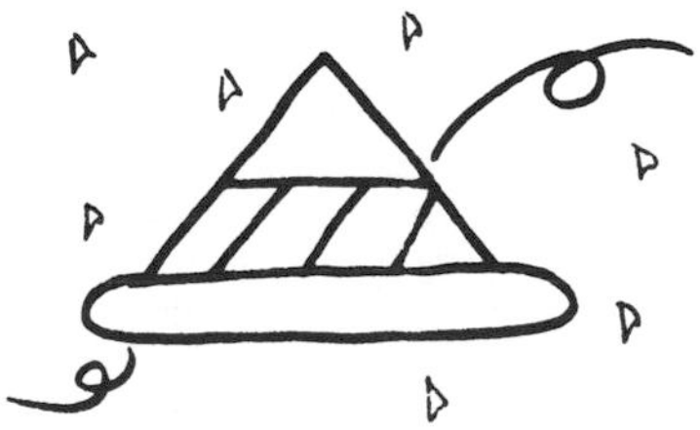

football

Name ____________________

WINTER FUN

Directions: Draw and color six things that you think are fun to do in the winter.

Name ______________________________

WORD HUNT

Directions: Circle the hidden words. You may go across and down.

a	m	n	o	v	e	m	b	e	r	j	s	t
u	w	o	c	t	o	b	e	r	a	u	a	h
f	e	b	r	u	a	r	y	i	p	l	t	u
r	d	e	c	e	m	b	e	r	r	y	u	r
i	n	a	u	g	u	s	t	r	i	t	r	s
d	e	s	u	n	d	a	y	l	l	m	d	d
a	s	e	p	t	e	m	b	e	r	a	a	a
y	d	x	n	p	j	a	n	u	a	r	y	y
m	a	v	q	s	u	y	i	g	h	c	e	d
i	y	f	m	o	n	d	a	y	j	h	k	l
s	u	n	t	u	e	s	d	a	y	m	u	a

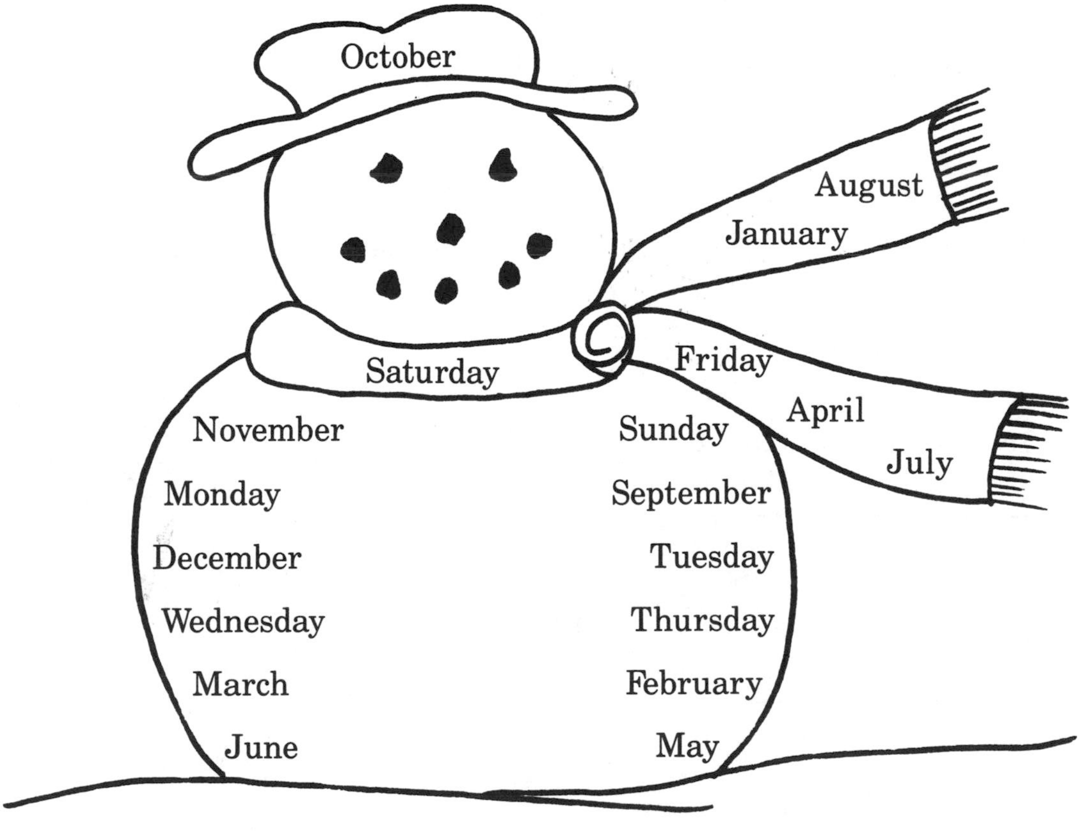

Name ______________________________

SH! IT'S A SECRET!

Directions: Use the following code to learn the secret. Write the letters on the correct line.

A	B	C	D	E	F	G	H	I	J	K	L	M
1	2	3	4	5	6	7	8	9	10	11	12	13
N	O	P	Q	R	S	T	U	V	W	X	Y	Z
14	15	16	17	18	19	20	21	22	23	24	25	26

10 1 14 21 1 18 25 / 9 19 / 20 8 5

___ ___ ___ ___ ___ ___ ___   ___ ___   ___ ___ ___

6 9 18 19 20 / 13 15 14 20 8 / 15 6

___ ___ ___ ___ ___   ___ ___ ___ ___ ___   ___ ___

20 8 5 / 25 5 1 18 / 9 20 / 9 19

___ ___ ___   ___ ___ ___ ___.   ___ ___   ___ ___

15 14 5 / 15 6 / 20 8 5

___ ___ ___   ___ ___   ___ ___ ___

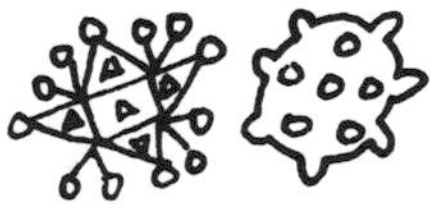

23 9 14 20 5 18 / 13 15 14 20 8 19

___ ___ ___ ___ ___ ___   ___ ___ ___ ___ ___ ___.

MISSING CONSONANT PUZZLE

Directions: Fill in the missing consonants.

1. ___ ___ o w
2. ___ o l ___
3. s ___ e ___
4. ___ ___ o ___ m a ___
5. ___ a ___ ___ y
6. ___ ___ o w f ___ a ___ e
7. ___ i ___ ___ e n
8. ___ a ___ u a ___ y
9. ___ o ___ ___ h
10. ___ ea ___ o ___

happy	year	snow	mitten
snowman	cold	season	January
new	snowflake	sleet	freezing
first	month	sled	fall

Name ________________________________

MISSING VOWEL PUZZLE

Directions: Fill in the missing vowels.

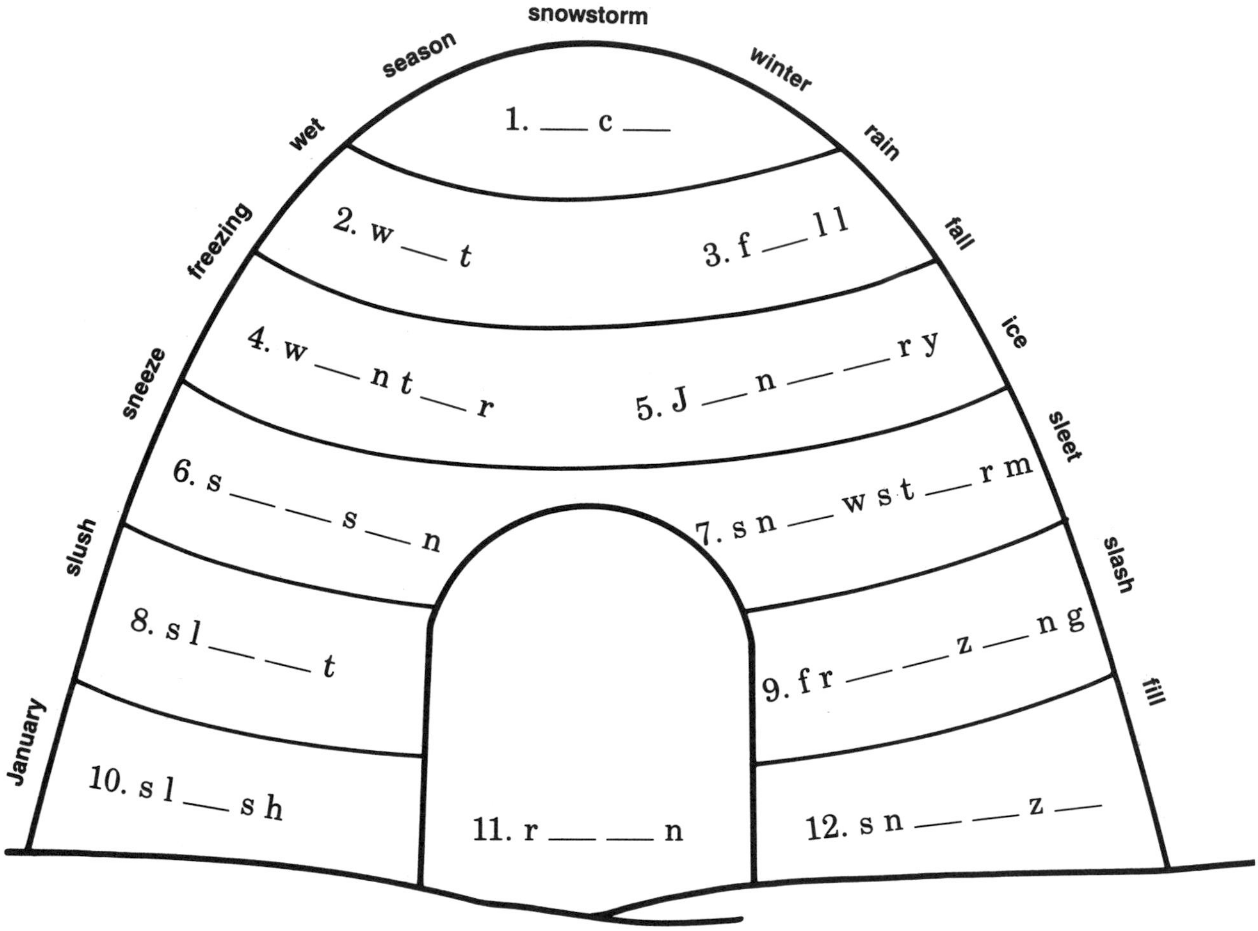

Name ________________________________

MAKE A WORD

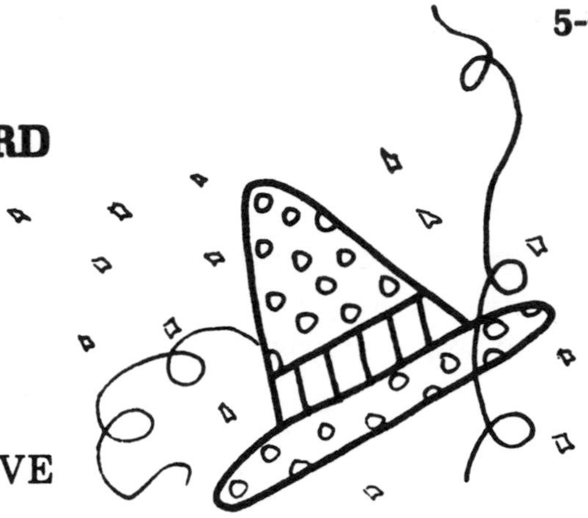

Directions: Use the letters in the words "New Year's Eve" to make as many different words as possible.

NEW YEAR'S EVE

Name ____________________

MAKE A WORD

Directions: Use the letters in the words "New Year's Day" to make as many different words as you can.

NEW YEAR'S DAY

ORDER! ORDER!

Directions: Write these special days in the correct order. The first one has been done for you.

New Year's Eve
Washington's Birthday
Fourth of July
Christmas
Easter Sunday
Memorial Day
Father's Day
April Fool's Day
New Year's Day

Mother's Day
Columbus Day
Labor Day
Halloween
St. Patrick's Day
Valentine's Day
Thanksgiving
Christmas Eve
Lincoln's Birthday

1. New Year's Eve
2. ____________________
3. ____________________
4. ____________________
5. ____________________
6. ____________________
7. ____________________
8. ____________________
9. ____________________
10. ____________________
11. ____________________
12. ____________________
13. ____________________
14. ____________________
15. ____________________
16. ____________________
17. ____________________
18. ____________________

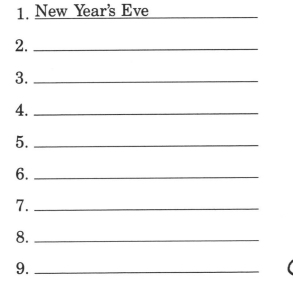

Name ______________________________

THE SNOWBALL FIGHT

Directions: Complete the story. Illustrate your story in the space below.

One day when I was walking home from school, I got hit in the back of the head with a snowball. I dropped my books and ______________________________

Name ______________________________

SNOW

Directions: Complete the story. Illustrate your story in the space below.

When it is snowing, I ______________________________

Name ______________________________

ICE

Directions: Complete the story. Illustrate your story in the space below.

One morning I looked out of the window and saw that everything was covered with ice. The sun made everything sparkle like magic. I got dressed in my warmest clothes and ______________________________

Name ______________________________

MARTIN LUTHER KING, JR. DAY

Directions: Fill in the blanks with words from the scroll.

Dr. Martin Luther King, Jr. was born on (1) ________________ 15, 1929. He was a civil (2) ________________ leader who believed in using nonviolent means to bring about social, political, and economic (3) ________________ for blacks. In 1964 he (4) ________________ the Nobel peace prize for his efforts.

Many (5) ________________ Americans did not agree with Dr. King's (6) ________________ methods. On April 4, 1968, Dr. King was (7) ________________ in Memphis, (8) ________________. Today, his birthday is (9) ________________ as a national holiday in order to honor a great leader.

assassinated	equality	won
celebrated	nonviolent	black
Tennessee	rights	
January		

Name ______________________________

MARTIN LUTHER KING, JR. WORD HUNT

Directions: Circle the hidden words. You may go across and down.

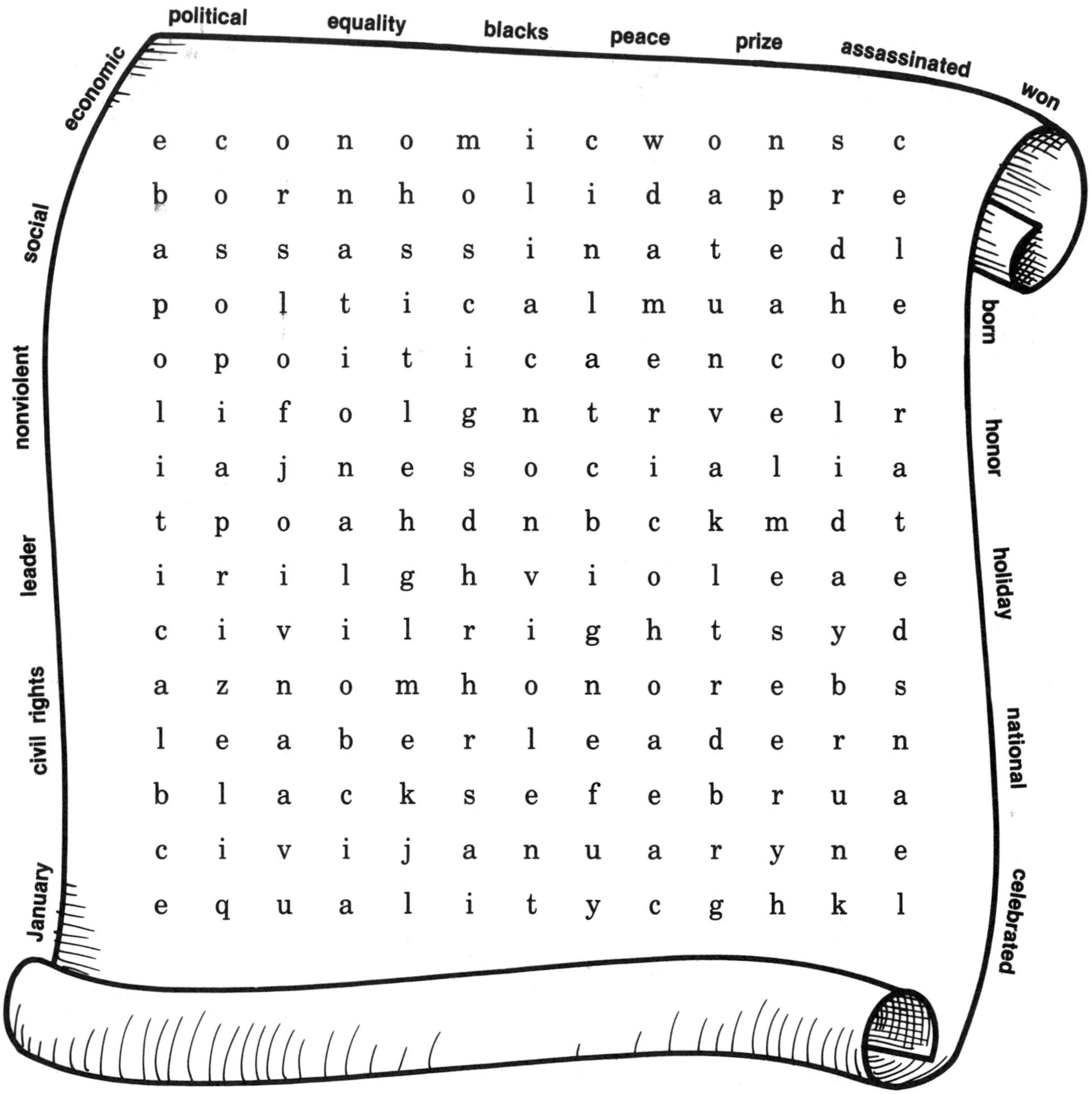

e	c	o	n	o	m	i	c	w	o	n	s	c
b	o	r	n	h	o	l	i	d	a	p	r	e
a	s	s	a	s	s	i	n	a	t	e	d	l
p	o	l	t	i	c	a	l	m	u	a	h	e
o	p	o	i	t	i	c	a	e	n	c	o	b
l	i	f	o	l	g	n	t	r	v	e	l	r
i	a	j	n	e	s	o	c	i	a	l	i	a
t	p	o	a	h	d	n	b	c	k	m	d	t
i	r	i	l	g	h	v	i	o	l	e	a	e
c	i	v	i	l	r	i	g	h	t	s	y	d
a	z	n	o	m	h	o	n	o	r	e	b	s
l	e	a	b	e	r	l	e	a	d	e	r	n
b	l	a	c	k	s	e	f	e	b	r	u	a
c	i	v	i	j	a	n	u	a	r	y	n	e
e	q	u	a	l	i	t	y	c	g	h	k	l

FEBRUARY

Activity Number and Title		Special Day
6-1	Groundhog Day	Groundhog Day
6-2	Groundhog Day Word Hunt	Groundhog Day
6-3	A Picture to Color	St. Valentine's Day
6-4	Same or Different	St. Valentine's Day
6-5	Alphabet Scramble	St. Valentine's Day
6-6	A Secret Pal	St. Valentine's Day
6-7	What Is It?	St. Valentine's Day
6-8	Valentine Maze	St. Valentine's Day
6-9	Valentine Maze	St. Valentine's Day
6-10	A Valentine Puzzle	St. Valentine's Day
6-11	Valentine Match	St. Valentine's Day
6-12	Word Hunt	St. Valentine's Day
6-13	Sh! It's a Secret!	St. Valentine's Day
6-14	Word Scramble	St. Valentine's Day
6-15	Make a Word	St. Valentine's Day
6-16	Valentine Puzzle	St. Valentine's Day
6-17	Sentence Completion	St. Valentine's Day
6-18	A Valentine Party	St. Valentine's Day
6-19	A Love Note	St. Valentine's Day
6-20	Surprise! Surprise!	St. Valentine's Day
6-21	A Love Potion	St. Valentine's Day
6-22	What's Cooking?	St. Valentine's Day
6-23	Saint Valentine	St. Valentine's Day
6-24	Love Lore	St. Valentine's Day
6-25	Abraham Lincoln	Lincoln's Birthday
6-26	Lincoln's Birthday	Lincoln's Birthday
6-27	George Washington	Washington's Birthday
6-28	Washington's Birthday	Washington's Birthday
6-29	Missing Consonant Puzzle	Washington's Birthday
6-30	Missing Vowel Puzzle	Washington's Birthday

A Heart Game

Make a "Broken Heart/Mended Heart" game for the Fun Box by cutting large red and pink hearts out of construction paper. Cut each heart into two separate puzzle pieces. On one half place a question about February, Saint Valentine, Groundhog Day, Abraham Lincoln, or George Washington. Place the answer on the other half of the broken heart. The student must answer each question correctly in order to mend the broken heart. The heart puzzle might look like the ones shown here.

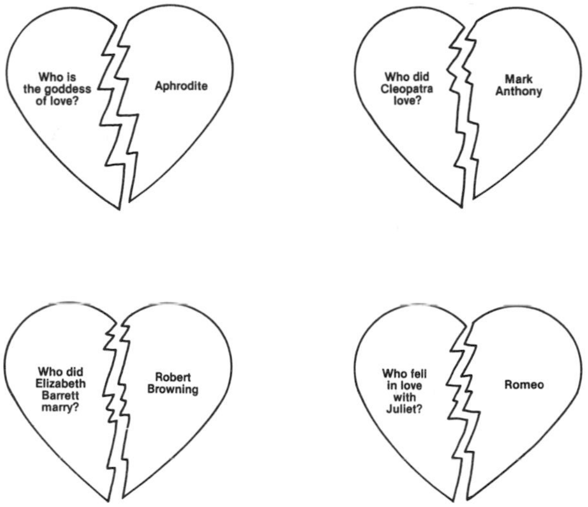

A Library Contest

Have a library contest to give students practice using the card catalog, encyclopedia, dictionary, atlas, almanac, and other reference materials. If you are planning to have the class spend an hour in the library working on the contest, you should have at least sixty questions prepared. Type the questions on a sheet of paper and cut it into strips so that only one question appears on each strip. Use one small box for the strips that are going to be handed out and another small box for holding the completed strips as they are handed in.

You can divide your class into teams or pit your class against another class. The winner is the team that answers the most questions correctly in the allotted time.

Here are some sample questions.

1. The Taj Mahal was built by a ruler in loving memory of his wife. Where is the Taj Mahal located? (India)
2. Who wrote *Romeo and Juliet*? (William Shakespeare)
3. Elizabeth Barrett Browning's most famous sonnet begins with "How do I love thee? Let me count the ways." This sonnet tells of her love for what person? (Robert Browning)

4. Barbara Cartland writes what kind of novel? Select the correct spelling: romanse, romance, romanese, romanes. (romance)
5. Who wrote *If This Is Love, I'll Take Spaghetti*? (Ellen Conford)
6. George Washington was born in 1732. When did he die? (1799)
7. How old was Abraham Lincoln when he was assassinated? (56 years old)
8. In what do groundhogs hibernate? Select the correct spelling: burrows, burros, barrows, barrels. (burrows)
9. What is the French word for "love"? Select the correct spelling: arroyo, armoire, armored, amour. (amour)

Vocabulary

The following five word lists will help develop your students' vocabularies in February.

Groundhog Day Word List	Valentine's Day Word List 1	Valentine's Day Word List 2
February	love	authorities
shadow	candy	truelove
legend	cards	dew
groundhog	party	pillow
spring	hearts	chant
early	February	rise
long	mailbox	husband
hibernate	pink	story
winter	friends	merged
cloudy	sweetheart	window
burrow	month	married
sleep	gift	dream
sunny	second	name
outside	flowers	future
weeks	true	destined
second	dear	legend
awakens	mailman	brave
supposed	kiss	sunrise
another	red	couples
according	notes	valentine

Lincoln's Birthday Word List	**Washington's Birthday Word List**
president	constitution
civil	confessed
inaugurated	army
born	truth
education	commander
firelight	wrote
schooling	chopped
formal	lie
farm	through
cabin	known
union	first
accomplished	trees
split	wonder
nation	convention
log	independence
fighting	revolutionary
chores	stories
preserve	famous
distances	elected
great	cherry

Game Boards

Here are two game board patterns for you to use in February. For the bingo style game board, don't forget to arrange the words on the other cards in a different order.

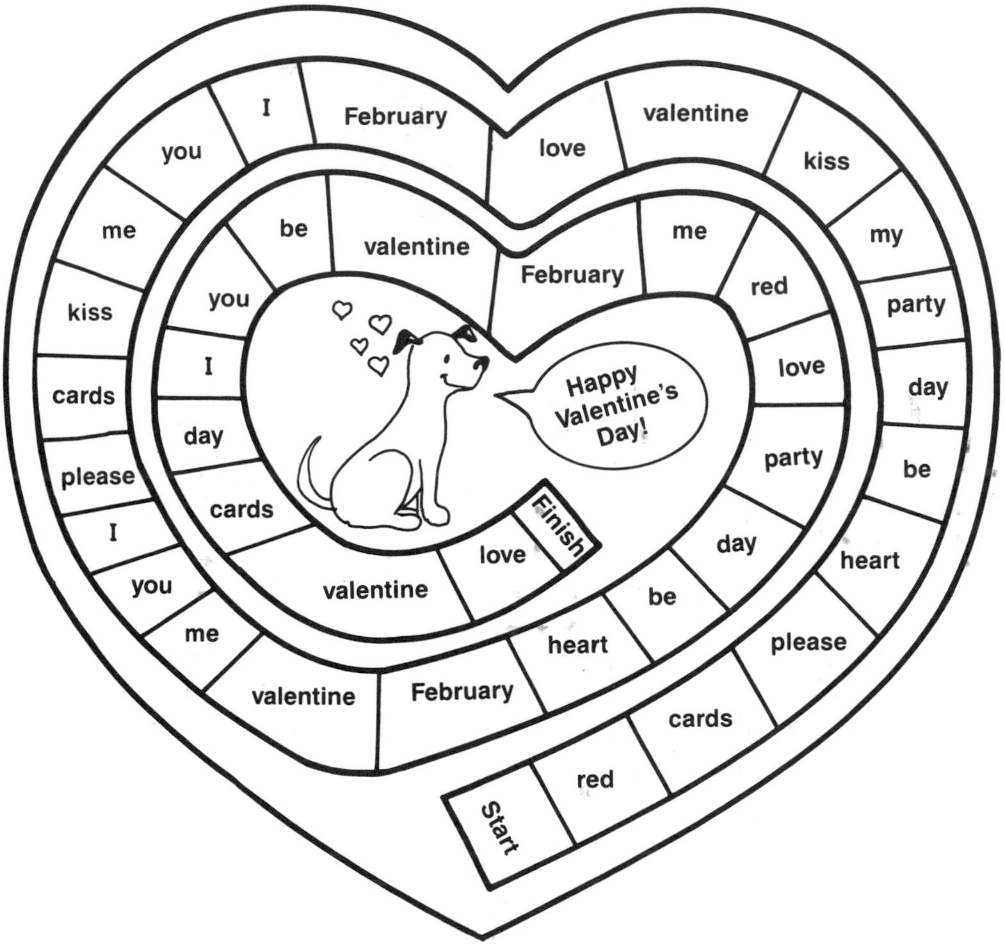

flowers	day	president	cards	February
be	you	heart	true	love
party	holidays		mine	sweet
United States	candy	month	red	me
please	second	valentine	my	kiss

Name ________________________________

GROUNDHOG DAY

Directions: Fill in the blanks with words from the sunglasses.

According to (1) ____________________, on the second day of February, the (2) ____________________ awakens from its (3) ____________________ winter (4) ______________________________ and comes out of its burrow to look for its (5) ______________. If the day is (6) ______________, it will see its shadow and go back in its (7) ______________________ to (8) ______________________ for another six weeks. This is supposed to mean that there will be six more weeks of (9) ______________. If the day is (10) ______________, it won't see its shadow and will stay outside. This means there will be an early (11) ________________.

Name ______________________________ 6-2

GROUNDHOG DAY WORD HUNT

Directions: Circle the hidden words. You may go across and down.

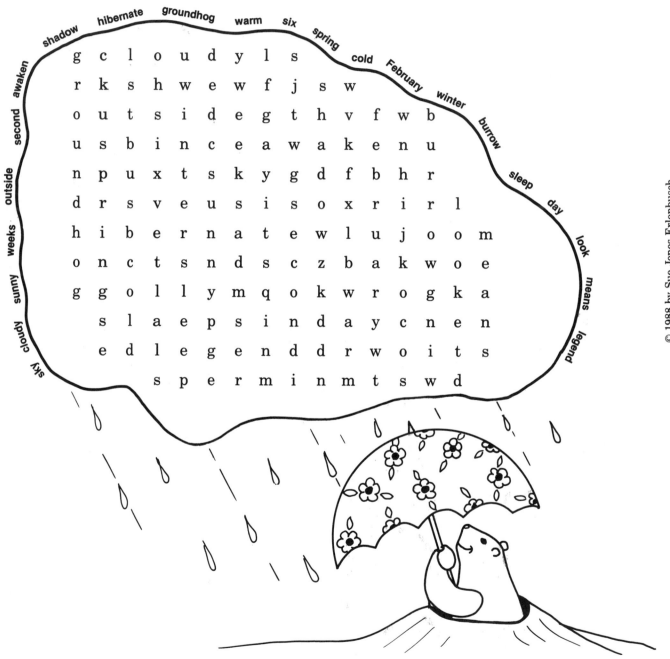

shadow
hibernate
groundhog
warm
six
spring
cold
February
winter
burrow
sleep
day
look
means
legend
sky
cloudy
sunny
weeks
outside
second
awaken

g	c	l	o	u	d	y	l	s							
r	k	s	h	w	e	w	f	j	s	w					
o	u	t	s	i	d	e	g	t	h	v	f	w	b		
u	s	b	i	n	c	e	a	w	a	k	e	n	u		
n	p	u	x	t	s	k	y	g	d	f	b	h	r		
d	r	s	v	e	u	s	i	s	o	x	r	i	r	l	
h	i	b	e	r	n	a	t	e	w	l	u	j	o	o	m
o	n	c	t	s	n	d	s	c	z	b	a	k	w	o	e
g	g	o	l	l	y	m	q	o	k	w	r	o	g	k	a
	s	l	a	e	p	s	i	n	d	a	y	c	n	e	n
	e	d	l	e	g	e	n	d	d	r	w	o	i	t	s
			s	p	e	r	m	i	n	m	t	s	w	d	

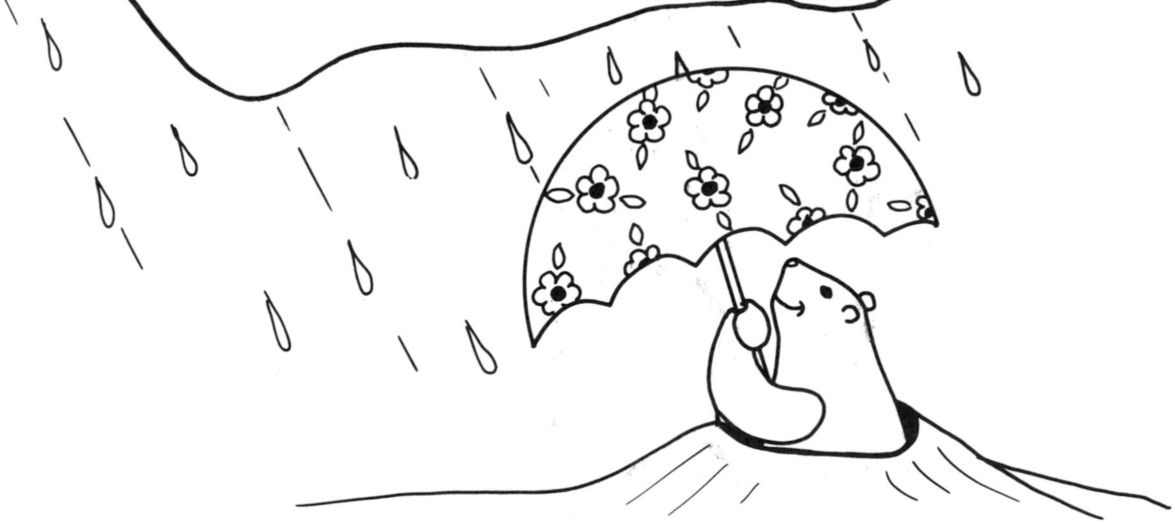

Name ____________________

A PICTURE TO COLOR

Directions: Color the picture.

Name ________________________________

SAME OR DIFFERENT

Directions: Look at the word on the left. Circle the word on the right that is like the one on the left.

heart	harte	heort	hearts	heart
valentines	valentines	valentine	valintines	valuntines
love	luve	loves	love	lowe
president	presudent	presadent	presidents	president
gifts	gifts	gifs	gitfs	giffs
birthday	birtday	birthday	birhday	birfday
flowers	flowers	flowurs	flower	flours
candy	candey	canby	candy	canbey
cards	cardes	cards	carbs	carbes
friends	friend	frienbs	frienb	friends

Name ______________________

ALPHABET SCRAMBLE

Directions: Write the letters of the alphabet in the correct order. Some of the letters have already been filled in for you.

A SECRET PAL

Directions: Connect the dots to find your secret pal. First, connect the capital letters from A to Z. Next, connect the lower case letters from a to z. Then, draw a face on your secret pal.

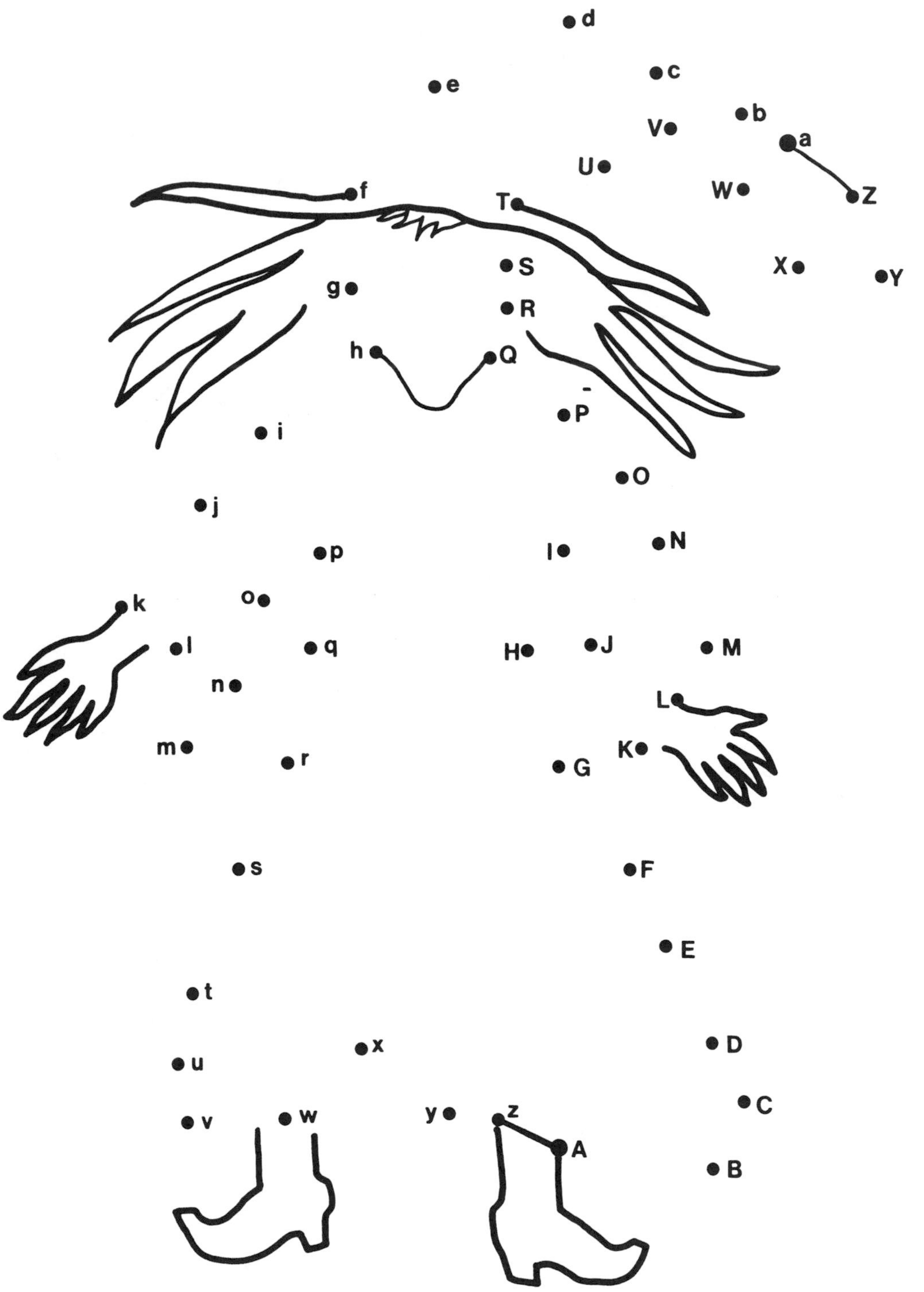

Name ______________________________

WHAT IS IT?

Directions: Connect the dots to find out what is in this picture. First, connect the capital letters from A to Z. Then, connect the lower case letters from a to z.

Name ______________________________

VALENTINE MAZE

Directions: Help the mailman find Susie's mailbox so he can deliver her Valentine cards. Draw a line from the mailman through the February words.

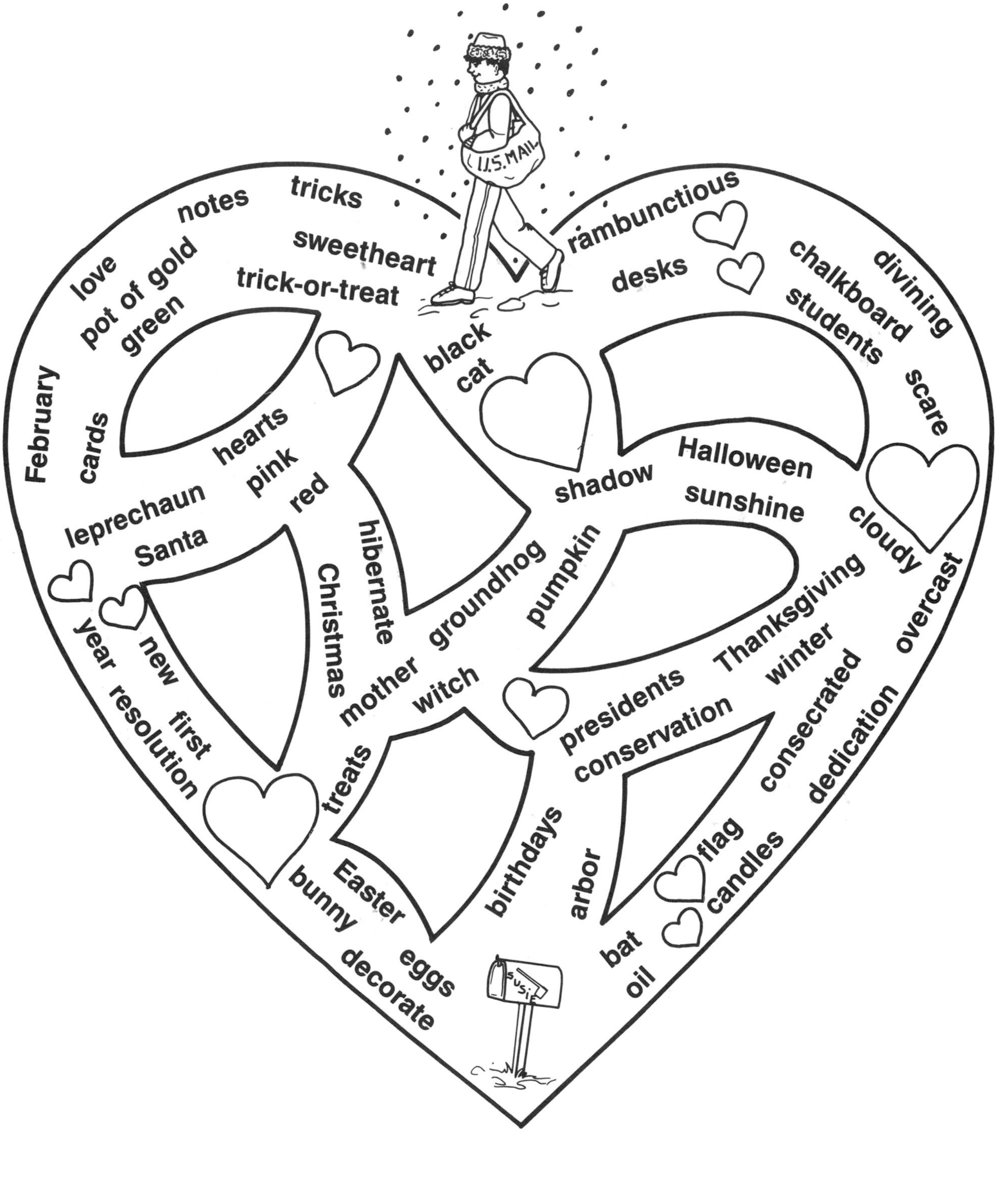

Name ______________________________

VALENTINE MAZE

Directions: Draw a line from the witch through the February words. Then, connect the dots to find out who will drink the love potion.

Hee! Heeee!
I'm making a love potion. Find out who will drink it.

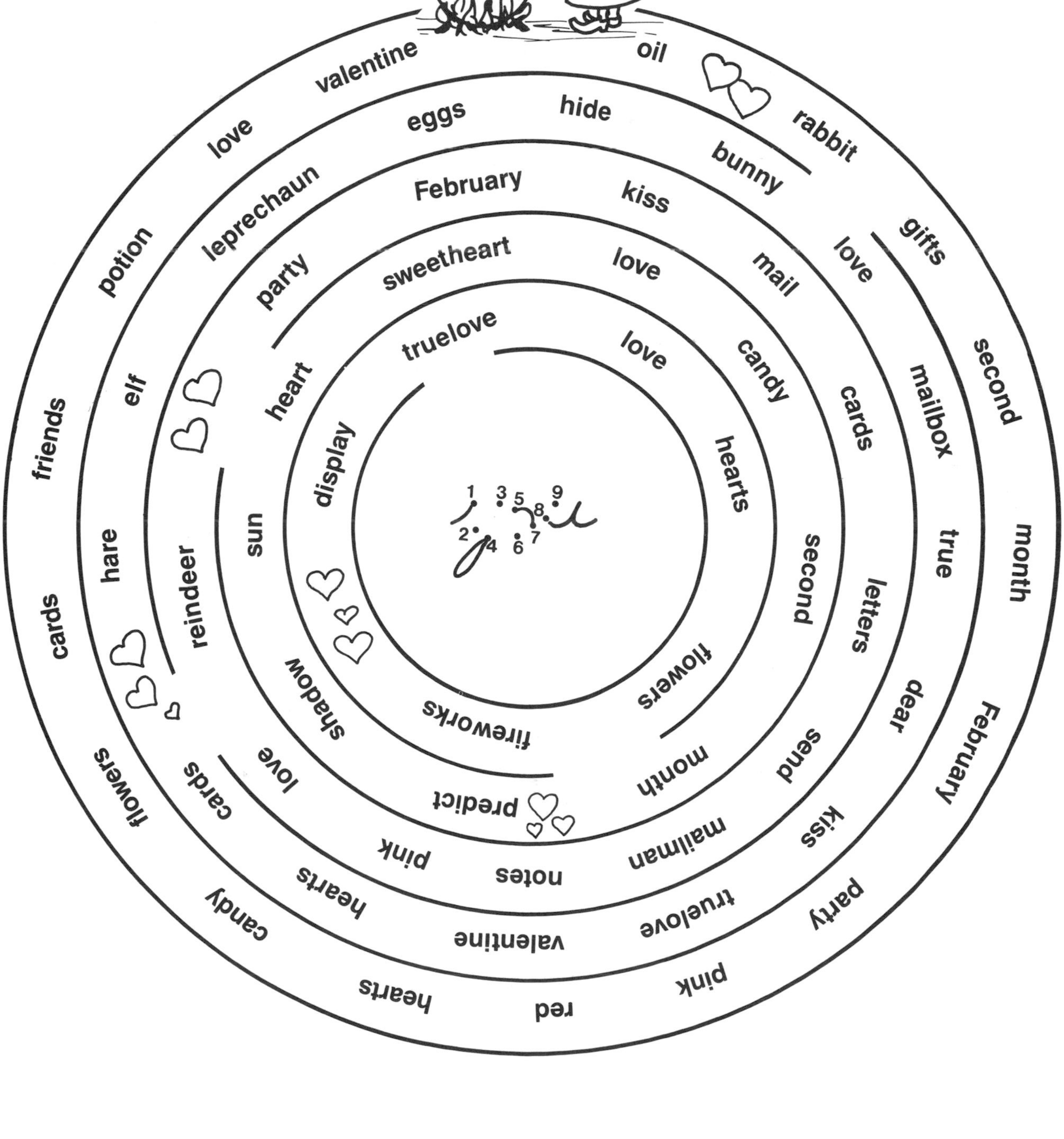

Name ________________________________

A VALENTINE PUZZLE

Directions: Color the vowels red. Color the consonants pink.

Name ______________________________

VALENTINE MATCH

Directions: Draw a line to match the pictures to the correct words.

flowers

love potion

gift

party

heart

ice cream

card

decorations

friend

cake

candy

Name ______________________________ 6-12

WORD HUNT

Directions: Find the Valentine words and circle them. You may go across and down.

v	a	l	e	n	t	i	n	e	i	n	g
s	u	o	b	o	d	w	s	r	l	t	k
f	w	v	k	t	p	m	o	n	t	h	l
l	r	e	d	e	c	c	a	n	d	y	e
o	p	r	e	s	e	n	t	s	i	q	t
w	l	r	z	f	u	q	k	e	h	p	t
e	y	p	g	t	w	m	i	n	e	a	e
r	r	s	l	q	c	a	r	d	s	r	r
s	l	x	a	a	p	h	e	a	r	t	s
k	r	e	c	e	i	v	e	c	u	y	j
u	g	m	e	d	p	i	n	k	e	i	t
t	p	s	o	f	e	b	r	u	a	r	y

SH! IT'S A SECRET!

Directions: Use the following code to learn the secret. Write the letters on the correct lines.

A	B	C	D	E	F	G	H	I	J	K	L	M
1	2	3	4	5	6	7	8	9	10	11	12	13
N	O	P	Q	R	S	T	U	V	W	X	Y	Z
14	15	16	17	18	19	20	21	22	23	24	25	26

4 5 1 18   22 1 12 5 14 20 9 14 5

__ __ __ __   __ __ __ __ __ __ __ __ __

16 12 5 1 19 5   2 5   13 9 14 5

__ __ __ __ __ __   __ __   __ __ __ __

9 6   25 15 21   4 15 14 ' 20   1 7 18 5 5

__ __   __ __ __   __ __ __ ' __   __ __ __ __ __

9 ' 12 12   20 21 18 14   25 15 21

__ ' __ __   __ __ __ __   __ __ __ .

9 14 20 15   1   6 12 5 1

__ __ __ __   __   __ __ __ __

Name ______________________

WORD SCRAMBLE

Directions: Unscramble the words.

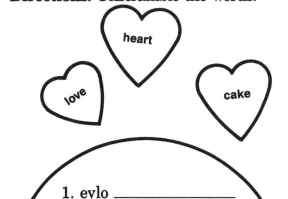

heart

love

cake

Valentine

1. evlo ____________ 2. rcda ____________

3. aetnVlnie ______________________

4. eruyFbar ______________________

5. traeh ______________________

6. yrpta ______________________

7. siks ______________________

8. dre ____________

red

February

party

card

kiss

dear

pink

Name ____________________________

MAKE A WORD

Directions: Use the letters in the words "Saint Valentine's Day" to make as many different words as possible.

SAINT VALENTINE'S DAY

VALENTINE PUZZLE

Directions: Choose the word that best completes each sentence. Write the word in the correct place.

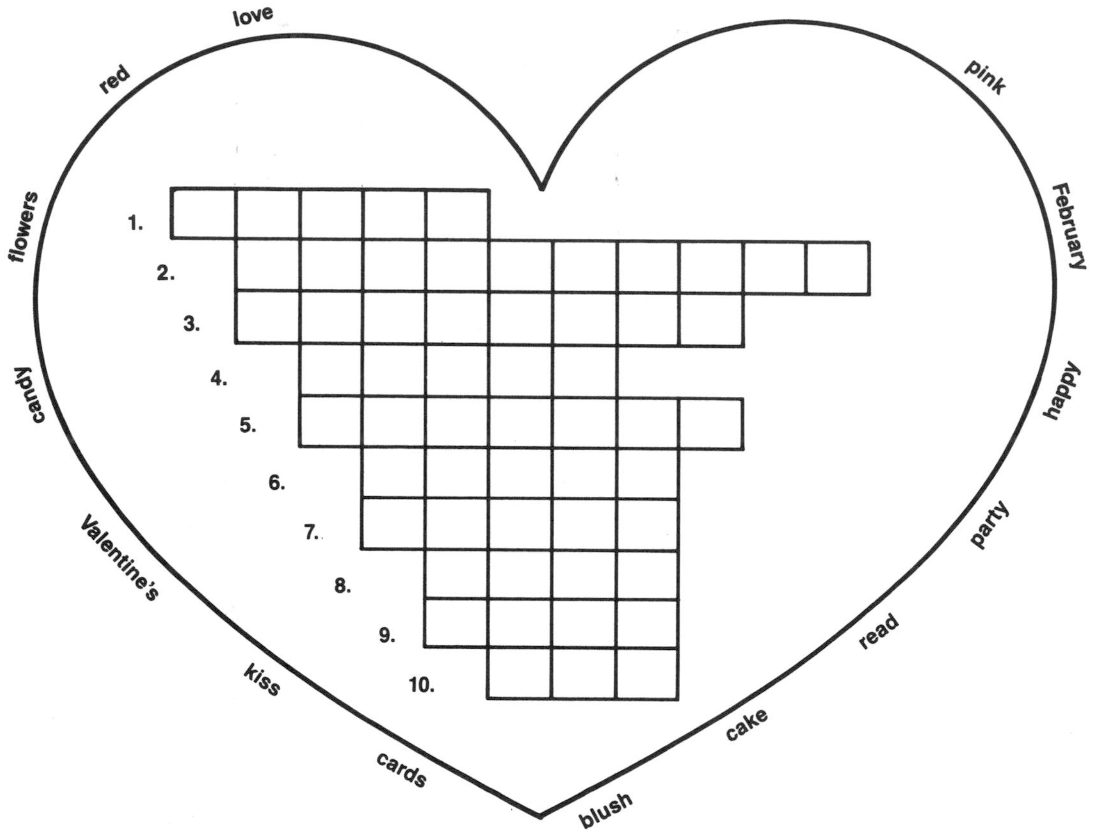

1. On Valentine's Day we give ________________ to our friends.
2. February 14th is ________________ Day.
3. Valentine's Day is in the month of ________________.
4. It is fun to have a Valentine's Day ________________.
5. Some people send ________________ to their sweethearts.
6. You can get fat from eating ________________.
7. Getting Valentine cards can make us ________________.
8. Sweethearts tell each other, "I ________________ you".
9. The boy gave his girlfriend a ________________.
10. Many Valentine cards are ________________.

Name ______________________________

SENTENCE COMPLETION

Directions: Complete the sentences.

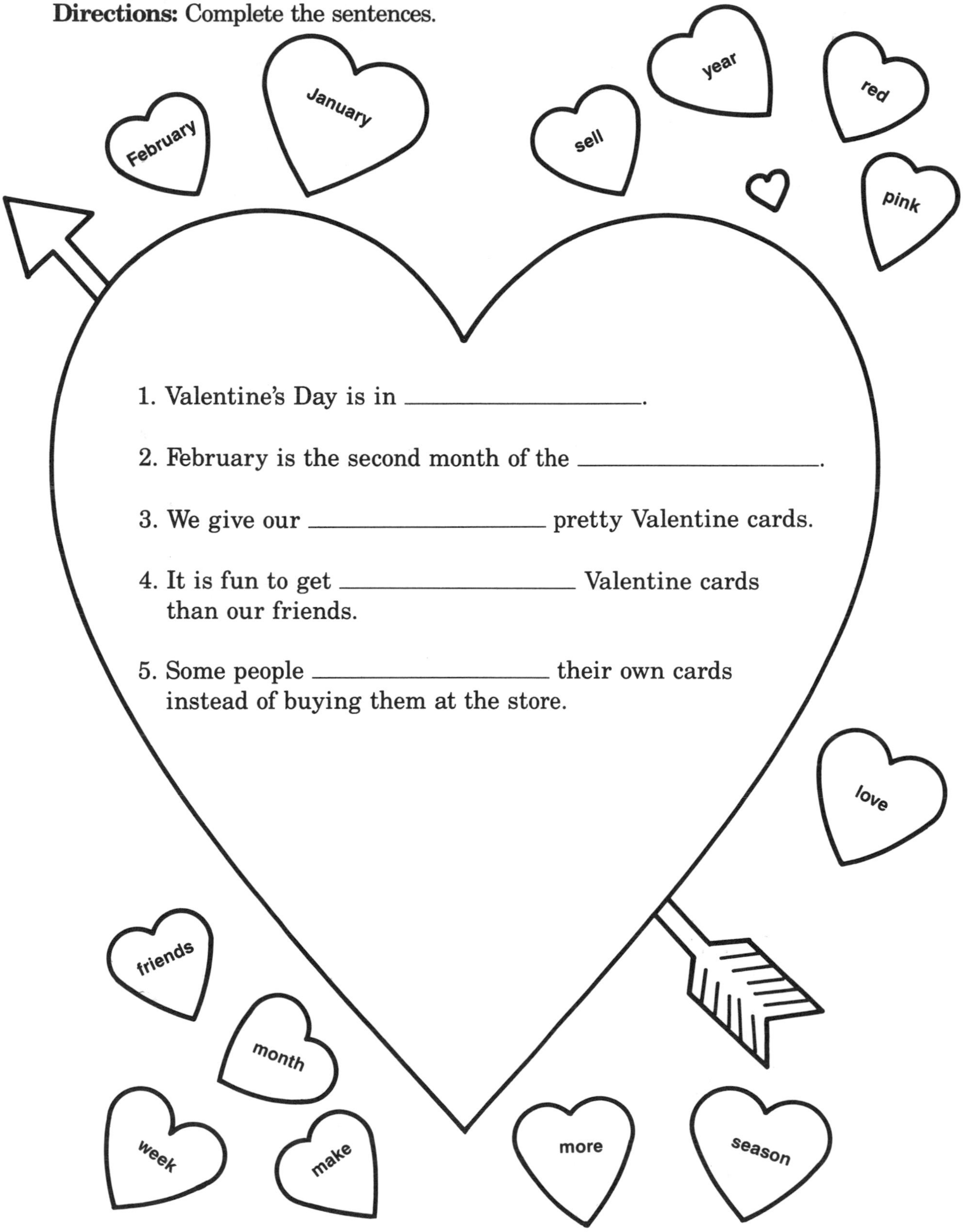

1. Valentine's Day is in ________________.
2. February is the second month of the ________________.
3. We give our ________________ pretty Valentine cards.
4. It is fun to get ________________ Valentine cards than our friends.
5. Some people ________________ their own cards instead of buying them at the store.

Name ________________________

A VALENTINE PARTY

Directions: Complete the story. Illustrate your story in the space below.

On Valentine's Day, I went to a party at my friend's house. We ____________

Name ______________________________

A LOVE NOTE

Directions: Write to someone special. Tell that person why he or she is special to you.

Heeee! Heee!
I hope someone
sends me a love
note. Heee!

Dear Valentine,

____

____

____

____

____

____

____

____

____

Love,

____

Name ______________________________

SURPRISE! SURPRISE!

Directions: Complete the story. Illustrate your story in the space below.

When I woke up on Valentine's Day, I found a surprise package in my room. The note on the package said to try to figure out what was in the box before I opened it.

I ____

Name ______________________________

A LOVE POTION

Directions: Write a recipe using at least six of the following ingredients.

Hi, Cutie!
This brew
is for you!

pucker powder	sheep eyes
kissing juice	porcupine lips
mushy mush	skunk spray
lovey dovey oil	elephant ears
throbbing heart	rotten eggs
poison candy	spoiled milk
snake venom	pig tails

Recipe Title: ______________________________

Ingredients: ______________________________

____

____

How to fix: ______________________________

____

____

____

____

How to cook: ______________________________

____

____

Name ______________________

WHAT'S COOKING?

Directions: Unscramble the ingredients. Write the name of the recipe on the line.

		Recipe ______________________
¾	cup	nworb gsrau ______
¾	cup	uasgr ______
1	cup	rettub ______
2		sgeg ______
2	tablespoons	limk ______
2½	teaspoons	kganib podwre ______
½	teaspoon	lsta ______
1	teaspoon	nillvaa ______
1	teaspoon	nnnmaioc ______
½	teaspoon	clsoev ______
½	teaspoon	etumgn ______

Place ingredients in a large bowl and beat until well mixed. Roll out and cut with Valentine cookie cutters. Bake at 350 degrees for 10 minutes. Makes 2 dozen.

Name ____________________

SAINT VALENTINE

Directions: Fill in the blanks with words from the hearts.

Some (1) ____________________ associate Valentine's Day with one or more (2) ____________________ of the early Christian Church. Over the years the various Valentines (3) ____________ into one. Many legends have been handed down about St. Valentine.

One (4) ______________ says that he (5) ______________ married young (6) ______________ even though the emperor (7) ______________ young men to marry. Another story says Valentine was a Christian who made (8) __________ with many children. When he was put in (9) ____________________ for refusing to (10) ______________ the Roman gods, the children tossed (11) ______________ notes into his (12) ______________.

Another legend says that Valentine (13) ____________________ the jailor's daughter of blindness and fell in love with her. Supposedly, he sent her a letter which he (14) ______________, "From your Valentine."

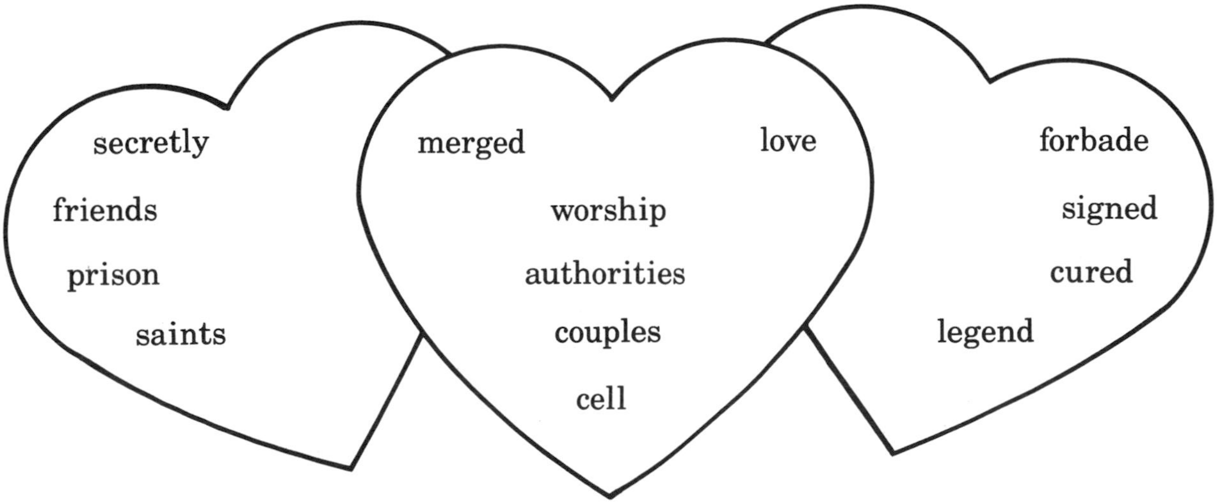

LOVE LORE

Directions: Fill in the blanks with words from the pillow.

Girls, would you like to know the (1) ____________________ of your truelove? If you're (2) ____________________, you can go to a (3) ____________________ on St. Valentine's Eve at midnight, sing a certain (4) ____________________, and run around the church twelve times. This is supposed to make your truelove (5) ______________.

If graveyards are not for you, you can write the names of boys on (6) __________ of paper, roll the pieces up in bits of clay and place them in (7) ______________. The first one to (8) ____________________ to the top will have the name of your truelove on it. If you would like to (9) ____________________ of your truelove, pin five bay (10) ____________________ on your pillow on St. Valentine's Eve. If you're an early (11) ______________, you can get up before (12) ____________________ on Valentine's Day and stand at your (13) ______________. The first man that you see, or someone who looks like him, is destined to be your (14) ______________ husband.

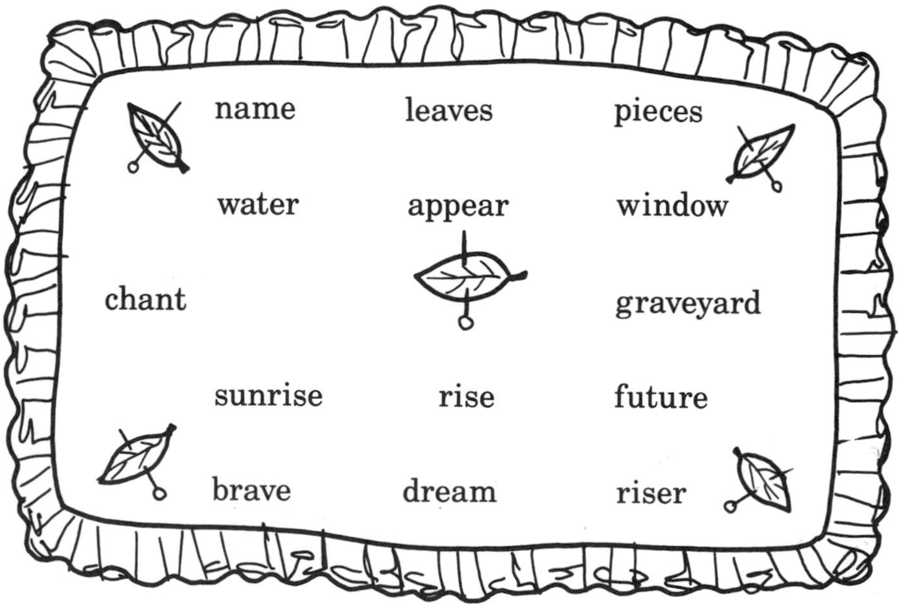

Name ______________________________

ABRAHAM LINCOLN

Directions: Fill in the blanks with words from the fireplace.

Abraham Lincoln was a (1) ____________ great man and (2) ____________. A month after he was (3) ________________ as the 16th President, this (4) ________________ began fighting the Civil War. Lincoln helped (5) ____________ the union. If the (6) ____________ had not been preserved, the United States would have (7) ________________ into two (8) ____________ nations.

Lincoln was (9) ________________ in a log cabin. When he could be (10) ____________ from farm (11) ____________, he attended school. His (12) ____________ schooling totaled less than a (13) ____________. He (14) ________________ most of his (15) ________________ on his own. Books were (16) ________________ and he was known to walk long (17) ____________ to (18) ____________ a book. After working on the (19) ____________ all day, he would sit and read by (20) ____________.

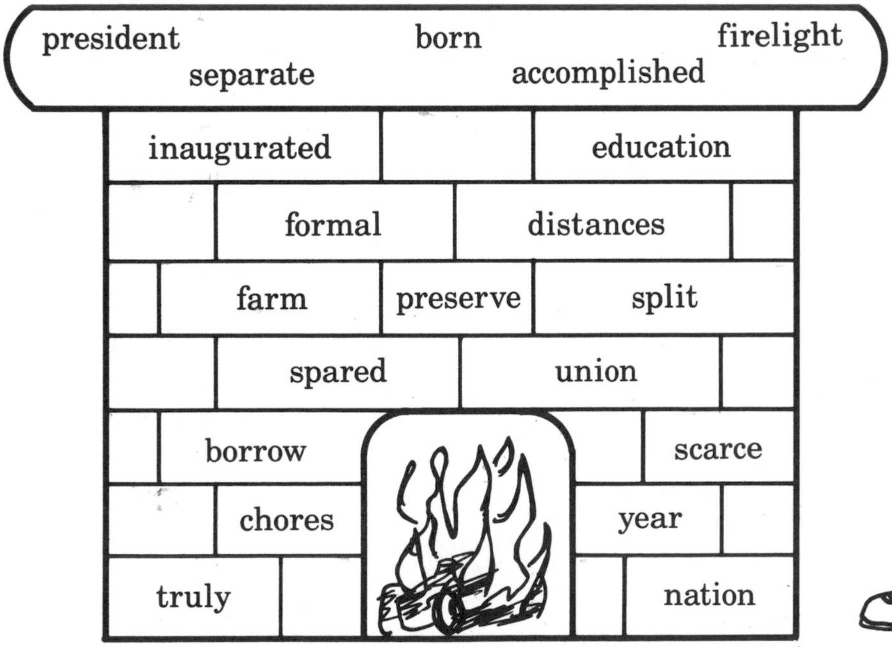

Name ______________________________

LINCOLN'S BIRTHDAY

Directions: Circle the hidden words. You may go across and down.

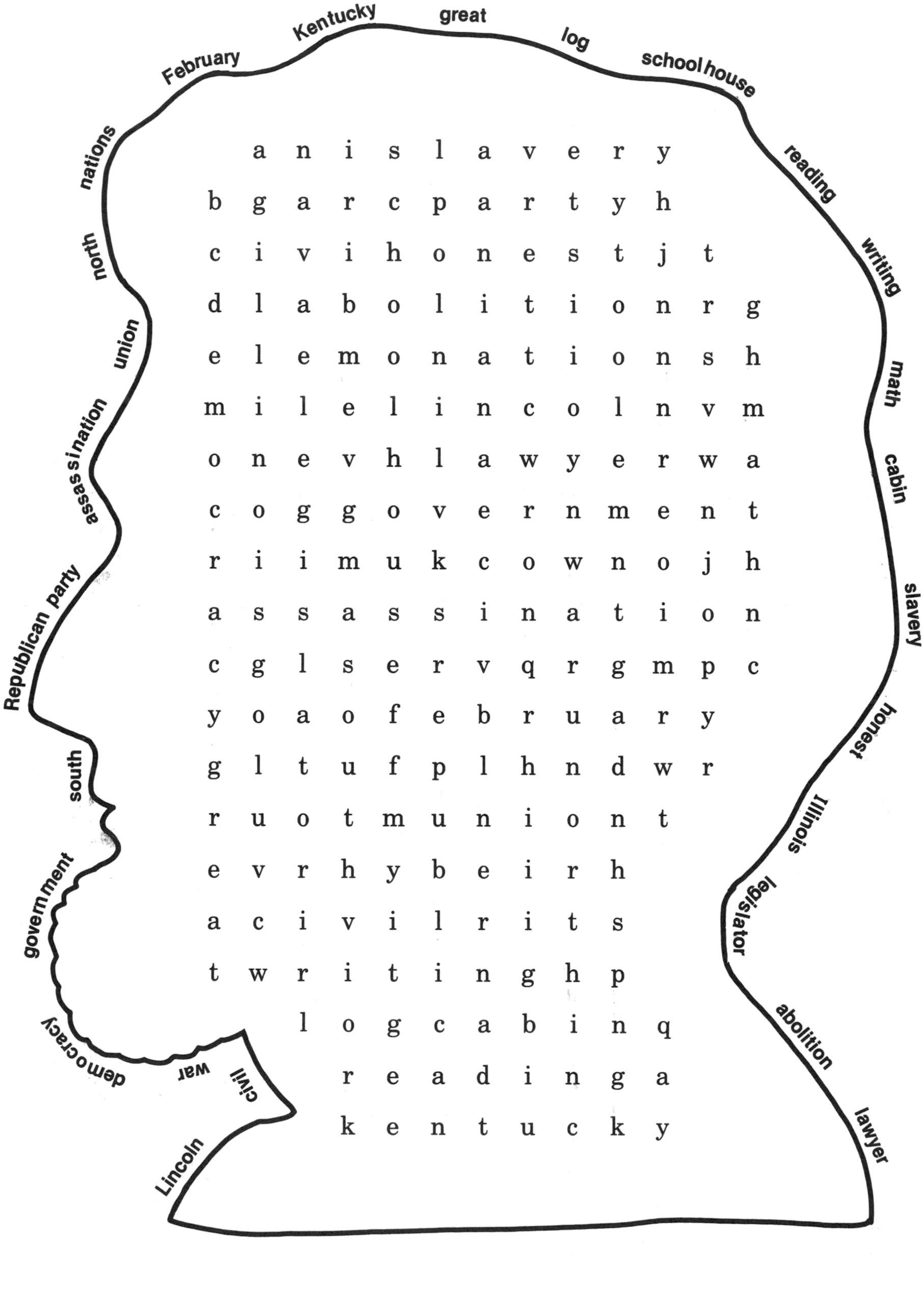

	a	n	i	s	l	a	v	e	r	y		
b	g	a	r	c	p	a	r	t	y	h		
c	i	v	i	h	o	n	e	s	t	j	t	
d	l	a	b	o	l	i	t	i	o	n	r	g
e	l	e	m	o	n	a	t	i	o	n	s	h
m	i	l	e	l	i	n	c	o	l	n	v	m
o	n	e	v	h	l	a	w	y	e	r	w	a
c	o	g	g	o	v	e	r	n	m	e	n	t
r	i	i	m	u	k	c	o	w	n	o	j	h
a	s	s	a	s	s	i	n	a	t	i	o	n
c	g	l	s	e	r	v	q	r	g	m	p	c
y	o	a	o	f	e	b	r	u	a	r	y	
g	l	t	u	f	p	l	h	n	d	w	r	
r	u	o	t	m	u	n	i	o	n	t		
e	v	r	h	y	b	e	i	r	h			
a	c	i	v	i	l	r	i	t	s			
t	w	r	i	t	i	n	g	h	p			
		l	o	g	c	a	b	i	n	q		
			r	e	a	d	i	n	g	a		
			k	e	n	t	u	c	k	y		

Name ______________________________

GEORGE WASHINGTON

Directions: Fill in the blanks with words from the hatchet.

George (1) ________________ is known as the "Father of Our Country." When we won our (2) __________________ from Great (3) ___________________ in the Revolutionary War, he was the (4) ______________________________ of our army. He was (5) ____________________ of the (6) ____________________ that wrote the United States (7) __________________. He was (8) __________________ the (9) ________________ President of the United States.

Many (10) _______________ have been told about George Washington through the years. One (11) ________________ story tells how he (12) _________________ down one of his father's cherry (13) _______________________________ and then (14) ________________ by saying, "Father, I cannot tell a lie."

Name ______________________________

WASHINGTON'S BIRTHDAY

Directions: Circle the hidden words. You may go across and down.

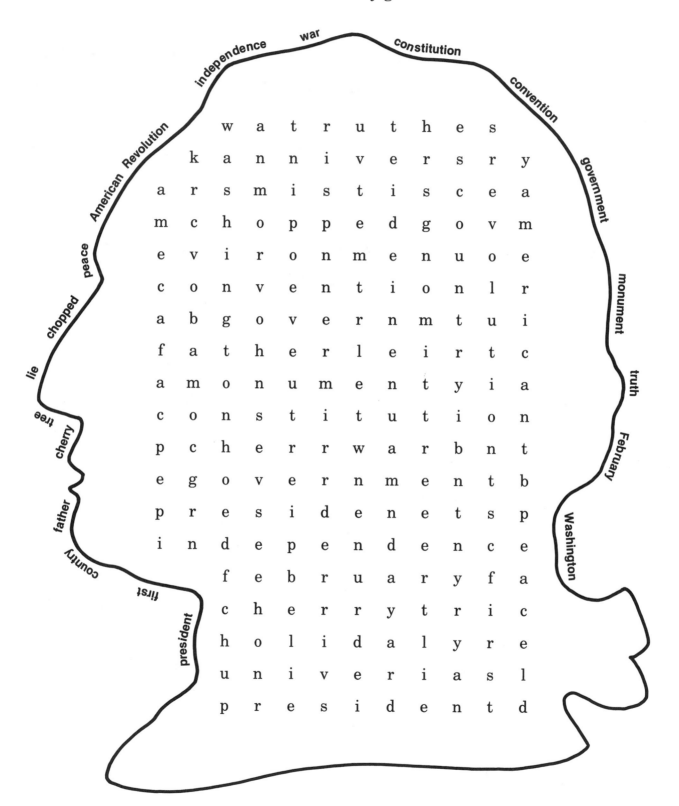

independence
war
constitution
convention
government
monument
truth
February
Washington
president
first
country
father
cherry
tree
lie
chopped
peace
American Revolution

		w	a	t	r	u	t	h	e	s	
	k	a	n	n	i	v	e	r	s	r	y
a	r	s	m	i	s	t	i	s	c	e	a
m	c	h	o	p	p	e	d	g	o	v	m
e	v	i	r	o	n	m	e	n	u	o	e
c	o	n	v	e	n	t	i	o	n	l	r
a	b	g	o	v	e	r	n	m	t	u	i
f	a	t	h	e	r	l	e	i	r	t	c
a	m	o	n	u	m	e	n	t	y	i	a
c	o	n	s	t	i	t	u	t	i	o	n
p	c	h	e	r	r	w	a	r	b	n	t
e	g	o	v	e	r	n	m	e	n	t	b
p	r	e	s	i	d	e	n	e	t	s	p
i	n	d	e	p	e	n	d	e	n	c	e
		f	e	b	r	u	a	r	y	f	a
		c	h	e	r	r	y	t	r	i	c
		h	o	l	i	d	a	l	y	r	e
		u	n	i	v	e	r	i	a	s	l
		p	r	e	s	i	d	e	n	t	d

Name ______________________________

MISSING CONSONANT PUZZLE

Directions: Fill in the missing consonants.

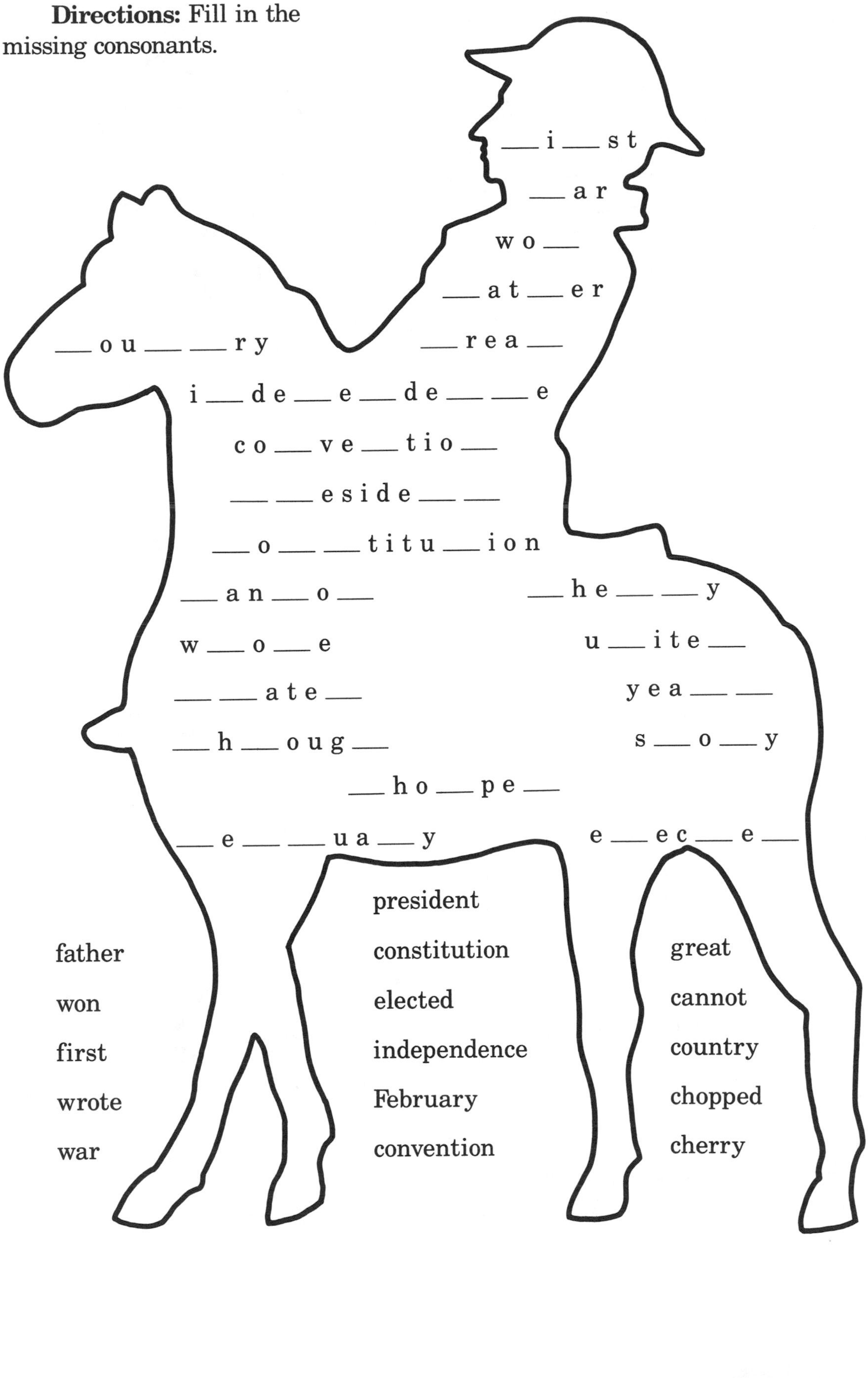

	president		
father	constitution	great	through
won	elected	cannot	united
first	independence	country	states
wrote	February	chopped	years
war	convention	cherry	story

Name ______________________________

MISSING VOWEL PUZZLE

Directions: Fill in the missing vowels.

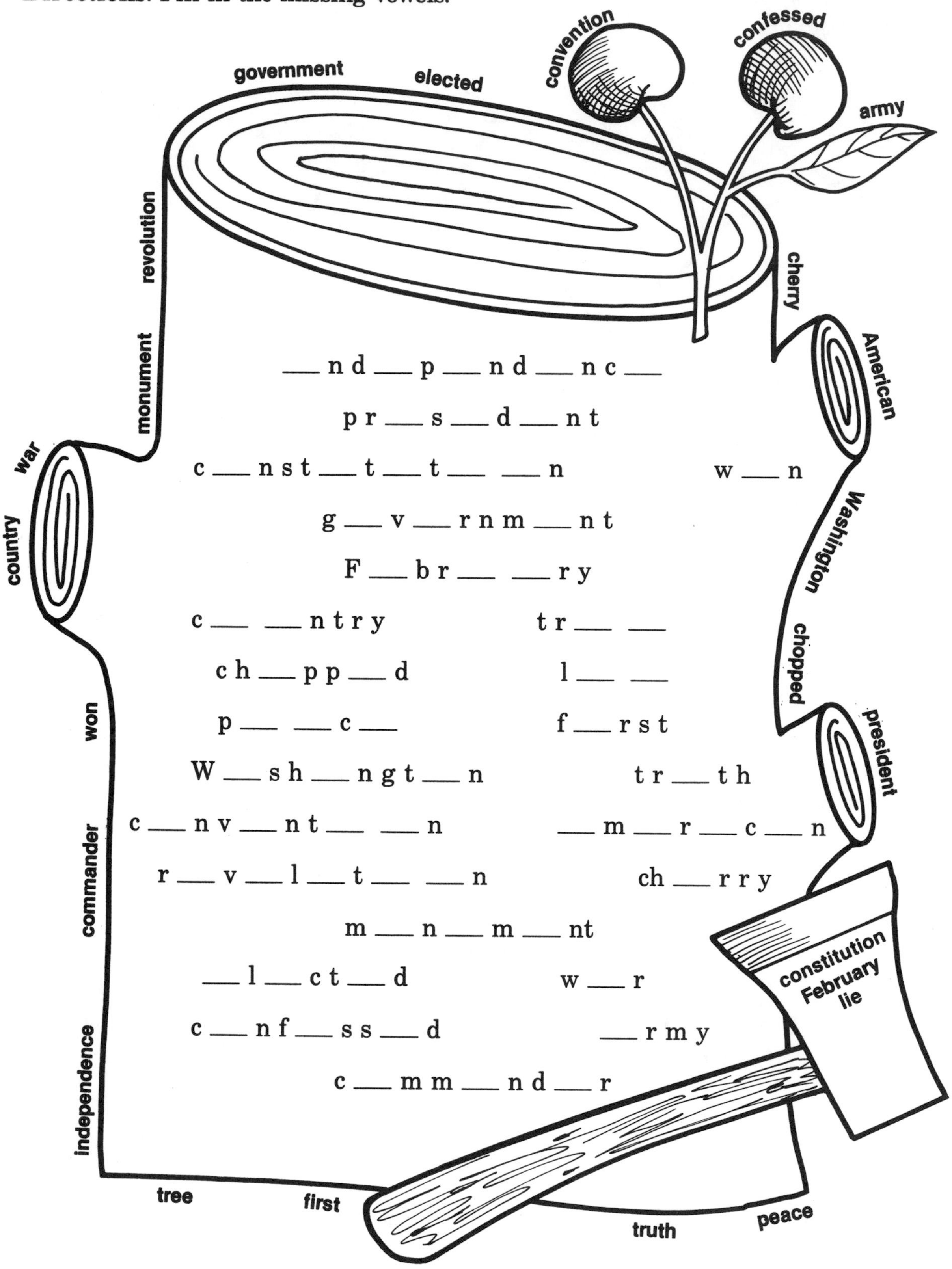

___ n d ___ p ___ n d ___ n c ___

p r ___ s ___ d ___ n t

c ___ n s t ___ t ___ t ___ ___ n   w ___ n

g ___ v ___ r n m ___ n t

F ___ b r ___ ___ r y

c ___ ___ n t r y   t r ___ ___

c h ___ p p ___ d   l ___ ___

p ___ ___ c ___   f ___ r s t

W ___ s h ___ n g t ___ n   t r ___ t h

c ___ n v ___ n t ___ ___ n   ___ m ___ r ___ c ___ n

r ___ v ___ l ___ t ___ ___ n   c h ___ r r y

m ___ n ___ m ___ nt

___ l ___ c t ___ d   w ___ r

c ___ n f ___ s s ___ d   ___ r m y

c ___ m m ___ n d ___ r

MARCH

Activity Number and Title		**Special Day**
7-1	A Picture to Color	St. Patrick's Day
7-2	Same or Different	St. Patrick's Day
7-3	Alphabet Scramble	St. Patrick's Day
7-4	Who Is It?	St. Patrick's Day
7-5	What Is It?	St. Patrick's Day
7-6	Shamrock Maze	St. Patrick's Day
7-7	Saint Patrick's Day Puzzle	St. Patrick's Day
7-8	Word Match	St. Patrick's Day
7-9	Shopping Spree	St. Patrick's Day
7-10	March Calendar	St. Patrick's Day
7-11	Word Hunt	St. Patrick's Day
7-12	Sh! It's a Secret!	St. Patrick's Day
7-13	Missing Consonant Puzzle	St. Patrick's Day
7-14	Missing Vowel Puzzle	St. Patrick's Day
7-15	Word Scramble	St. Patrick's Day
7-16	Rhyme Time	St. Patrick's Day
7-17	Make a Word	St. Patrick's Day
7-18	My Three Wishes	St. Patrick's Day
7-19	The Pot of Gold	St. Patrick's Day
7-20	Legend of the Leprechaun	St. Patrick's Day
7-21	Saint Patrick	St. Patrick's Day
7-22	The Last Snake	St. Patrick's Day

A Listening Lesson

Make a listening lesson for March. Write twenty true-false questions about Ireland, St. Patrick, leprechauns, and so on.

Ask the students to get a pencil and sheet of notebook paper. Say, "We are going to have a listening lesson. There are twenty true-false questions. You won't know all of the answers, but take your best guess. This lesson should help you become a better listener. Now, put your name at the top of the paper and number from 1 to 20."

Next, read the items aloud to the students. When you are finished, say, "Now I am going to reread all of the questions and give you the answers. Check your own paper. Pay close attention because we'll have a test on this material later this week."

You can also make listening lessons using questions that are multiple choice, fill-in-the-blanks, or fact and opinion. Another way to present a listening lesson is to read a short story first and then ask questions about it. Whichever format you choose, be sure to collect the papers at the end of the first session.

Vocabulary

The following two word lists will help develop your students' vocabularies in March.

St. Patrick's Day Word List 1	St. Patrick's Day Word List 2
leprechaun	Ireland
pot	honor
March	authorities
green	refused
coin	missionary
month	snake
Irish	slavery
lucky	water
shillelagh	escaped
celebrate	drove
third	anniversary
shamrock	famous
happy	stories
trick	captured
wish	finally
charm	monastery

St. Patrick's Day
Word List 1

gold
jig
mushroom
parade

St. Patrick's Day
Word List 2

sold
legends
converted
religious

Game Boards

Here are three game board patterns for you to use in March. For the bingo style game board, don't forget to arrange the words in a different order on the other cards.

Ireland	charm	celebration	trick	March
pinch	island	lucky	parade	wish
green	laddies		St. Patrick's Day	hat
saint	pot of gold	Irish	jig	shillelagh
shamrock	leprechaun	elf	lassies	holiday

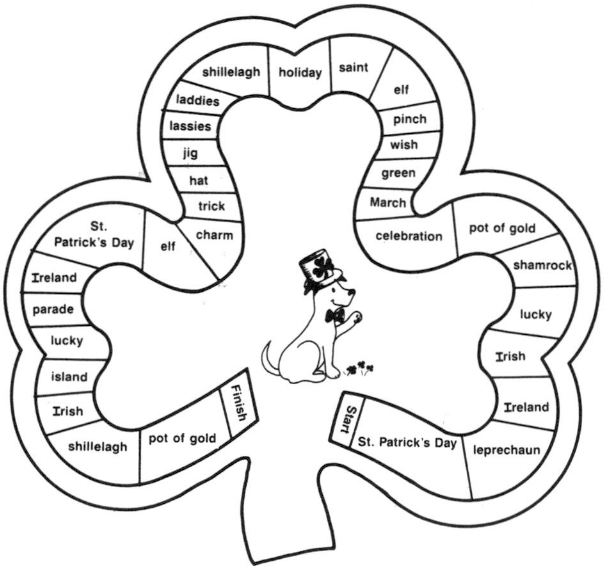

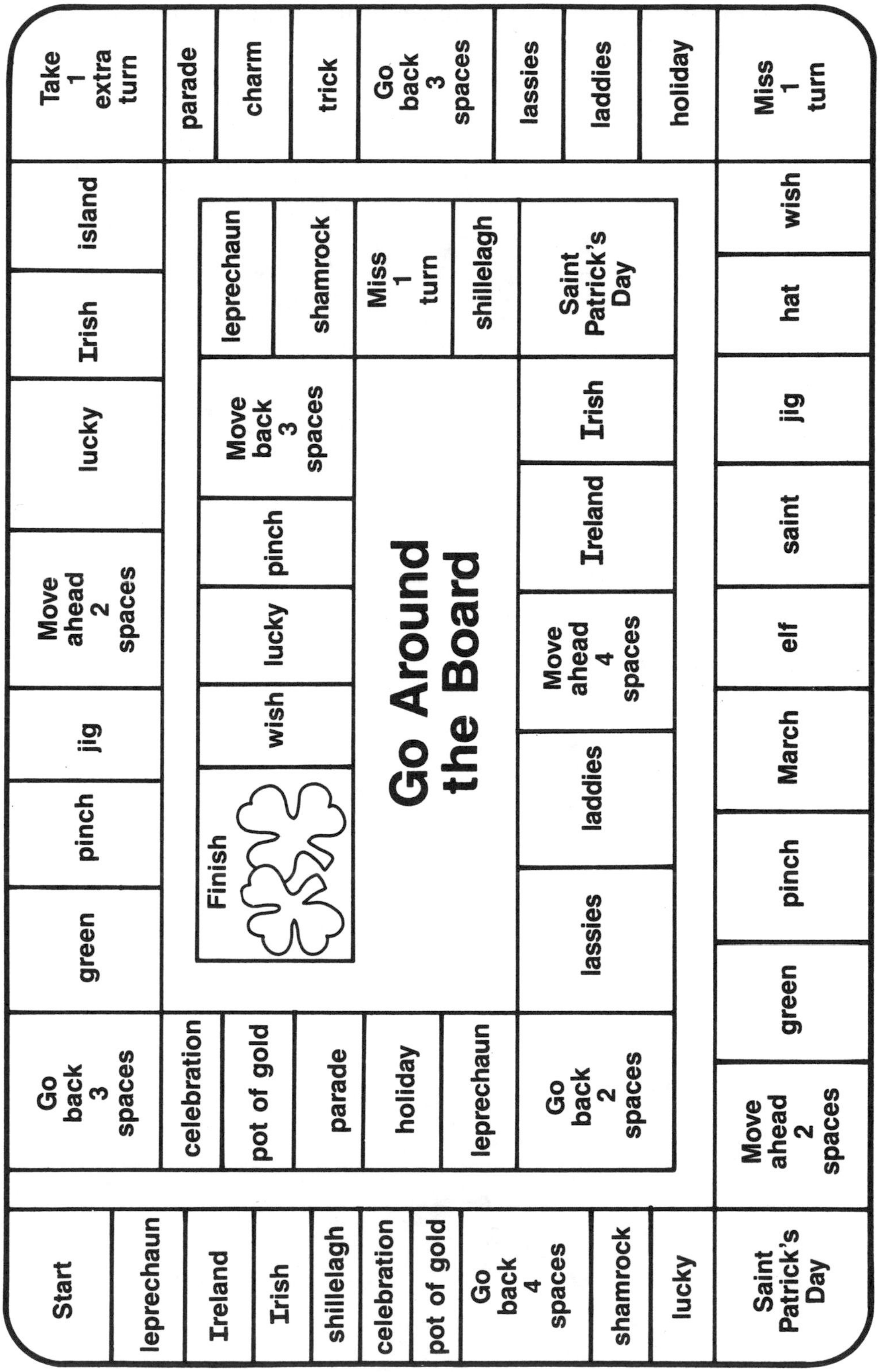
Go Around the Board
Start
leprechaun
Ireland
Irish
shillelagh
celebration
pot of gold
Go back 4 spaces
shamrock
lucky
Saint Patrick's Day
Move ahead 2 spaces
green
pinch
March
elf
saint
jig
hat
wish
Miss 1 turn
holiday
laddies
lassies
Go back 3 spaces
trick
charm
parade
Take 1 extra turn
island
Irish
lucky
Move ahead 2 spaces
jig
pinch
green
Go back 3 spaces
celebration
pot of gold
parade
holiday
leprechaun
Go back 2 spaces
lassies
laddies
Move ahead 4 spaces
Ireland
Irish
Saint Patrick's Day
shillelagh
Miss 1 turn
shamrock
leprechaun
Move back 3 spaces
pinch
lucky
wish
Finish

A PICTURE TO COLOR

Directions: First, connect the capital letters beginning with A. Then, connect the lower case letters beginning with a. Now, color the picture.

Name ______________________________

SAME OR DIFFERENT

Directions: Look at the word on the left. Circle the word on the right that is like the one on the left.

leprechaun	lepruchaun	liprechaun	leprechaun	leprachaun
shamrock	shammrock	shamrock	shamerock	shamrocks
trick	tricks	truck	tricke	trick
parade	parade	parabe	parude	porade
jig	jug	jog	jag	jig
coin	coin	cain	coine	coins
charm	charn	charm	charms	sharm
third	thirb	thurd	third	thord
lucky	lucky	ducky	luckey	locky
wish	dish	fish	wish	wash

Name ________________________________

ALPHABET SCRAMBLE

Directions: Write the letters of the alphabet in the correct order. Some of the letters have already been filled in for you.

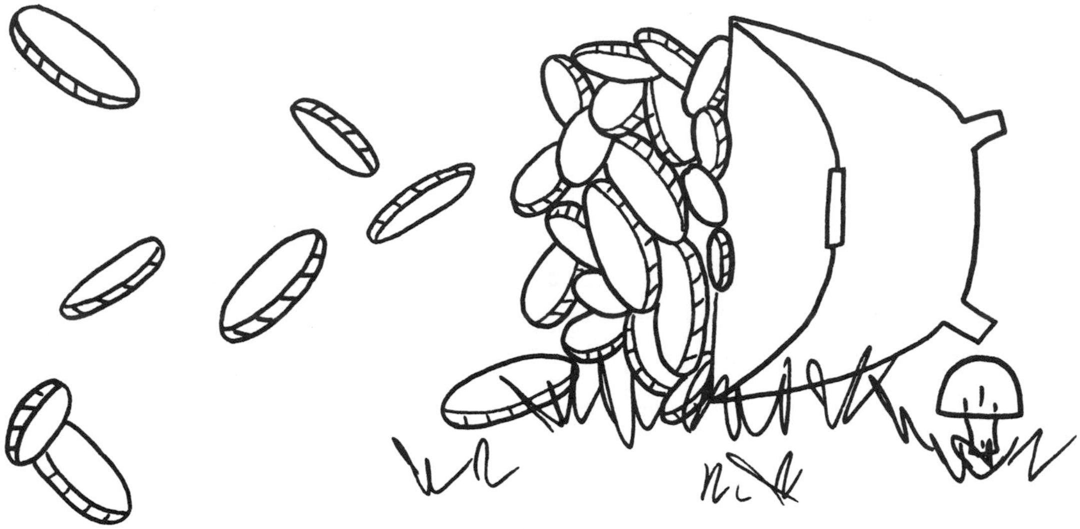

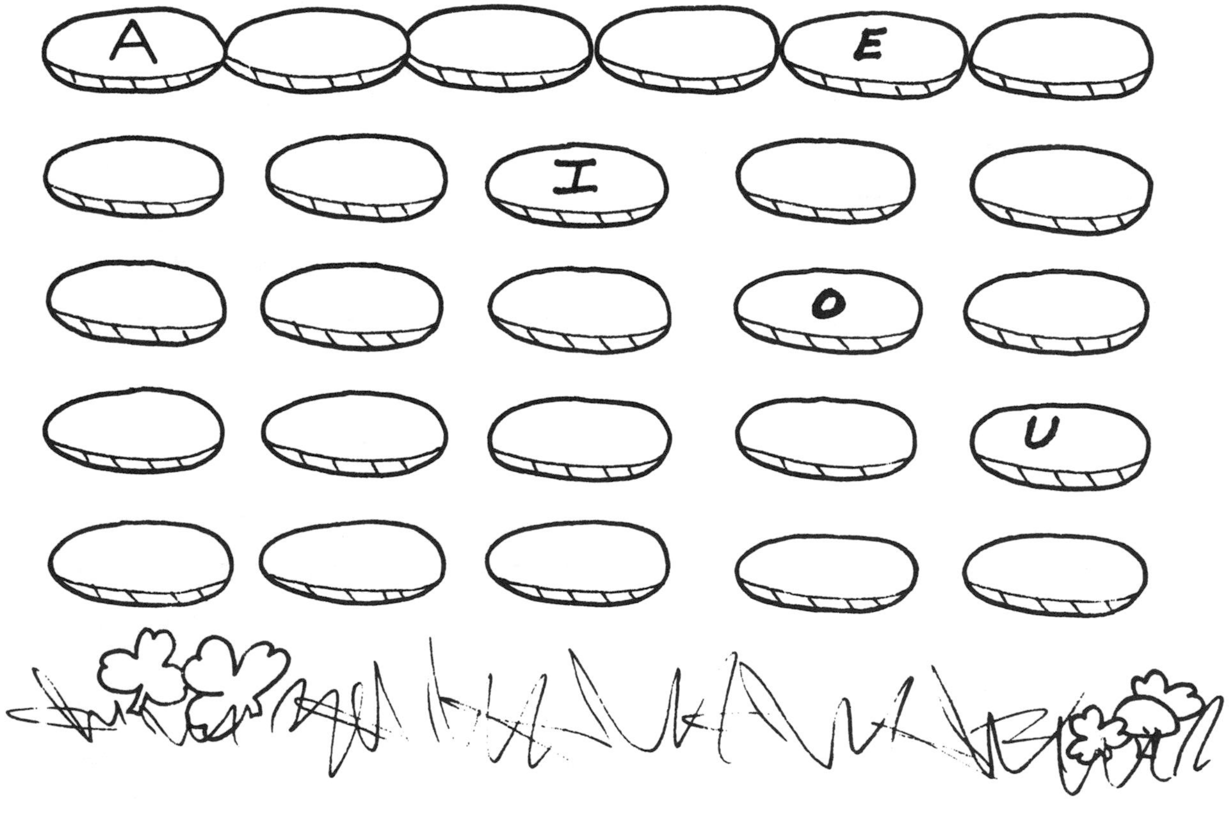

Name ______________________________

WHO IS IT?

Directions: Connect the dots to find out who is in this picture. Start with the first letter of the alphabet. First, connect the lower case letters. Then, connect the capital letters.

WHAT IS IT?

Directions: Connect the dots to find out what is in this picture. Start with the first letter of the alphabet. First, connect the lower case letters. Then, connect the capital letters.

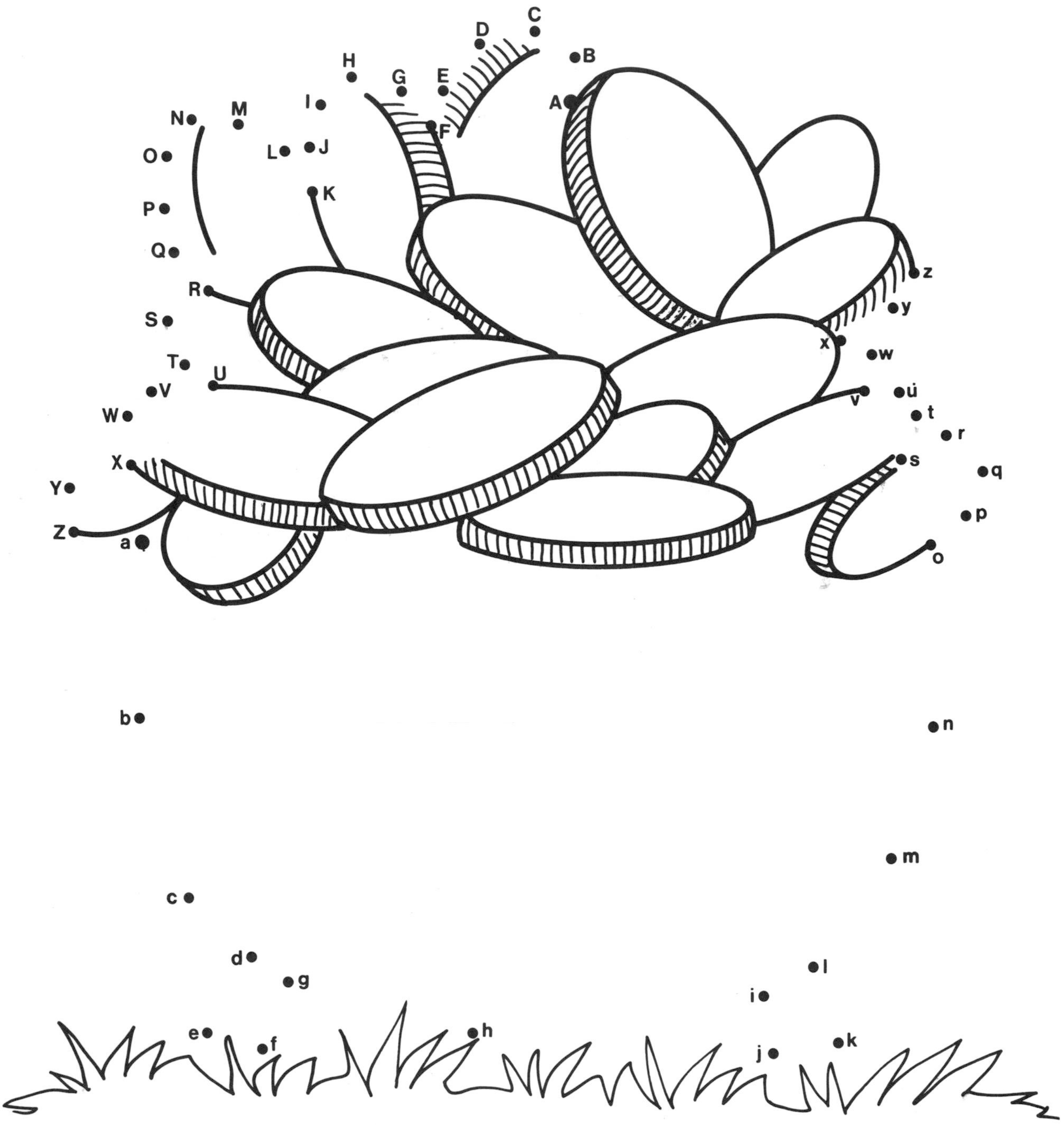

Name ______________________________

SHAMROCK MAZE

Directions: Help the little leprechaun find the pot of gold by drawing a line from him through the March words.

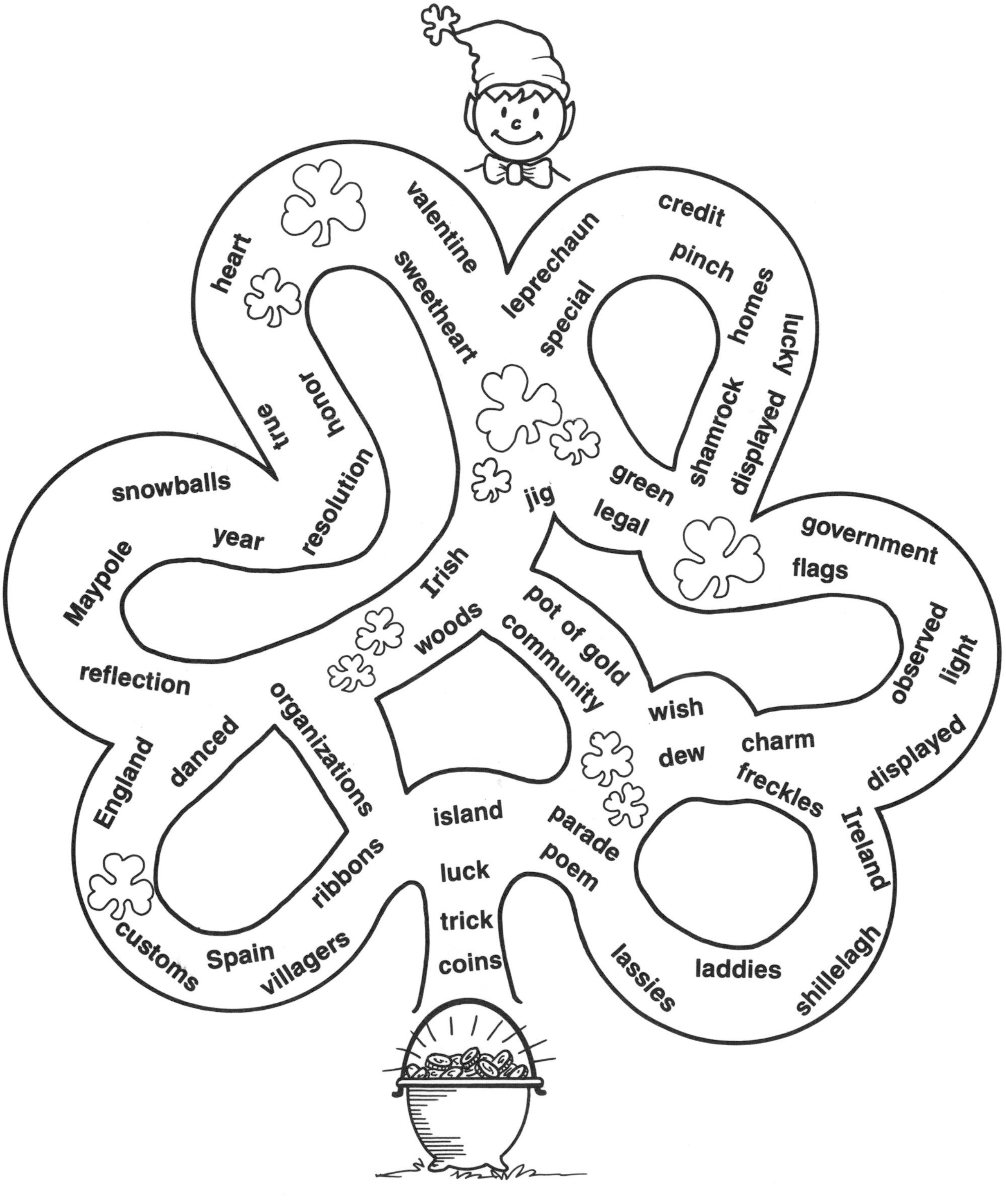

Name ______________________

SAINT PATRICK'S DAY PUZZLE

Directions: Color the vowels light green. Color the consonants dark green.

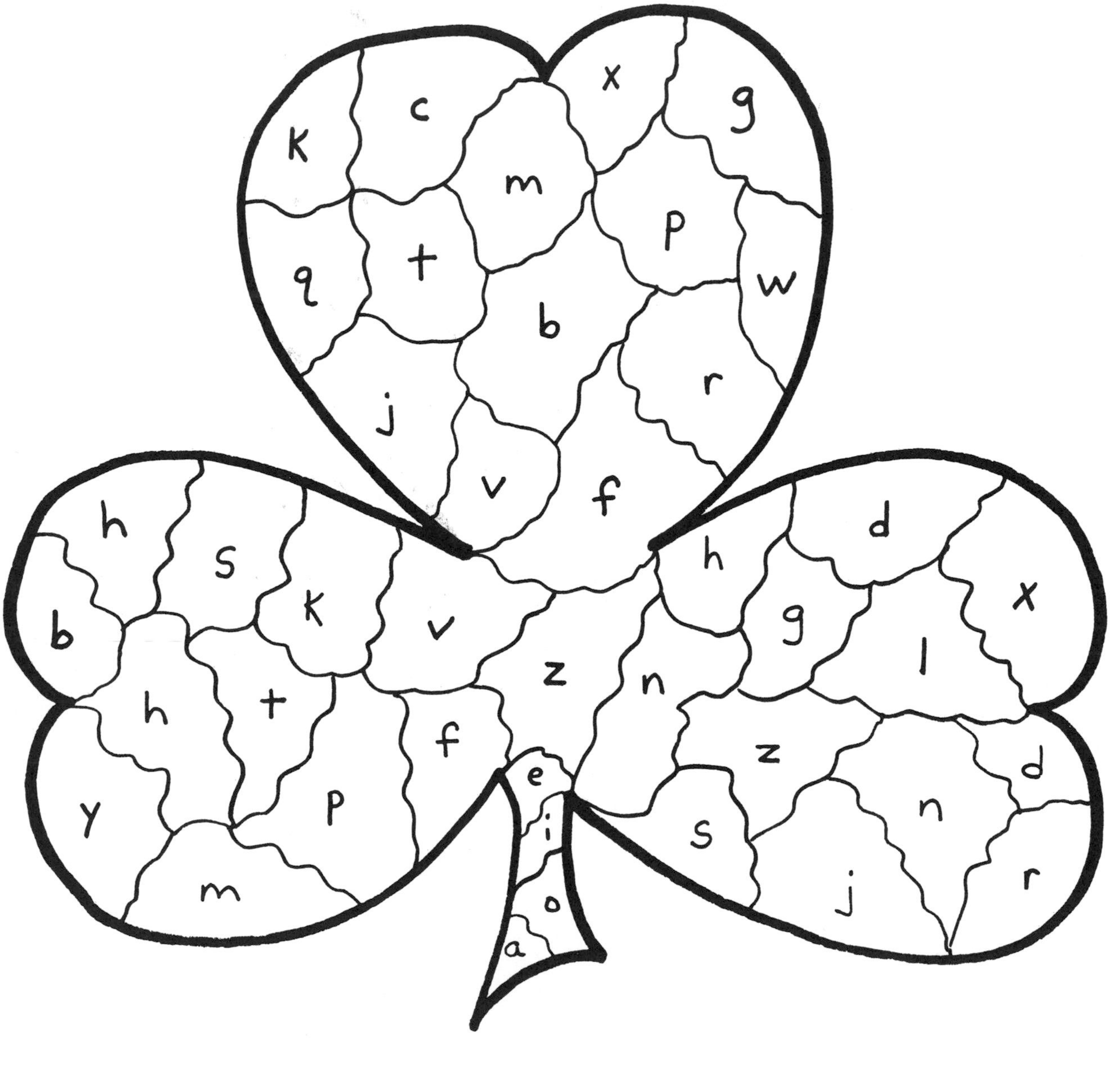

Name ______________________________

WORD MATCH

Directions: Draw a line to match the pictures to the correct words.

pot of gold

parade

shamrock

jig

leprechaun

trick

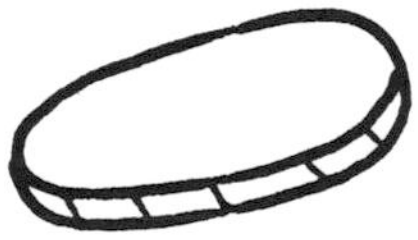

shillelagh

party

coin

mushroom

Name ______________________________

SHOPPING SPREE

Directions: Draw and color six things that you would buy if you found a pot of gold. Write the name of each item.

Name ______________________________

MARCH CALENDAR

Directions: Fill in the days of the month. Draw a shamrock to indicate St. Patrick's Day.

Sunday	Monday	Tuesday	Wednesday	Thursday	Friday	Saturday
			1	2	3	4
5	6	7	8	9	10	11
12	13	14	15	16		18
19	20	21	22	23	24	25
26	27	28	29	30	31	

Name ______________________________ 7-11

WORD HUNT

Directions: Circle the hidden words. You may go across and down.

l	e	p	r	e	c	h	a	u	n	q	c	s
u	b	p	a	r	a	d	e	g	r	e	e	n
c	h	a	r	m	i	n	p	w	u	t	l	b
k	e	i	r	i	s	h	k	i	h	h	e	a
y	d	f	k	j	p	i	g	s	c	i	b	n
i	p	u	l	m	a	r	c	h	o	r	r	d
s	t	p	a	t	r	i	c	k	s	d	a	y
h	o	m	o	n	t	h	r	s	t	u	t	w
g	h	a	p	p	y	m	n	o	p	q	e	i
p	o	u	p	o	t	o	f	g	o	l	d	s
z	d	c	e	f	s	h	a	m	r	o	c	k

SH! IT'S A SECRET!

Directions: Use the following code to learn the secret. Write the letters on the correct lines.

A	B	C	D	E	F	G	H	I	J	K	L	M
1	2	3	4	5	6	7	8	9	10	11	12	13
N	**O**	**P**	**Q**	**R**	**S**	**T**	**U**	**V**	**W**	**X**	**Y**	**Z**
14	15	16	17	18	19	20	21	22	23	24	25	26

16 5 15 16 12 5   23 5 1 18

__ __ __ __ __ __   __ __ __ __

7 18 5 5 14   15 14   19 20

__ __ __ __ __   __ __   __ __.

16 1 20 18 9 3 11 19   4 1 25

__ __ __ __ __ __ __ ' __   __ __ __

1 14 4   3 5 12 5 2 18 1 20 5

__ __ __   __ __ __ __ __ __ __ __ __

23 9 20 8   16 1 18 1 4 5 19

__ __ __ __   __ __ __ __ __ __ __.

Name ______________________________

MISSING CONSONANT PUZZLE

Directions: Fill in the missing consonants.

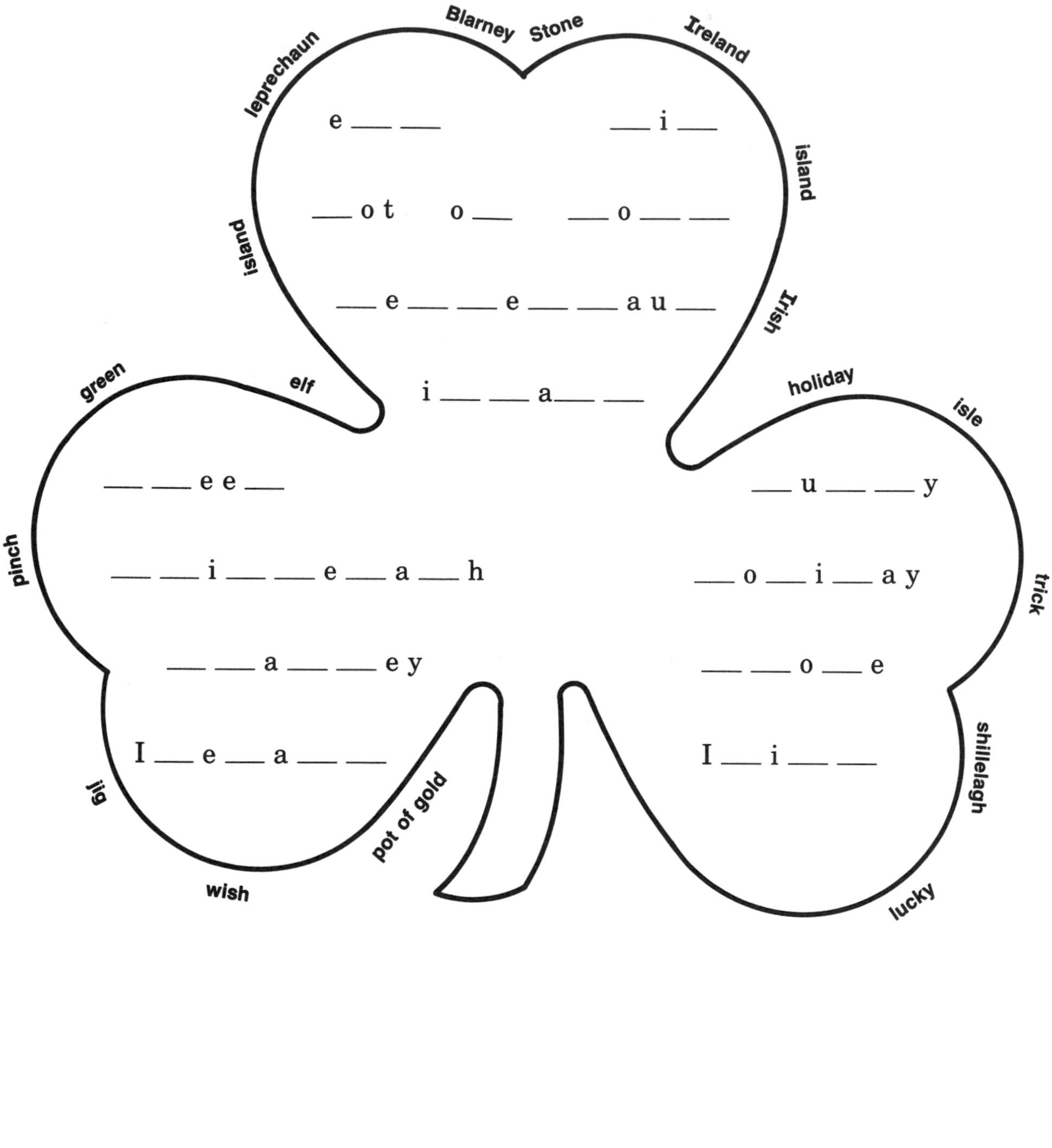

MISSING VOWEL PUZZLE

Directions: Fill in the missing vowels.

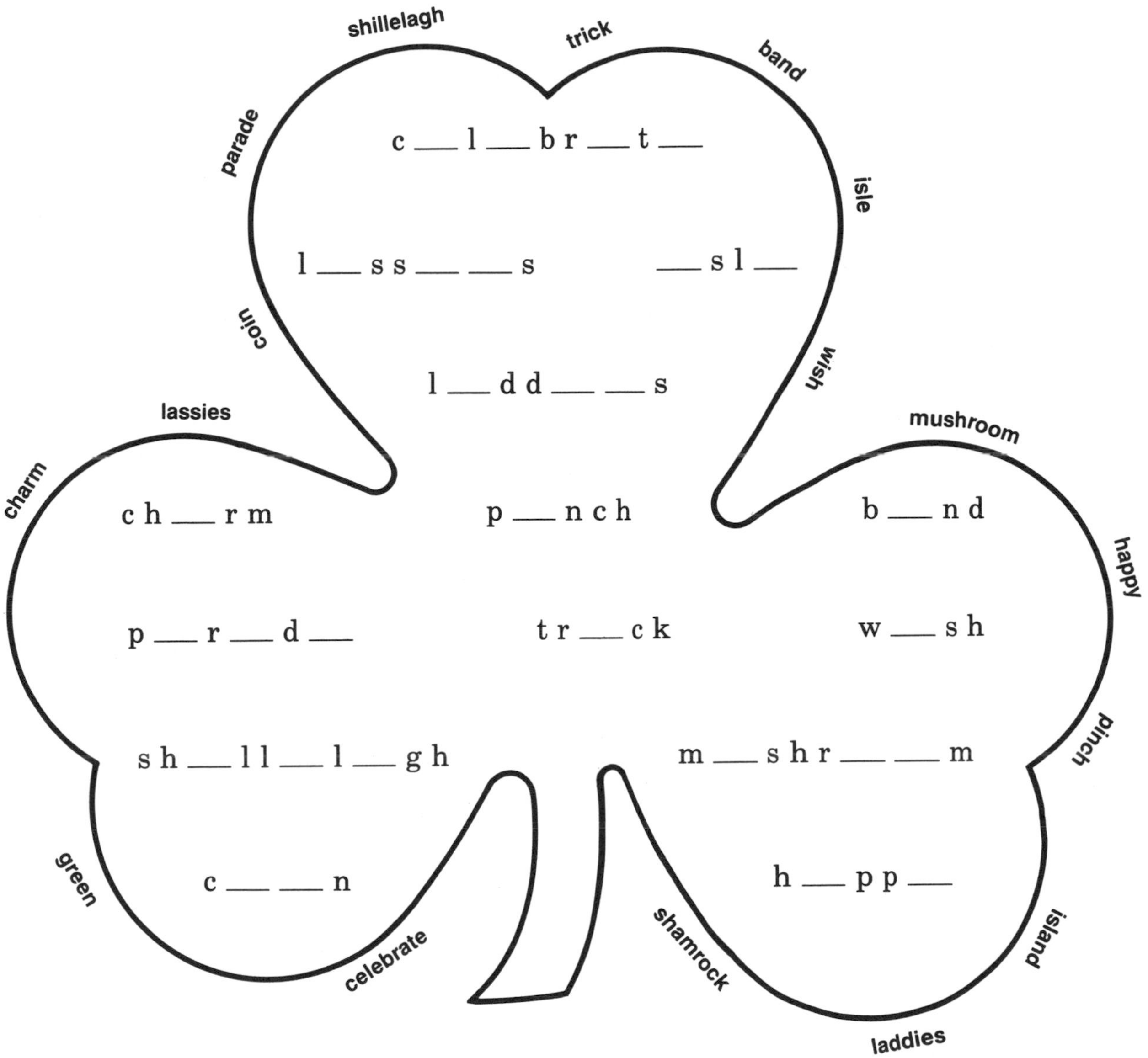

WORD SCRAMBLE

Directions: Unscramble each word and write it in the correct place.

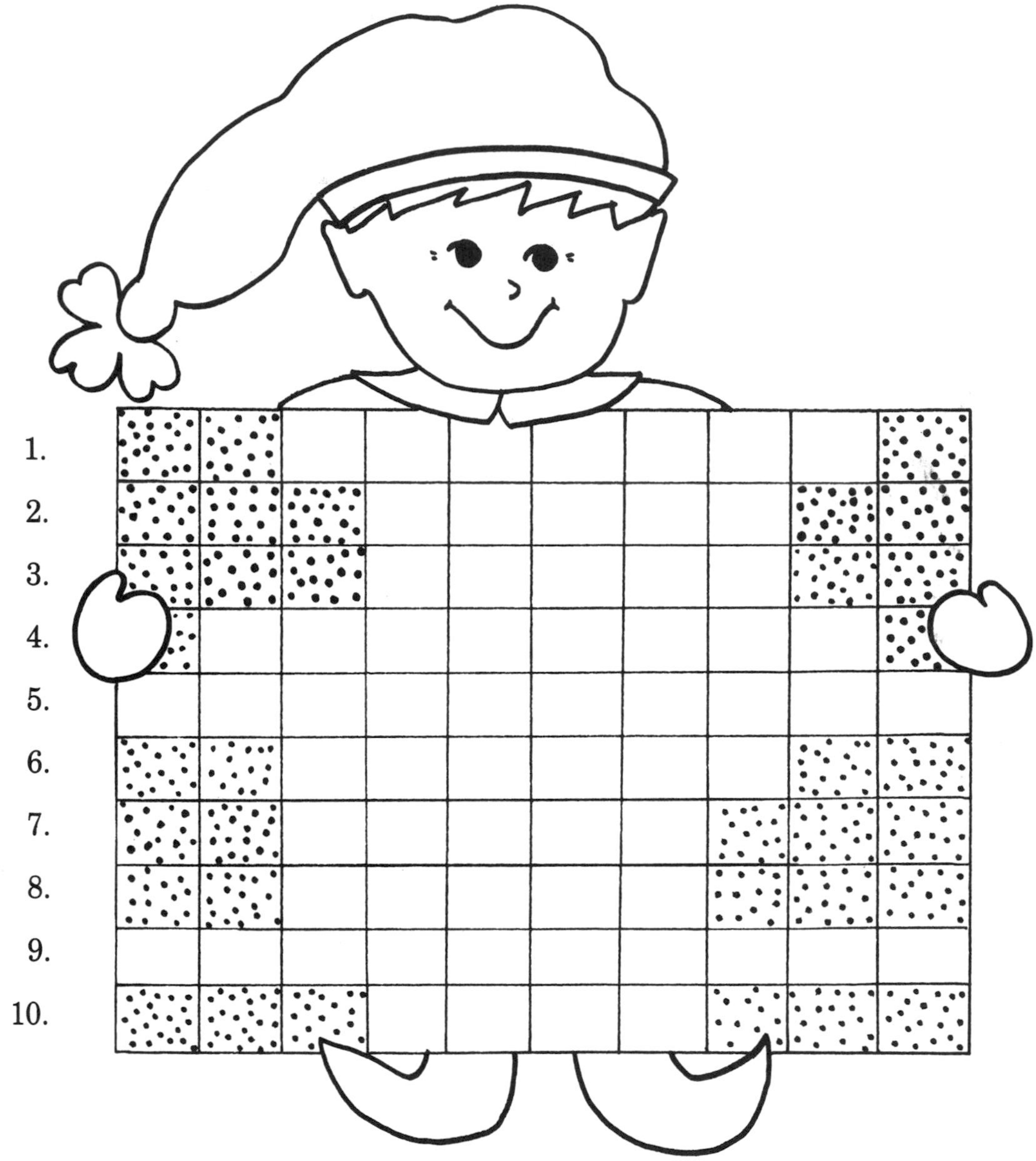

1. rlndIea
2. ykcul
3. enreg
4. shkcamor
5. chaunlepre
6. raedap
7. acmhr
8. Mrcha
9. shilllghea
10. whis

Name ______________________________

RHYME TIME

WORD BANK
pot of gold
green
pinch
trick
saint
hat
parade
charm
March
wish
jig
lucky
elf
coin

Directions: Write a St. Patrick's Day word that rhymes with each word. Use the word bank.

seen ____________________

big and bold ____________________

charade ____________________

Bucky ____________________

big ____________________

that ____________________

dish ____________________

shelf ____________________

inch ____________________

sick ____________________

alarm ____________________

paint ____________________

starch ____________________

Name ________________________________

MAKE A WORD

Directions: Use the letters in the words "Saint Patrick's Day" to make as many different words as possible.

SAINT PATRICK'S DAY

Name ______________________________

MY THREE WISHES

Directions: Complete the story. Illustrate your story in the space below.

Wow! I just caught a leprechaun. Now I get to make three wishes. I think I will

Name ________________________________

THE POT OF GOLD

Directions: Complete the story. Illustrate your story in the space below.

If I could find the pot of gold at the end of the rainbow, I would ____________

Name ______________________

LEGEND OF THE LEPRECHAUN

Directions: Complete the story. Illustrate your story in the space below.

A legend is a story that has been told for many years. Many people may think a legend is true, but they can't prove that it's true. The legend of the leprechaun tells us

Name ______________________________

SAINT PATRICK

Directions: Fill in the blanks with words from the shamrocks.

Saint Patrick is the patron saint of Ireland. Some (1) ____________________ say that he was born in Scotland in the year 385. When he was sixteen years old, he was (2) ________________ by a band of Irish (3) ________________ and sold into (4) ________________. Six years later, he (5) ________________ and went to Britain where he entered a (6) ________________ in order to prepare himself to do religious work.

Around 432, he (7) ______________________ to Ireland and began trying to (8) ______________ the Irish to Christianity. He used the (9) ______________ to explain the idea of the Trinity. He converted thousands of Irishmen and founded many churches and (10) ________________.

After working as a (11) ______________________ for many years, he died on March 17, 461. The (12) ________________________________ of his death is a (13) ____________ holiday in Ireland. People honor St. Patrick in special religious (14) ________________ and by (15) ________________ shamrocks.

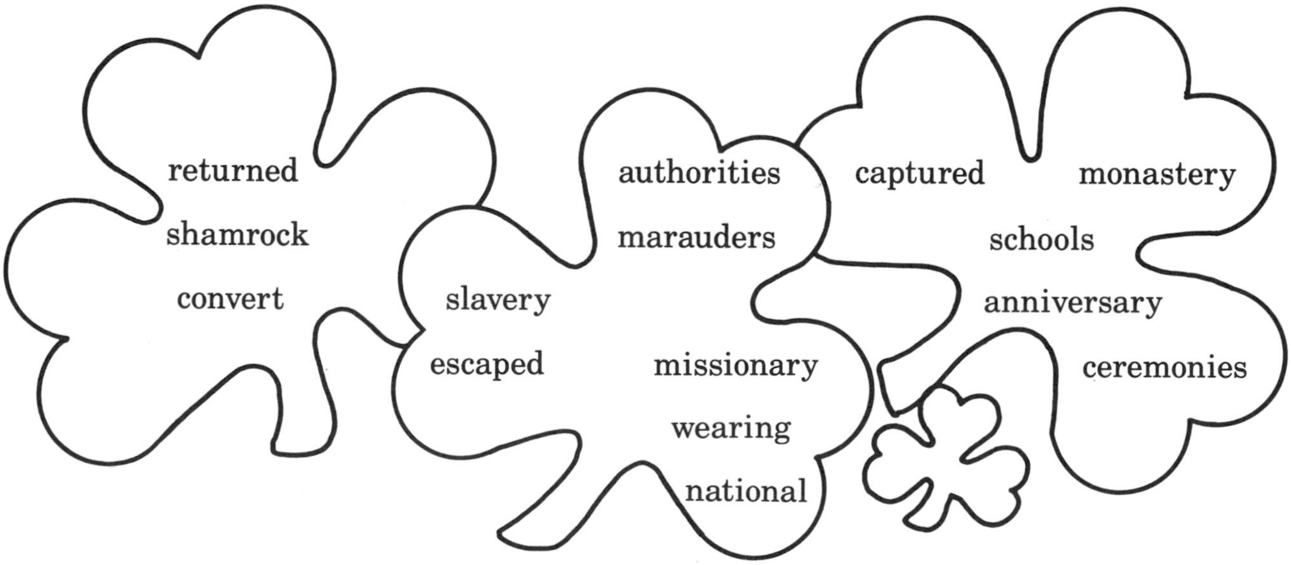

Name ______________________________

THE LAST SNAKE

Directions: Fill in the blanks with words from the snake.

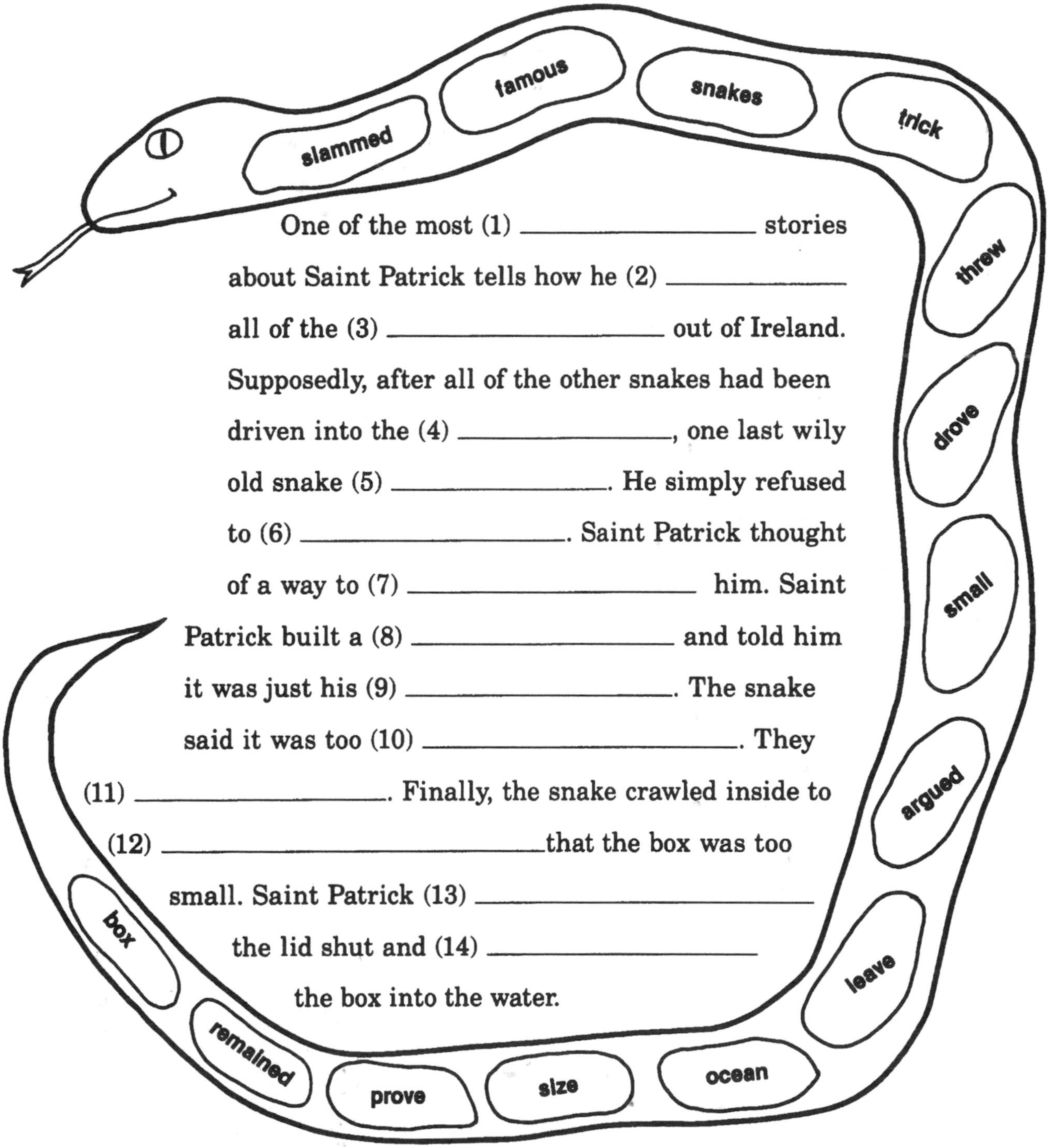

One of the most (1) ______________ stories about Saint Patrick tells how he (2) ______________ all of the (3) ______________ out of Ireland. Supposedly, after all of the other snakes had been driven into the (4) ______________, one last wily old snake (5) ______________. He simply refused to (6) ______________. Saint Patrick thought of a way to (7) ______________ him. Saint Patrick built a (8) ______________ and told him it was just his (9) ______________. The snake said it was too (10) ______________. They (11) ______________. Finally, the snake crawled inside to (12) ______________ that the box was too small. Saint Patrick (13) ______________ the lid shut and (14) ______________ the box into the water.

APRIL

Activity Number and Title		Special Day
8-1	April Fool's Day	April Fool's Day
8-2	Arbor Day	Arbor Day
8-3	Arbor Day Word Hunt	Arbor Day
8-4	A Picture to Color	Easter
8-5	Same or Different	Easter
8-6	Alphabet Scramble	Easter
8-7	Who Is It?	Easter
8-8	The Lost Bonnet	Easter
8-9	Easter Maze	Easter
8-10	Easter Puzzle	Easter
8-11	Easter Puzzle	Easter
8-12	Easter Match	Easter
8-13	Easter Word Hunt	Easter
8-14	Easter Sentences	Easter
8-15	Sh! It's a Secret!	Easter
8-16	Easter Consonant Puzzle	Easter
8-17	Easter Vowel Puzzle	Easter
8-18	Word Scramble	Easter
8-19	Word Scramble	Easter
8-20	Make a Word	Easter
8-21	An Easter Story	Easter
8-22	Easter Morning	Easter
8-23	New Clothes for an Old Witch	Easter
8-24	Easter	Easter
8-25	Word Hunt	Easter

A Scrambled Egg Game

Make a "Scrambled Egg" game for the Fun Box. Cut large egg shapes out of construction paper. Decorate one side with a design that is different from any of the other eggs used for this game. Cut each egg in half. On the undecorated side, put a question about Easter, April Fool's Day, or Arbor Day on one half and the answer on the other half.

The student has to match the correct answer to each question. The answer is correct if the design on the decorated side of the egg matches.

Here is an example showing both sides of a "Scrambled Egg":

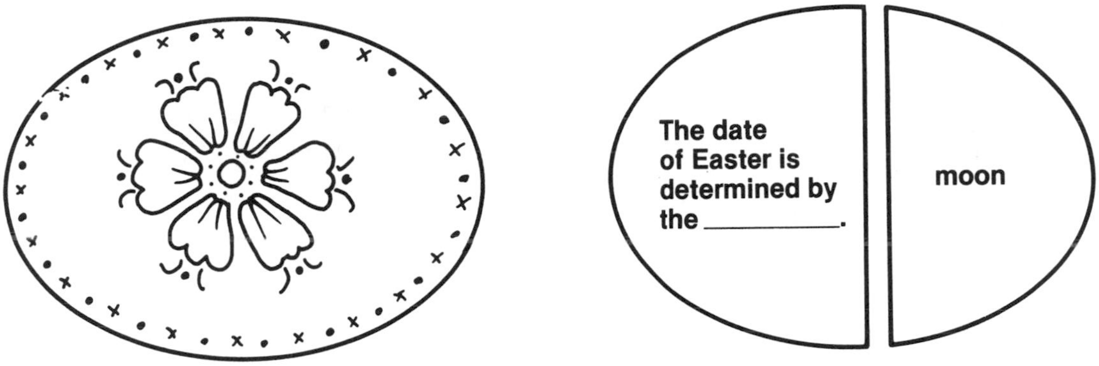

Fun with Quotation Marks

Present a lesson on quotation marks by cutting cartoons out of the comic section of the Sunday newspaper. Explain that the balloons in the cartoons contain words that are being spoken by the characters. Have the students write the dialogue on a sheet of notebook paper using quotation marks.

Vocabulary

The following three word lists will help develop your students' vocabularies in April.

April Fool's Day Word List	**Arbor Day Word List**	**Easter Word List**
celebrated	arbor	Sunday
tradition	tree	hunting
jokes	observed	new
April	persuaded	flowers
fourth	civic	clothes

April Fool's Day Word List	Arbor Day Word List	Easter Word List
custom	conserve	March
origin	groups	symbol
time	proposed	churches
practical	school	relationship
break	proclaim	bunny
first	enrich	represent
people	climate	excitement
reformed	soil	life
began	beautify	eggs
fools	legislature	outfits
lost	moisture	lilies
refused	planting	April
customary	erosion	Easter
continued	treeless	hare
day	celebrating	basket

Game Boards

Here are three game board patterns for you to use in April. For the bingo style game board, don't forget to arrange the words on the other cards in a different order.

Sunday	bunny	Easter	eggs	April
basket	hunting	new	flowers	rabbit
candy	clothes		hare	moon
church	March	spring	lilies	decorate
card	chicks	sunshine	rain	cake

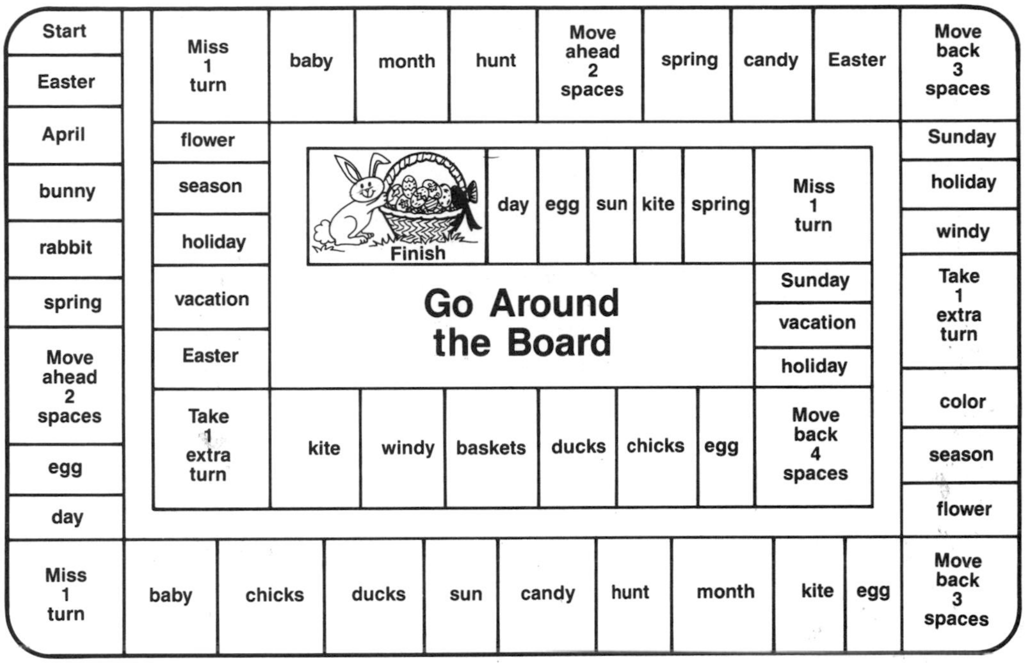
Start
Easter
April
bunny
rabbit
spring
Move ahead 2 spaces
egg
day
Miss 1 turn
baby
chicks
ducks
sun
candy
hunt
month
kite
egg
Move back 3 spaces
flower
season
color
Take 1 extra turn
windy
holiday
Sunday
Move back 3 spaces
Easter
candy
spring
Move ahead 2 spaces
hunt
month
baby
Miss 1 turn
flower
season
holiday
vacation
Easter
Take 1 extra turn
kite
windy
baskets
ducks
chicks
egg
Move back 4 spaces
holiday
vacation
Sunday
Miss 1 turn
spring
kite
sun
egg
day
Finish
Go Around the Board

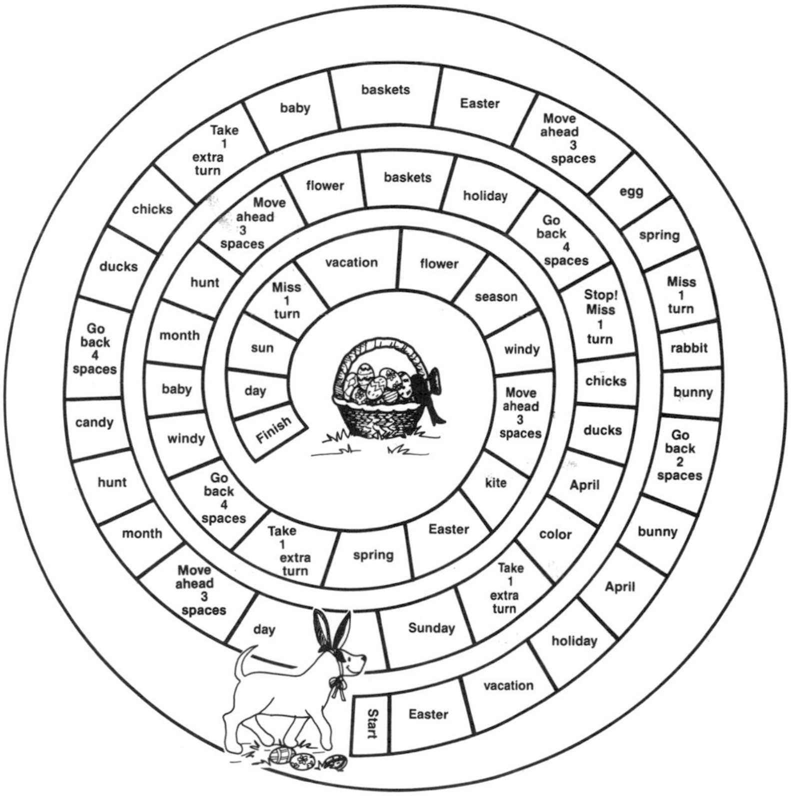
Start
Easter
vacation
holiday
April
bunny
Go back 2 spaces
bunny
rabbit
Miss 1 turn
spring
egg
Move ahead 3 spaces
Easter
baskets
baby
Take 1 extra turn
chicks
ducks
Go back 4 spaces
candy
hunt
month
Move ahead 3 spaces
day
Sunday
Take 1 extra turn
color
April
ducks
chicks
Stop! Miss 1 turn
Go back 4 spaces
holiday
baskets
flower
Move ahead 3 spaces
hunt
month
baby
windy
Go back 4 spaces
Take 1 extra turn
spring
Easter
kite
Move ahead 3 spaces
windy
season
flower
vacation
Miss 1 turn
sun
day
Finish

Name ________________________________

APRIL FOOL'S DAY

Directions: Fill in the blanks with words from the envelope.

April Fool's Day is the (1) ________________ day of (2) ________________. On this day, it is (3) ________________ to play practical (4) ________________ on people. This custom is so old that the (5) ________________ has been (6) ________________. Some people think the (7) ________________ began in (8) ________________ after their king, Charles IX, adopted the reformed (9) ________________ which (10) ________________ the date of New Year's Day to January 1.

Up to that (11) ________________ it had been (12) ________________ on April 1. Some people refused to break with (13) ________________ and (14) ________________ to celebrate New Year's Day on April 1. These people were called April (15) ________________.

Name ________________________________

ARBOR DAY

Directions: Fill in the blanks with words from the tree.

In Latin the word "arbor" means "tree." Arbor Day is a day set aside for (1) ________________ trees. It is especially observed by school (2) ________________, Boy Scouts, Girl Scouts, and civic and (3) ____________ groups.

The (4) ____________ who proposed Arbor Day was Julius Sterling Morton. He lived on the (5) ______________ plains of Nebraska where (6) ____________ was a problem. He realized that trees would enrich the soil, conserve (7) ______________, and beautify the state. He persuaded the Nebraska (8) ______________ to proclaim the first Arbor Day in 1872. Nebraska celebrates Arbor Day on April 22, his (9) ____________.

Other states (10) __________ the value of (11) ________ planting and began (12) __________ Arbor Day at (13) ____________ times depending on the climate. Most Northern states (14) ____________ Arbor Day in April or May. The Southern states observe Arbor Day (15) ____________ December and March.

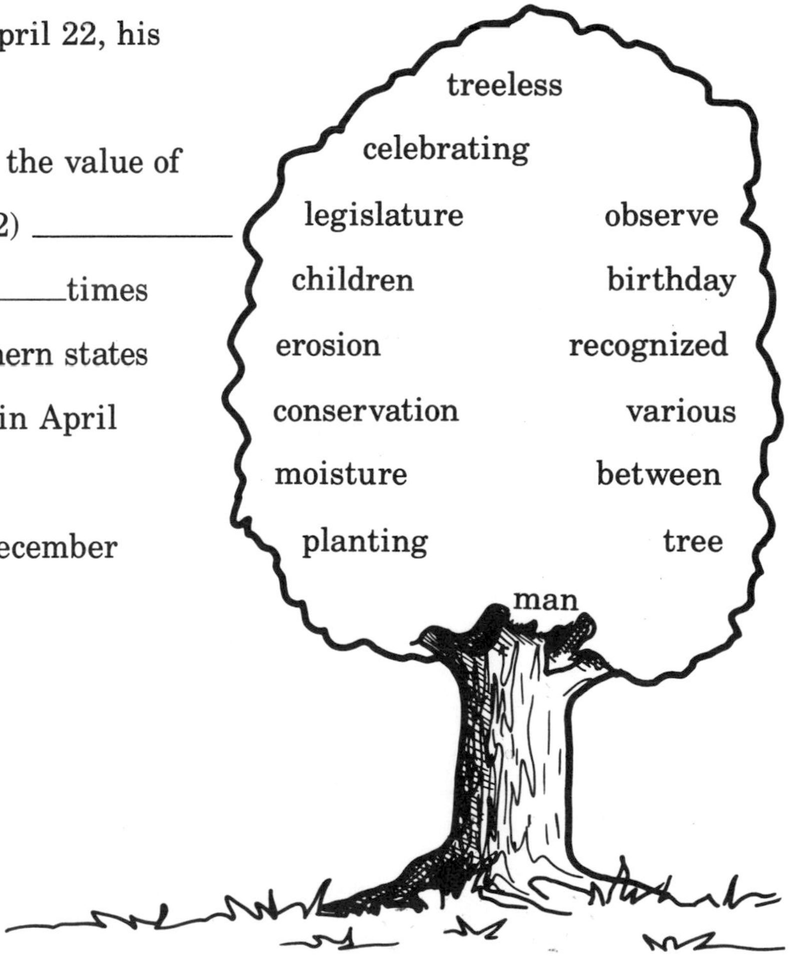

Name ______________________________

ARBOR DAY WORD HUNT

Directions: Circle the hidden words. You may go across and down.

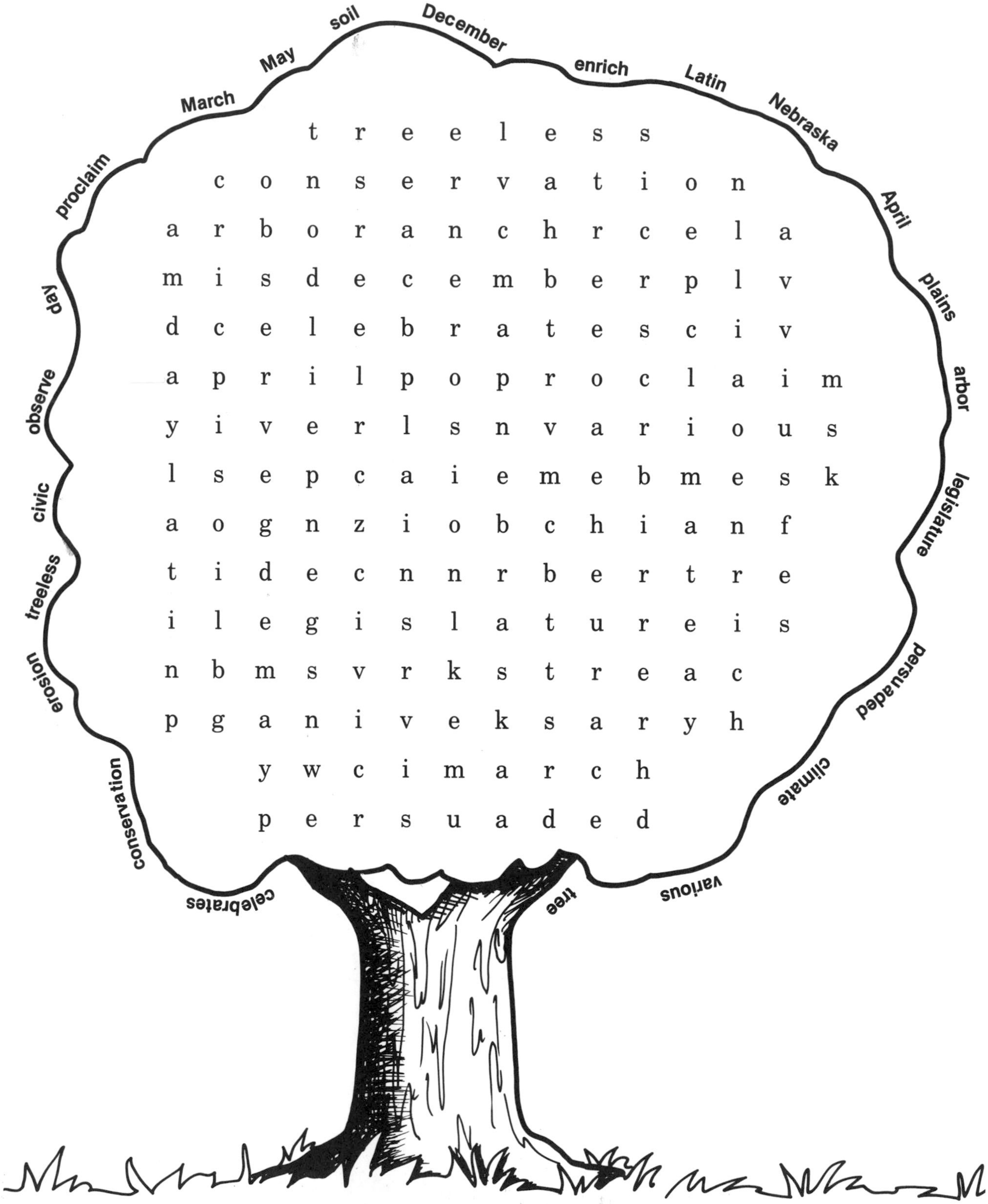

			t	r	e	e	l	e	s	s				
	c	o	n	s	e	r	v	a	t	i	o	n		
a	r	b	o	r	a	n	c	h	r	c	e	l	a	
m	i	s	d	e	c	e	m	b	e	r	p	l	v	
d	c	e	l	e	b	r	a	t	e	s	c	i	v	
a	p	r	i	l	p	o	p	r	o	c	l	a	i	m
y	i	v	e	r	l	s	n	v	a	r	i	o	u	s
l	s	e	p	c	a	i	e	m	e	b	m	e	s	k
a	o	g	n	z	i	o	b	c	h	i	a	n	f	
t	i	d	e	c	n	n	r	b	e	r	t	r	e	
i	l	e	g	i	s	l	a	t	u	r	e	i	s	
n	b	m	s	v	r	k	s	t	r	e	a	c		
p	g	a	n	i	v	e	k	s	a	r	y	h		
		y	w	c	i	m	a	r	c	h				
		p	e	r	s	u	a	d	e	d				

Name ______________________________

A PICTURE TO COLOR

Directions: Color the picture.

Name ______________________________

SAME OR DIFFERENT

Directions: Look at the word on the left. Circle the word on the right that is like the one on the left.

bunny	buny	dunny	bunny	bunney
April	Aqril	April	Aprul	Agril
clothes	clothes	clathes	cluthes	clothe
basket	baskets	basket	dasket	baskut
showers	showurs	showirs	shower	showers
eggs	egg	epps	eggs	aggs
new	niw	nuw	newe	new
hide	hid	hibe	hade	hide
decorate	decurate	decorate	decorat	becorate
candy	candy	cindy	canby	caendy

Name ____________________

ALPHABET SCRAMBLE

Directions: Someone tipped over the Easter basket. All the letters of the alphabet spilled out. Write them in the correct order. The first three are done for you.

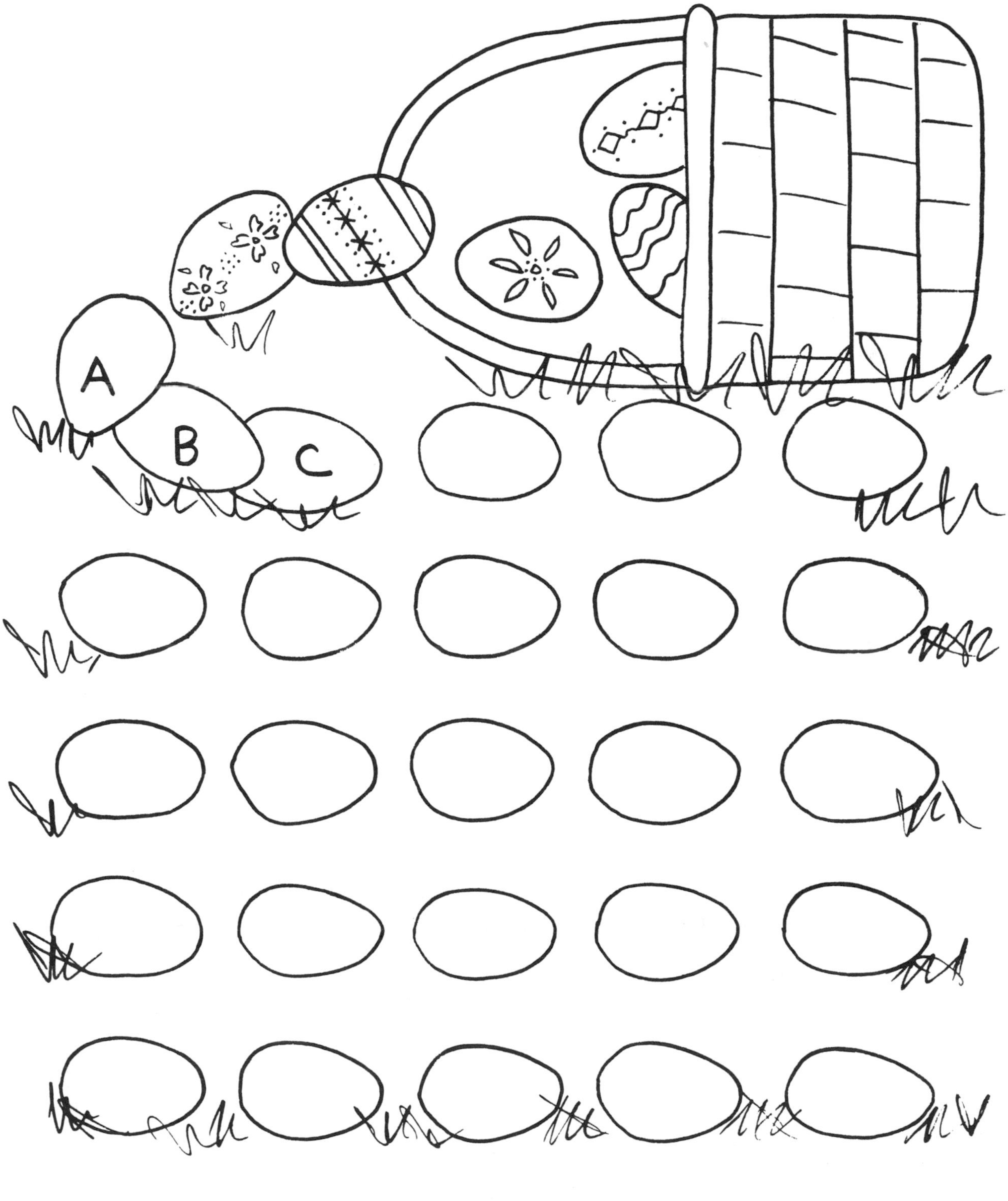

Name ______________________________

WHO IS IT?

Directions: Connect the dots to find out who is in this picture. Start with the first letter of the alphabet. First, connect the lower case letters. Then, connect the capital letters.

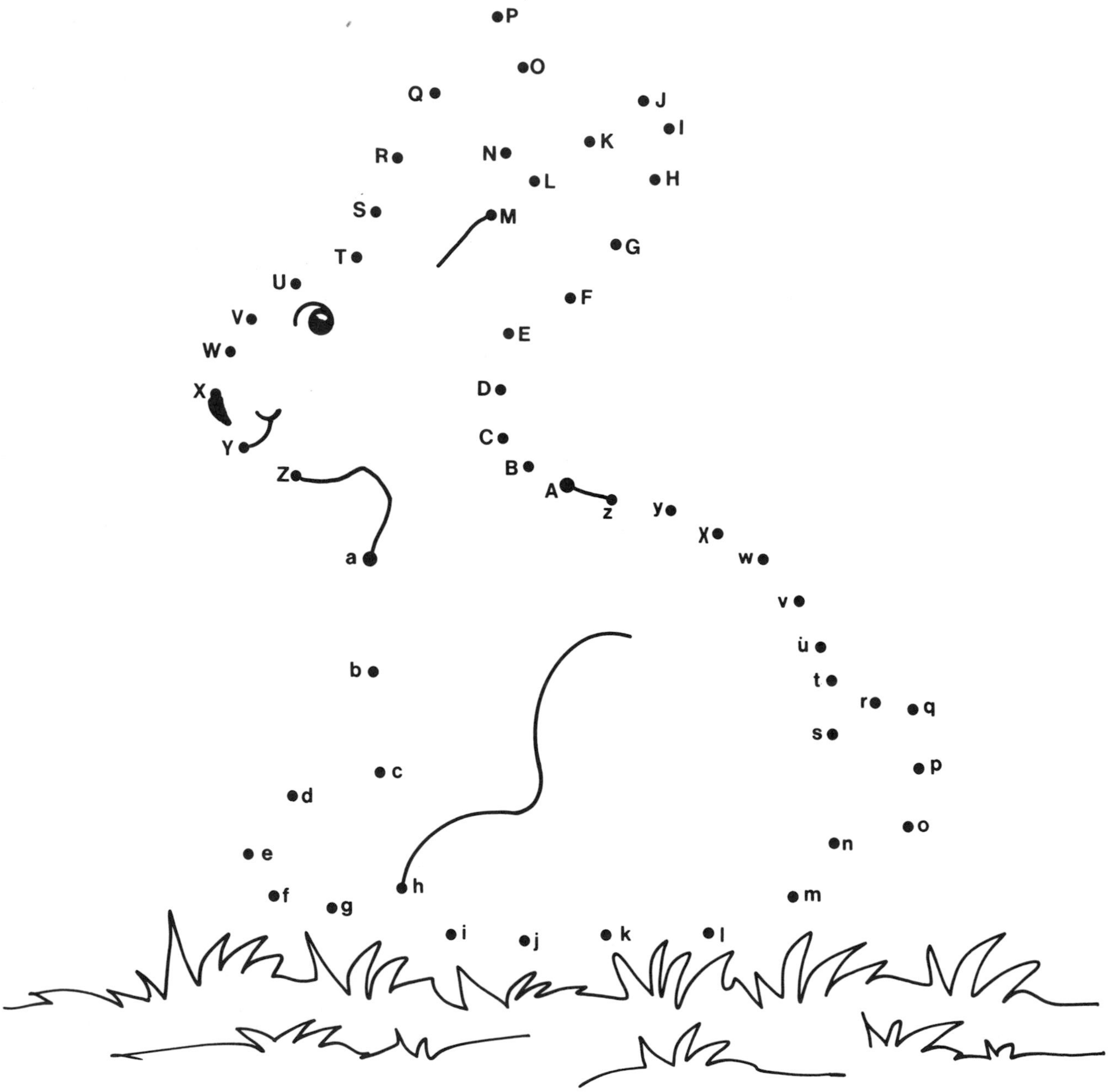

Name ________________________________

THE LOST BONNET

Directions: Help the witch find her new Easter bonnet by drawing a line to connect all the Easter words. Start near the witch.

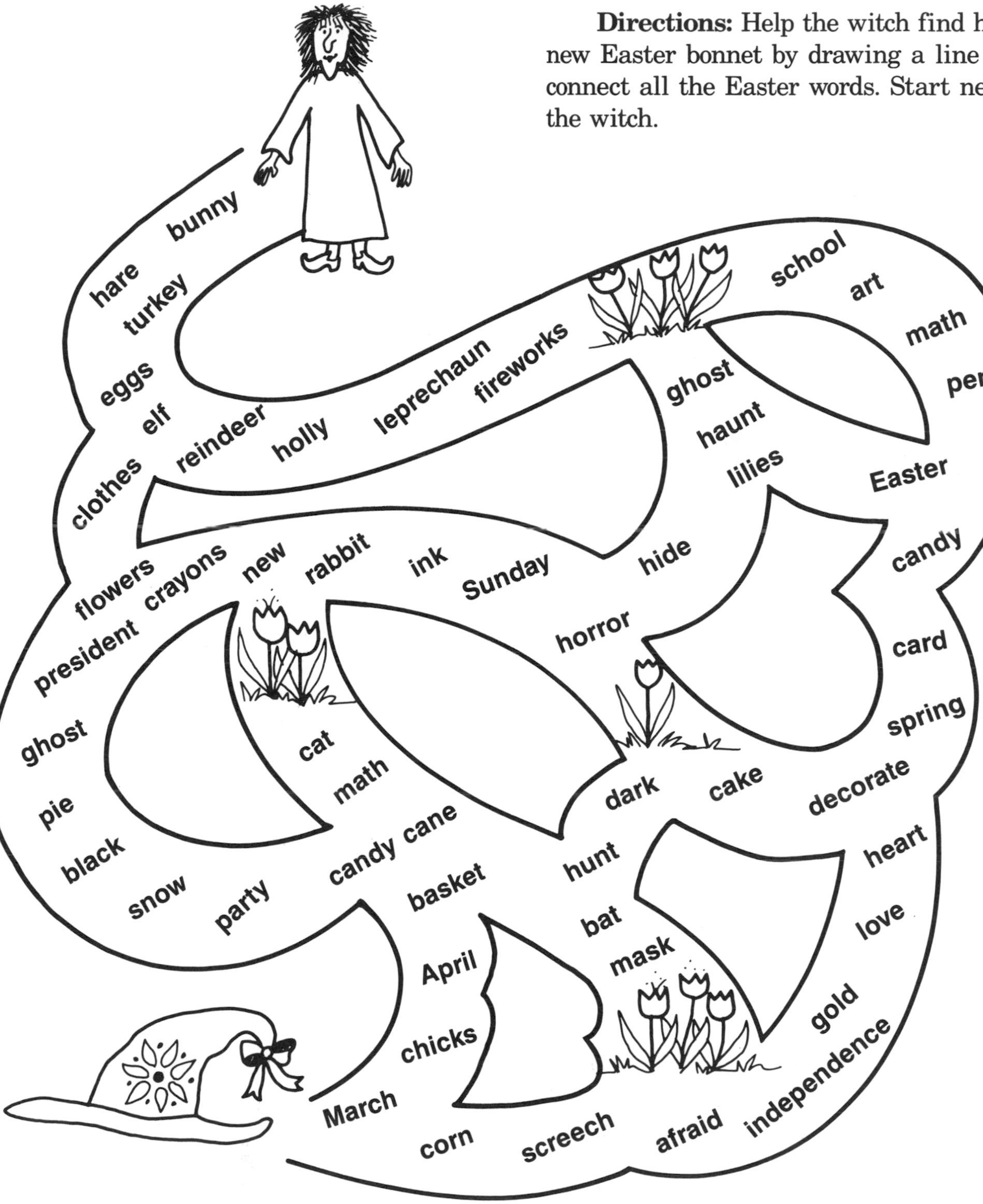

Name ______________________________

EASTER MAZE

Directions: The Easter Bunny can't find any Easter eggs. Can you help? Draw a line from him through all of the Easter words.

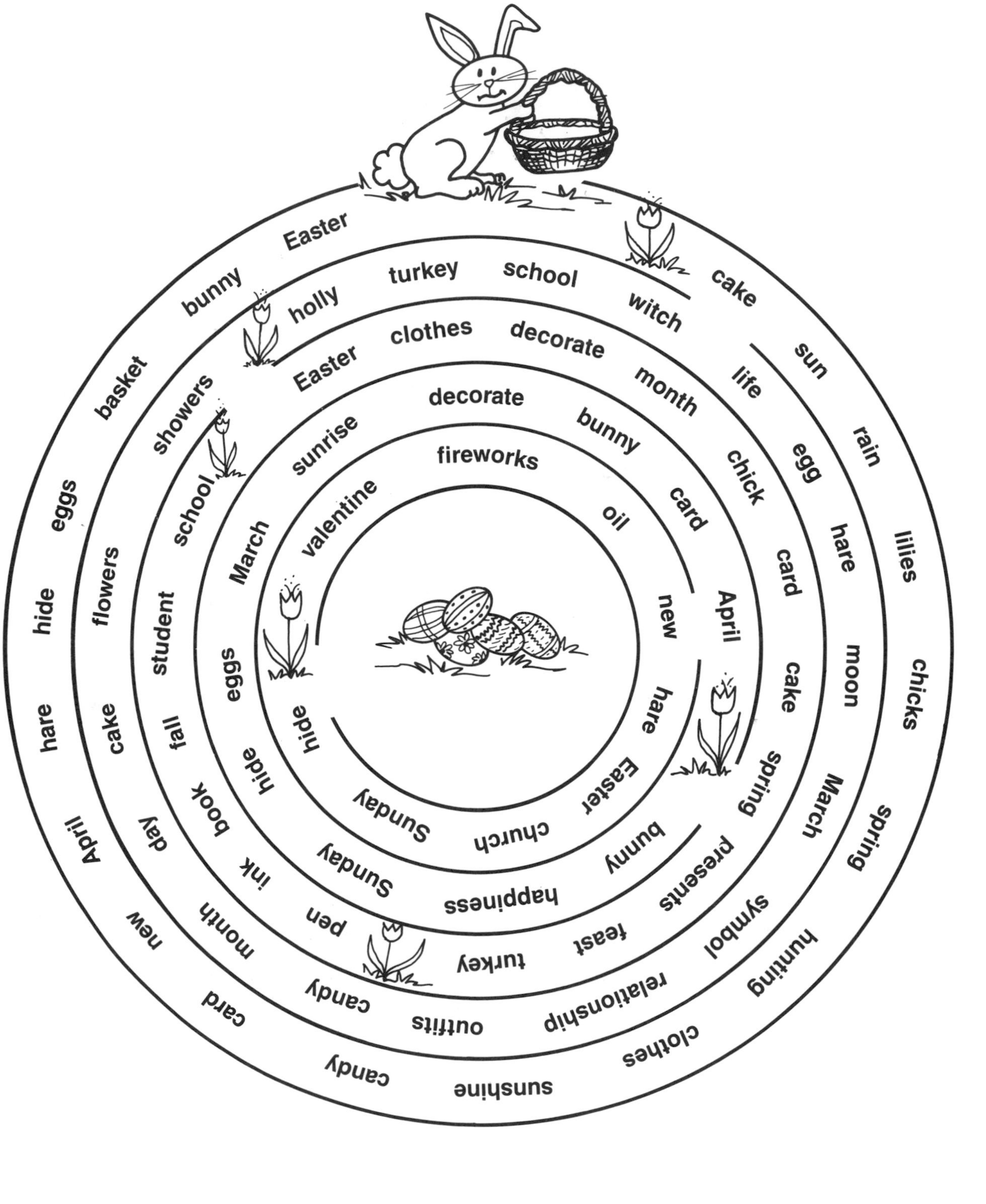

Name ______________________________

EASTER PUZZLE

Directions: Color the vowels pink. Color the consonants yellow. Color the rest of the egg your favorite color!

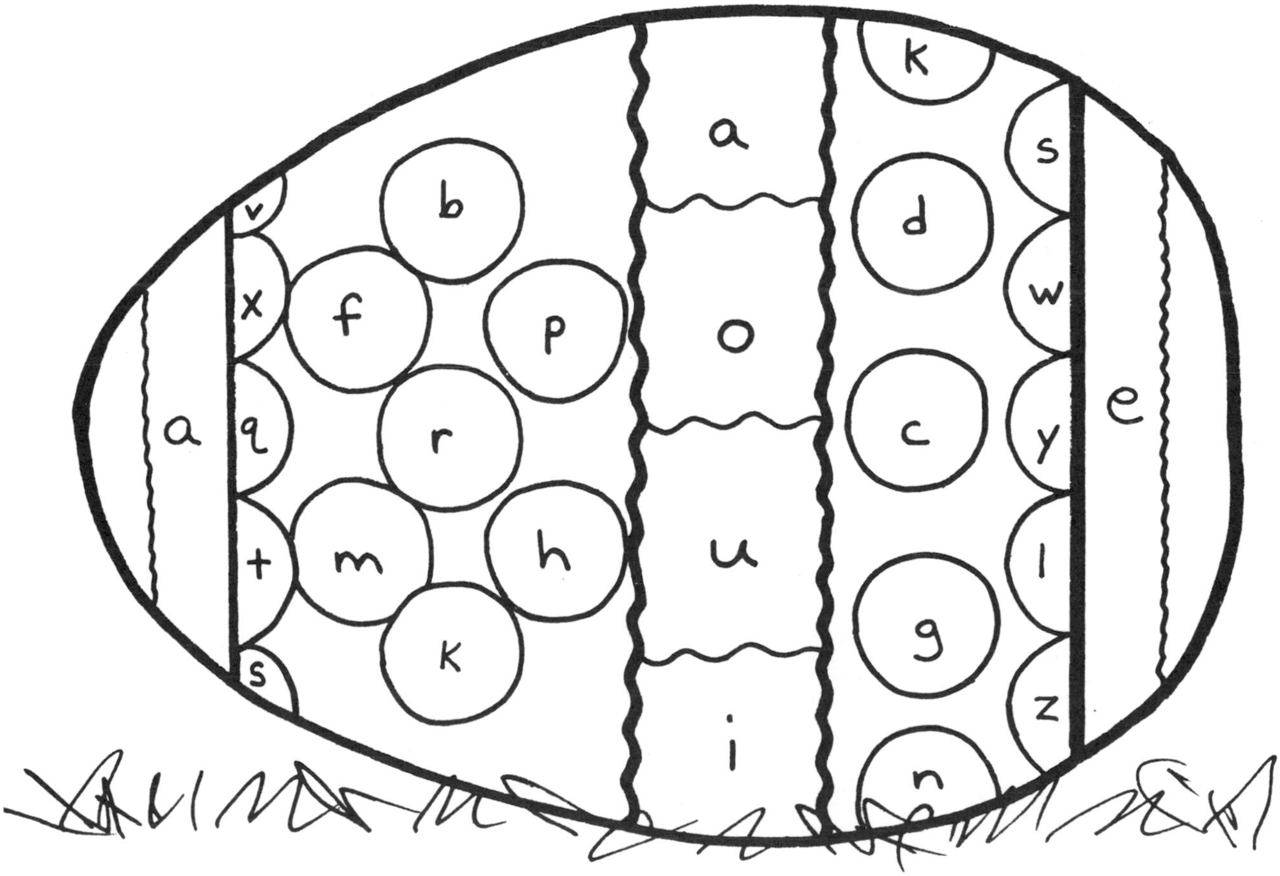

Name ______________________________

EASTER PUZZLE

Directions: Color the vowels pink. Color the consonants gray.

EASTER MATCH

Directions: Draw a line to match the pictures to the correct words.

card

showers

flowers

cake

basket

candy

bunny

chicks

eggs

church

Name ______________________________

EASTER WORD HUNT

Directions: Circle the hidden words. You may go across and down.

e	a	s	t	e	r	x	s	u	n	d	a	y
q	a	p	r	i	l	j	u	z	l	k	r	s
c	a	r	d	n	m	o	n	t	h	b	d	h
e	f	i	g	m	o	q	s	k	m	z	x	a
b	u	n	n	y	i	c	h	i	c	k	s	p
k	e	g	g	s	x	h	i	d	e	a	z	p
m	a	r	c	h	s	p	n	e	w	r	i	y
e	h	j	b	a	s	k	e	t	l	p	u	v
c	l	o	t	h	e	s	k	m	r	a	i	n
d	c	h	u	r	c	h	g	s	p	k	m	o
c	h	u	r	c	d	e	c	o	r	a	t	e

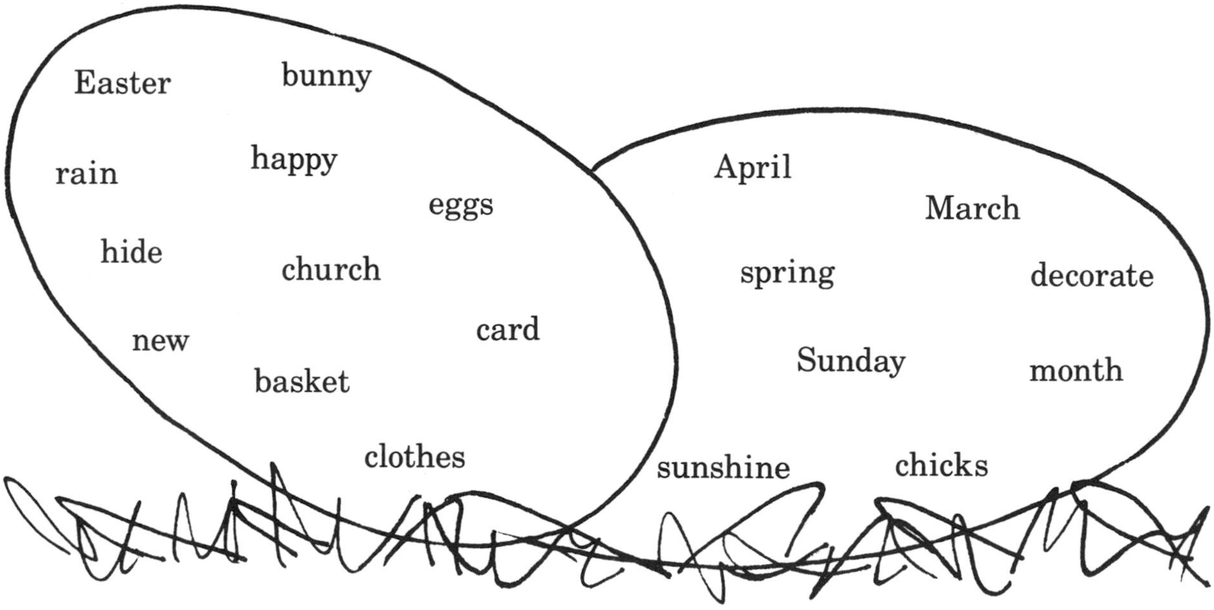

EASTER SENTENCES

Directions: Capitalize and punctuate the sentences correctly.

1. easter is a special day

____

____

2. it comes in the spring

____

____

3. on easter morning we get an easter basket filled with pretty eggs and candy

____

____

____

4. it is fun to hide the easter eggs and then have an easter egg hunt

____

____

____

5. for dessert we always have a cake that looks like the easter bunny

____

____

____

Name ____________________

SH! IT'S A SECRET!

Directions: Use the following code to learn the secret. Write the letters on the correct lines.

Are you ready to hunt for Easter eggs?

A	B	C	D	E	F	G	H	I	J	K	L	M
1	2	3	4	5	6	7	8	9	10	11	12	13
N	O	P	Q	R	S	T	U	V	W	X	Y	Z
14	15	16	17	18	19	20	21	22	23	24	25	26

1 12 12   15 6   20 8 5

__ __ __   __ __   __ __ __

5 1 19 20 5 18   5 7 7 19

__ __ __ __ __ __   __ __ __ __

1 18 5   8 9 4 4 5 14

__ __ __   __ __ __ __ __ __

21 14 4 5 18   20 8 5

__ __ __ __ __   __ __ __

12 9 12 1 3   2 21 19 8 5 19

__ __ __ __ __   __ __ __ __ __ __.

EASTER CONSONANT PUZZLE

Directions: Fill in the missing consonants.

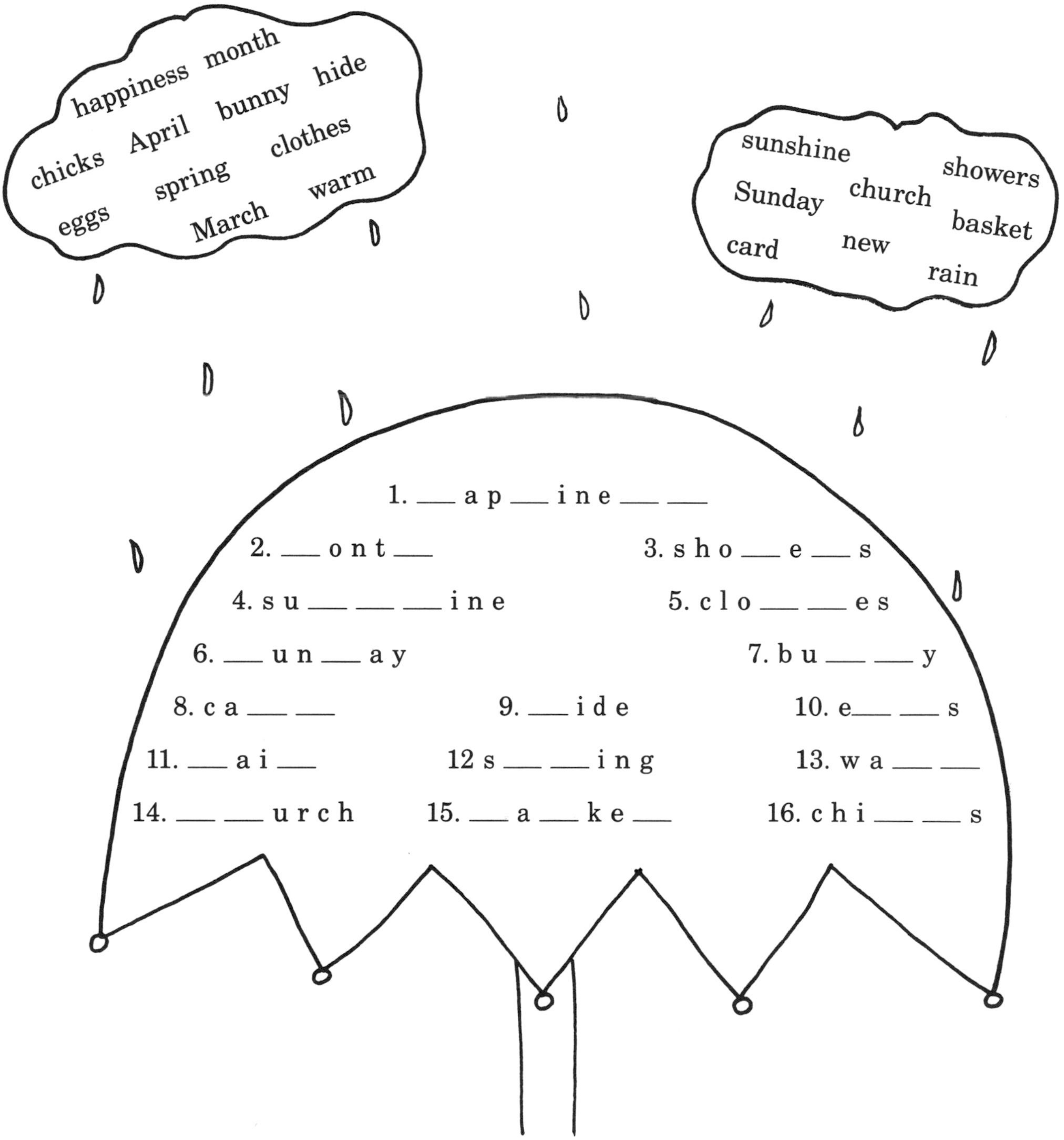

Name ______________________________

EASTER VOWEL PUZZLE

Directions: Fill in the missing vowels.

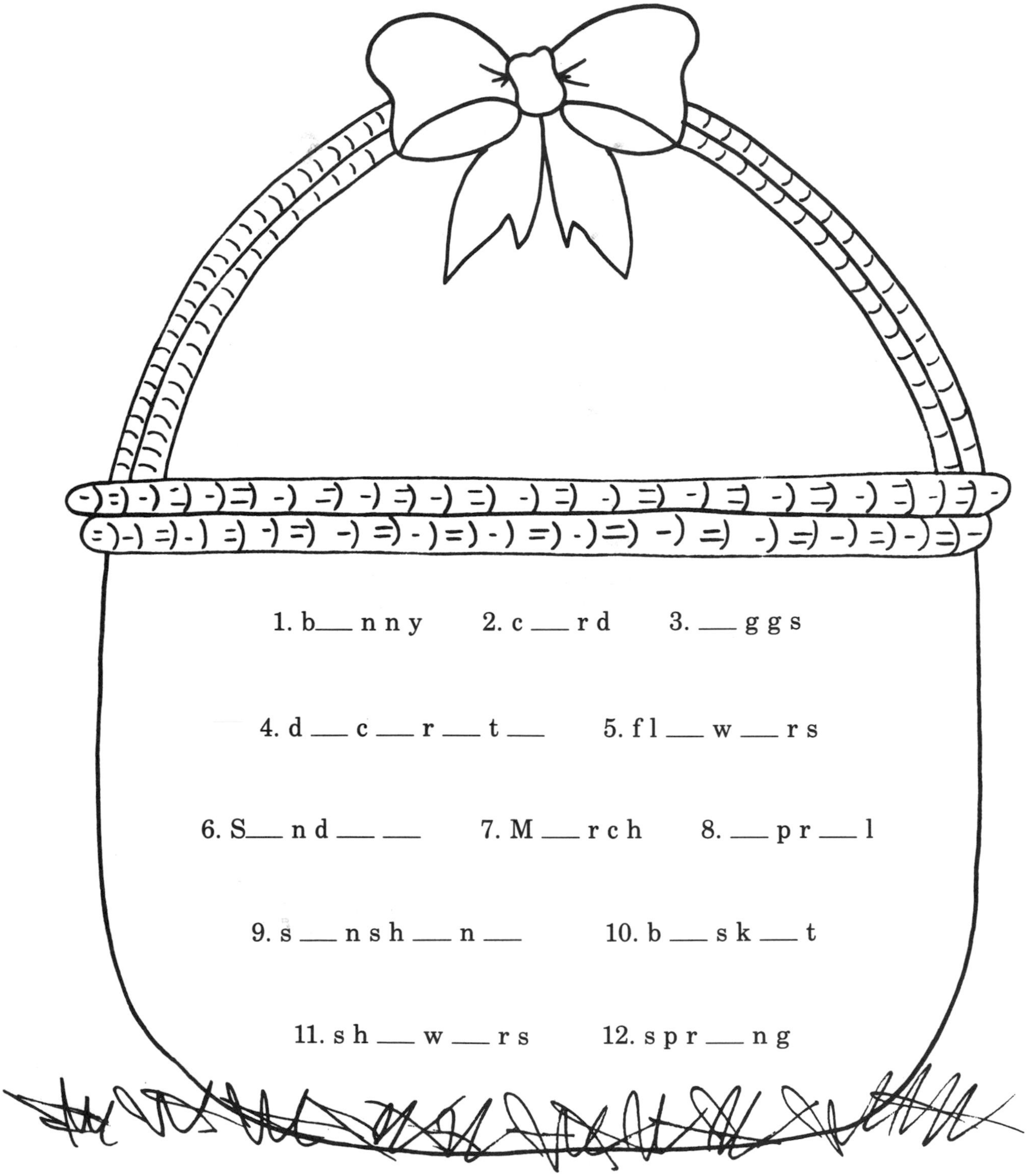

1. b___nny 2. c___rd 3. ___ggs

4. d___c___r___t___ 5. fl___w___rs

6. S___nd______ 7. M___rch 8. ___pr___l

9. s___nsh___n___ 10. b___sk___t

11. sh___w___rs 12. spr___ng

Name ______________________________

WORD SCRAMBLE

Directions: Unscramble the words. Write the words on the lines.

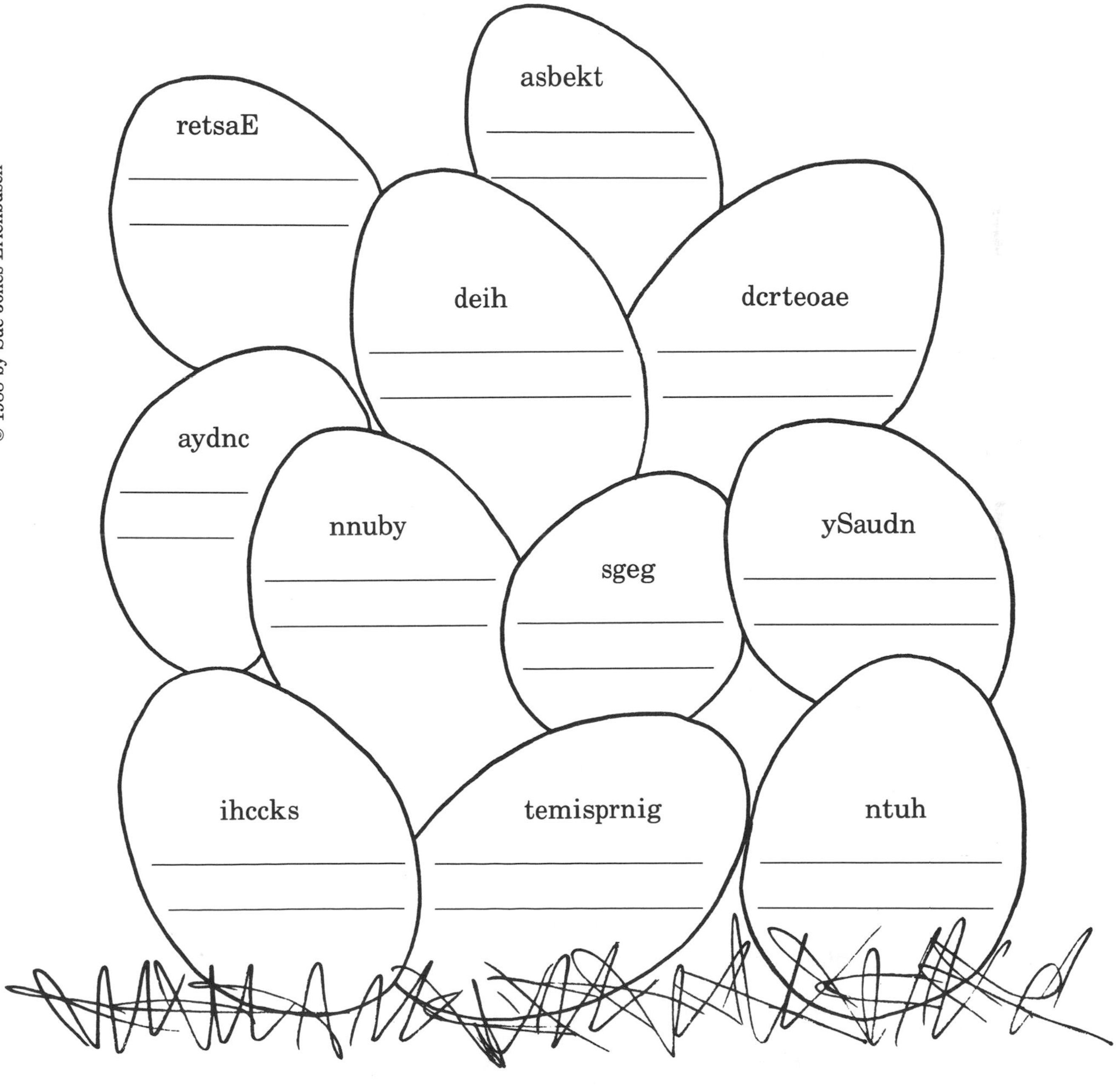

Name ______________________________

WORD SCRAMBLE

Directions: Unscramble each word and write it in the correct place.

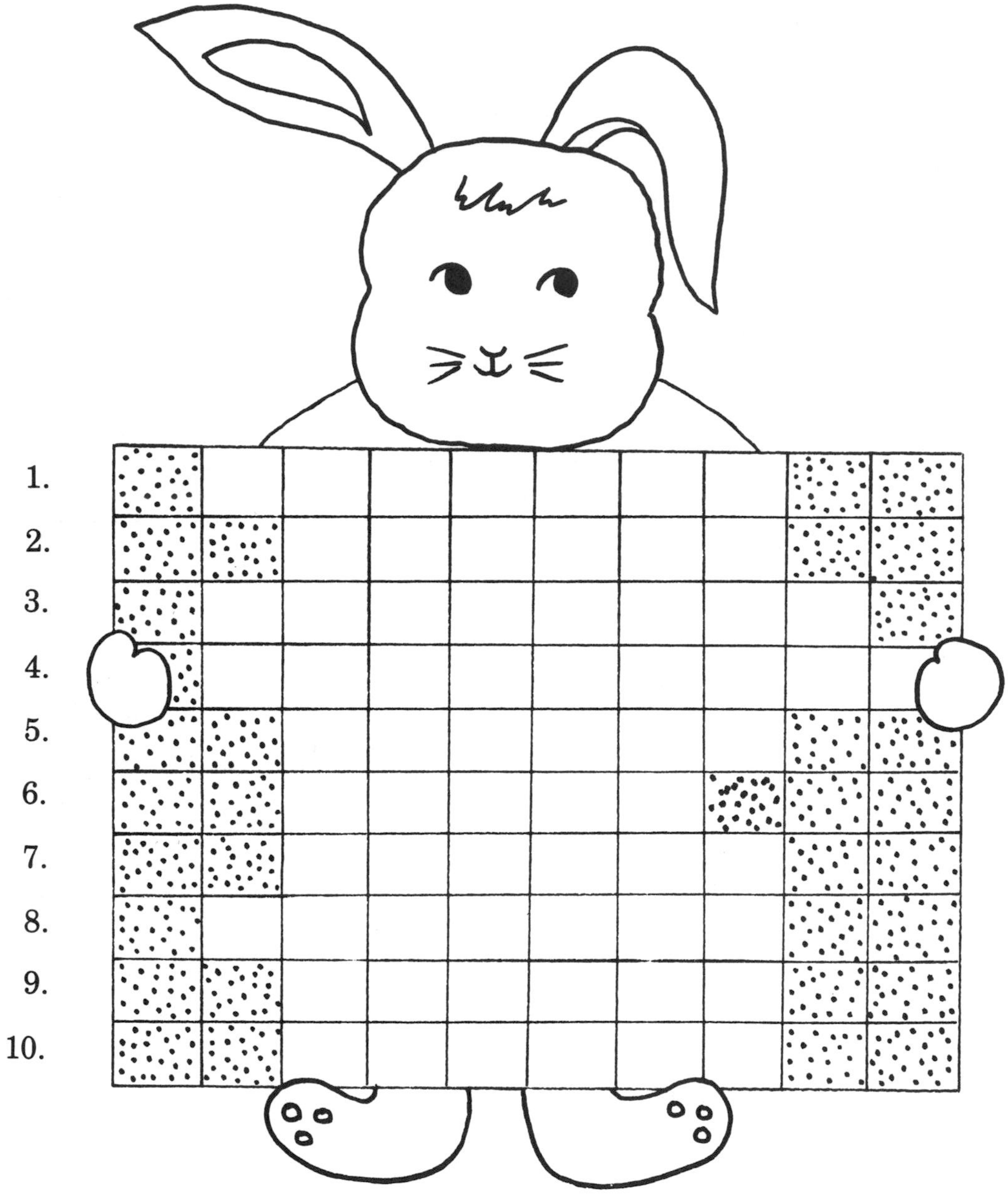

1. foeslwr
2. nnierd
3. shunsien
4. inhaespsp
5. ruhchc
6. irAlp
7. yadunS
8. iaygpln
9. oaenss
10. ketbsa

Name ______________________________

MAKE A WORD

Directions: Use the letters in the word "Easter" to make as many different words as possible.

EASTER

______	______	______
______	______	______
______	______	______
______	______	______
______	______	______
______	______	______
______	______	______
______	______	______
______	______	______
______	______	______
______	______	______
______	______	______
______	______	______
______	______	______
______	______	______
______	______	______
______	______	______
______	______	______
______	______	______

Name ______________________________

AN EASTER STORY

Directions: Complete the story. Illustrate your story in the space next to the witch.

The old witch cast a spell on the Easter Bunny. Easter will be a little different this year because ____

____

____

____

____

____

____

____

____

____

____

____

____

____

____

Name ______________________________

EASTER MORNING

Directions: Complete the story. Illustrate your story in the space below.

On Easter morning, I am going to ____________________________________

Name ______________________________

NEW CLOTHES FOR AN OLD WITCH

Directions: Complete the story. Illustrate your story in the space below.

I wanted some new clothes for Easter, so I decided to cast some spells. Something went wrong with every spell. I tried to turn a rock into a new purse, but ______________________________

Name ______________________________

EASTER

Directions: Fill in the blanks with words from the egg.

Christians (1) ________________ the resurrection of Christ on Easter Sunday. Many churches hold Easter (2) ______________________ services. Churches are decorated with (3) _________________________ lilies and are filled with people (4) ____________________ new Easter outfits. The choir and congregation join in (5) ________________ special hymns of joy.

For many children, the excitement of receiving an Easter (6) ______________ filled with goodies and hunting for eggs (7) ___________________ by the Easter rabbit is topped only by the excitement of receiving gifts from (8) ______________ at Christmas. Did you ever wonder why the Easter (9) ________________________ brings the eggs instead of the Easter chicken? After all, (10) ________________, not rabbits, lay eggs.

Since eggs represent new life, Christians adopted eggs as an Easter (11) ________________ because Easter also represents new life. The date of Easter is (12) ________________ by the moon. The hare is a symbol of the (13) ____________________. Because of this relationship, the hare came to represent (14) ________________. Hares and rabbits are (15) ________________ related. In America, we (16) ________________ the rabbit instead of the hare for our Easter symbol.

sunrise
Santa bunny
closely singing
hidden determined
chickens wearing
celebrate symbol
Easter basket
chose white
moon

Name ______________________________ 8-25

WORD HUNT

Directions: Circle the hidden words. You may go across and down.

excitement children topped lilies relationship represent outfits sunrise

wonder rabbit white congregation life chicken hidden Christians people America resurrection

b a s k e t o p p e
r e p r e s e n t a d i n g h
j k a h i y j e t s u c h u r c h e s
s i m g s y m b o l a c r o s c h o i r u
r a b b i t m e n y r s h a r e h u v d j n k
e n e n f e n t a b e t i m i r r u r d u d o s
c s t a c t r s c b a c g l e d f i l h e j a k m
h u a b b s m q o r s e t d r n e s v x n p y w o
i r e l a t i o n s h i p r i s x t w a s y z h o
k r b w s c o h g o e v e e c e c i f h u n t i n g
e e d h k p i p r t t i o n a r i a r o n i d e k
n c h i c k e n e o d n p v e v t n a n r
s t a t t a c l g p s g l i l i e s o f i f
l i f e g o s o a p t m e o n c m q u i s k
o e s o p d a t e f a b e l e e g g s e s
n r e c e i v i d g o o n a s n u p d
p u v a d o p t e d c o u t f i t s
m a w o n d e r f i l l a m i n
d e c o r a t e d h u s

basket
symbol

hunting
receiving
adopted

hare
gifts
Santa

joy
moon
date

services
hymns

eggs

MAY

Activity Number and Title		Special Day
9-1	May Day Customs	May Day
9-2	May Day Superstitions	May Day
9-3	Mother's Day	Mother's Day
9-4	Memorial Day	Memorial Day

Resource Idea

If some of the activity sheets that utilize the cloze procedure are too difficult for your students to do independently, try this: first, go over the vocabulary words; next, ask the students to put their pencils down and look at the sheet as you read the story to them out loud; then ask them to reread the story silently to themselves and fill in the blanks.

Vocabulary

The following three word lists will help develop your students' vocabularies in May.

May Day Word List	**Mother's Day Word List**	**Memorial Day Word List**
superstitions	May	proclaimed
dew	second	honored
sunrise	nationwide	birthday
May	colored	memorial
festivals	proclamation	decorate
husband	custom	flag
Maypole	president	sponsor
magic	living	community
future	red	cemeteries
reflection	observance	May
month	began	display
mirror	designated	parades
danced	mother	graves
fifth	campaign	citizens
dawn	country	civil
predict	honored	organizations
angle	white	flowers
associate	Sunday	patriotic
village	issued	military
customs	carnation	war

Name ______________________________

MAY DAY CUSTOMS

Directions: Fill in the blanks with words from the basket.

Many of the (1) ______________ that we associate with (2) ______________ Day began in medieval (3) ________________. May Day was one of the villagers' favorite (4) _______________. The villagers went into the (5) ________________ before dawn to gather flowers to (6) ________________________ their homes and (7) ____________. They danced around a Maypole holding onto (8) _____________ that streamed from the top. As they (9) ________________, they wove the ribbons around the (10) _____________. They chose a pretty village (11) ______________ to be their May (12) _______________.

In (13) ____________ in the 1800s, young girls filled May (14) _____________ with flowers and hung them on the (15) ________________________ doors of their friends' homes. Suitors gathered (16) ___________________ to fill May baskets for their (17) ________________.

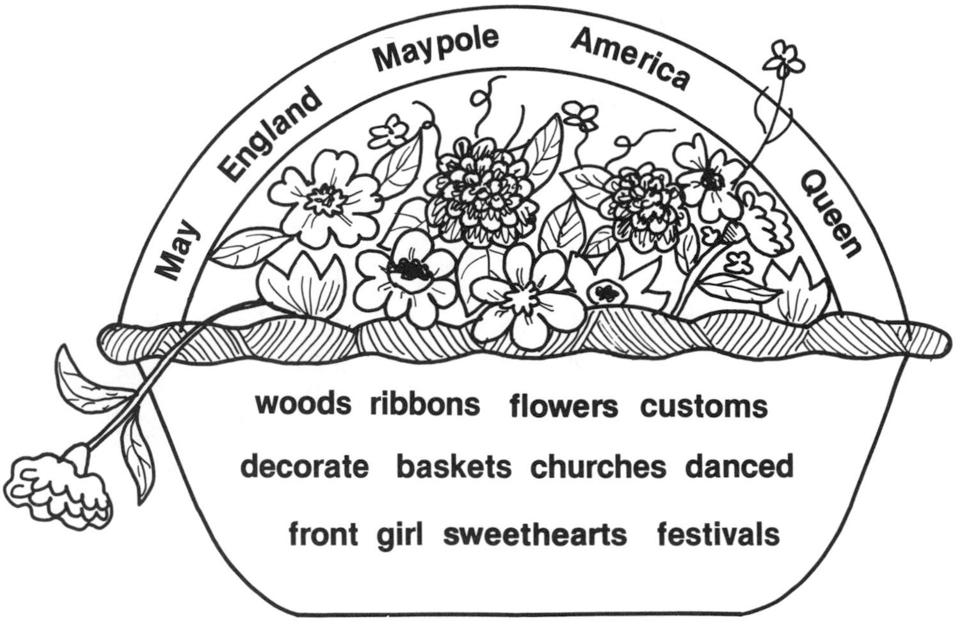

Name ______________________________

MAY DAY SUPERSTITIONS

Directions: Fill in the blanks with words from the hand mirror.

People used to believe there was (1) ______________________ in certain (2) ______________________ performed on May Day. These acts were supposed to (3) ________________ who a girl's future (4) ________________ would be.

If a girl went into the country before (5) ________________ on May Day and washed her face in the morning (6) ______________________ just as the sun was (7) ________________, she was supposed to have a lovely complexion that wouldn't get (8) ________________. If she also said a certain (9) ________________ as she washed her face in the dew, she would (10) ______________________ soon. At dawn on May Day, a girl could hold up a (11) ______________________ full of water and see the outline of her truelove. When she first woke up, she could hold her (12) ______________ at an angle to see the initial or (13) ______________ of her truelove. At noon, she could use the mirror to reflect light into a (14) ________ and see her sweetheart's face in the (15) ____________________ .

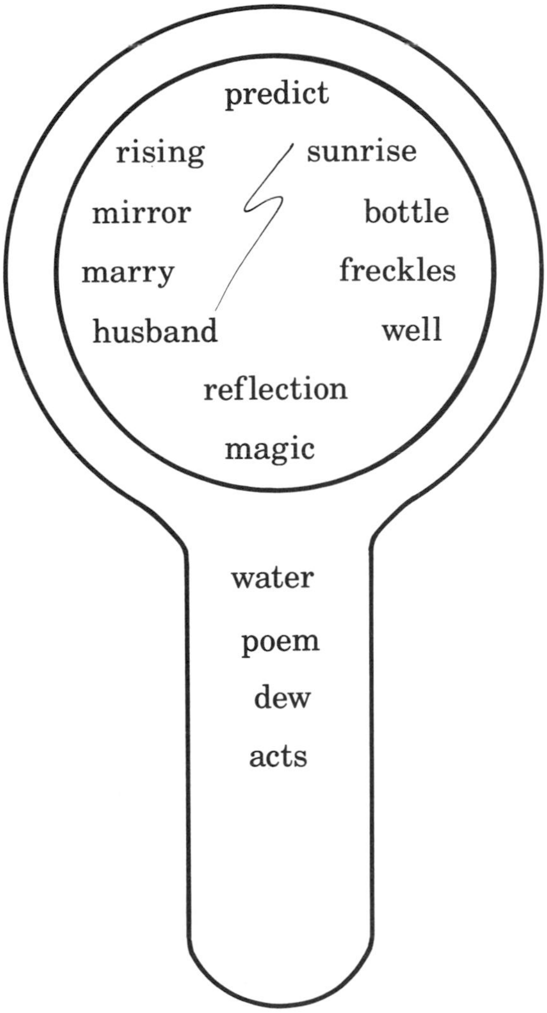

MOTHER'S DAY

Directions: Fill in the blanks with words from the scroll.

Anna Jarvis is (1) ____________________ as the (2) ____________________ of Mother's Day. In 1907, she began a (3) ________________ for a (4) ________________ observance of Mother's Day. She chose the (5) ________________________________ Sunday in May as the day on which mothers would be (6) __________________.

She also began the (7) ____________________ of wearing a carnation on Mother's Day. A colored (8) ____________________ means that your mother is still living. A (9) ________________ carnation means that your mother is (10) ________________.

In 1914, (11) ____________________ Woodrow Wilson (12) ____________________ a Mother's Day (13) ____________________ that designated the second Sunday in May as a day when the (14) ____________________ would honor the mothers of our country.

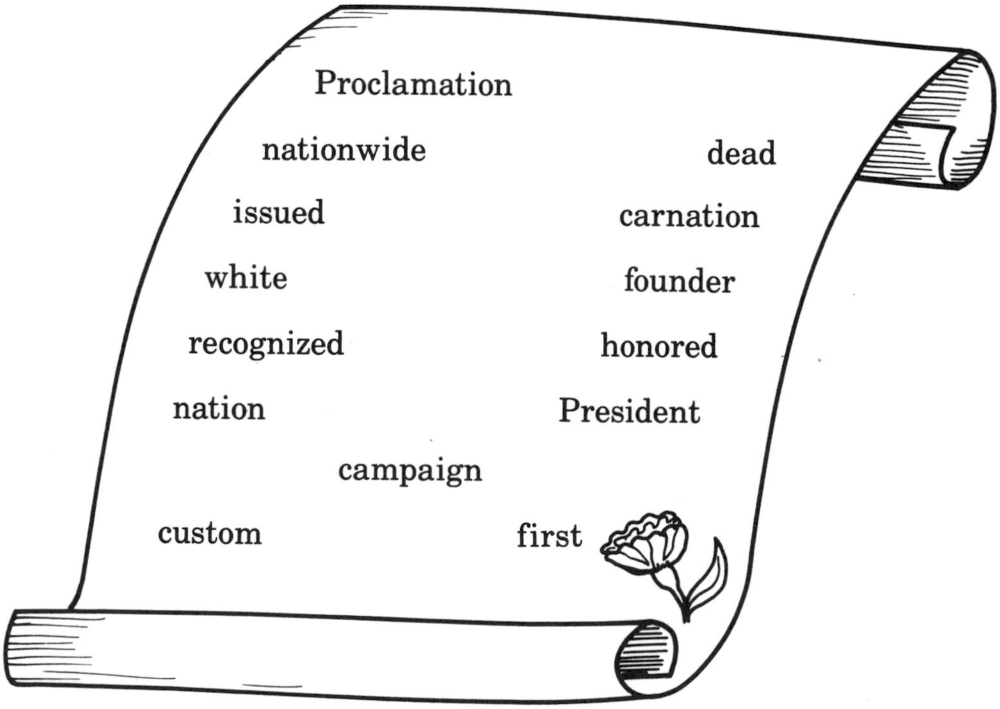

Name ______________________________

MEMORIAL DAY

Directions: Fill in the blanks with words from the flag.

Memorial Day was begun right after the Civil War. The (1) ________________ of Waterloo, New York, has been proclaimed the (2) ________________ of Memorial Day. On May 5, 1866, the people of Waterloo (3) ________________ the war dead of both the North and South by placing (4) ________________ on their graves.

At first, Memorial Day honored the men who (5) ________________ during the Civil War. As time (6) ________________ and this country (7) ________________ in more wars, this (8) ________________ holiday was (9) ________________ to honor the men and women who died during the Spanish-American War, World War I, World War II, Korean War, and Vietnam War. Special (10) ________________ ceremonies are held at Arlington National Cemetery and other cemeteries around the (11) ________________. Veterans' (12) ________________ sponsor (13) ________________ and flags are flown at half-staff.

Today, private (14) ________________ decorate the graves of their (15) ________________ ones on Memorial Day and many people (16) ________________ the flag on their homes.

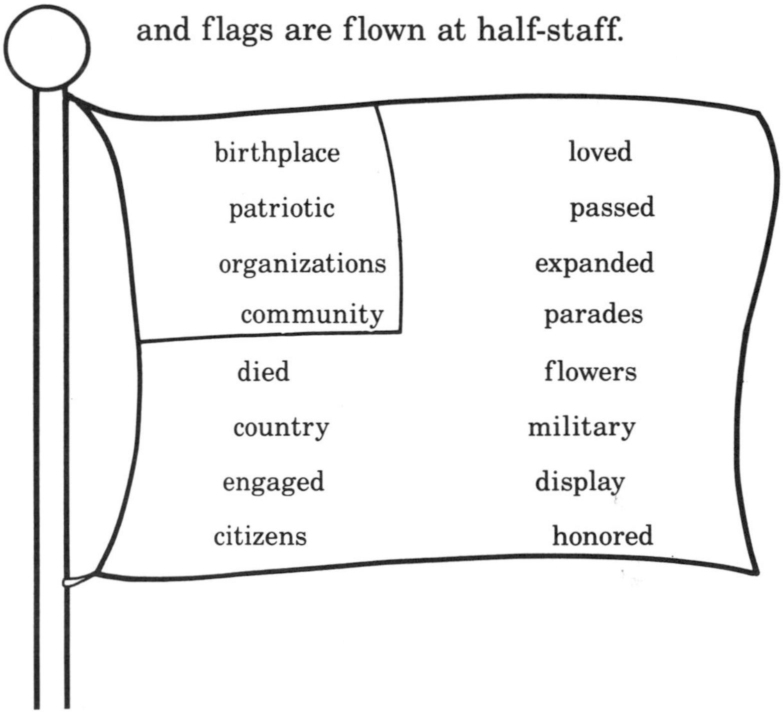

birthplace
patriotic
organizations
community
died
country
engaged
citizens
loved
passed
expanded
parades
flowers
military
display
honored

JUNE

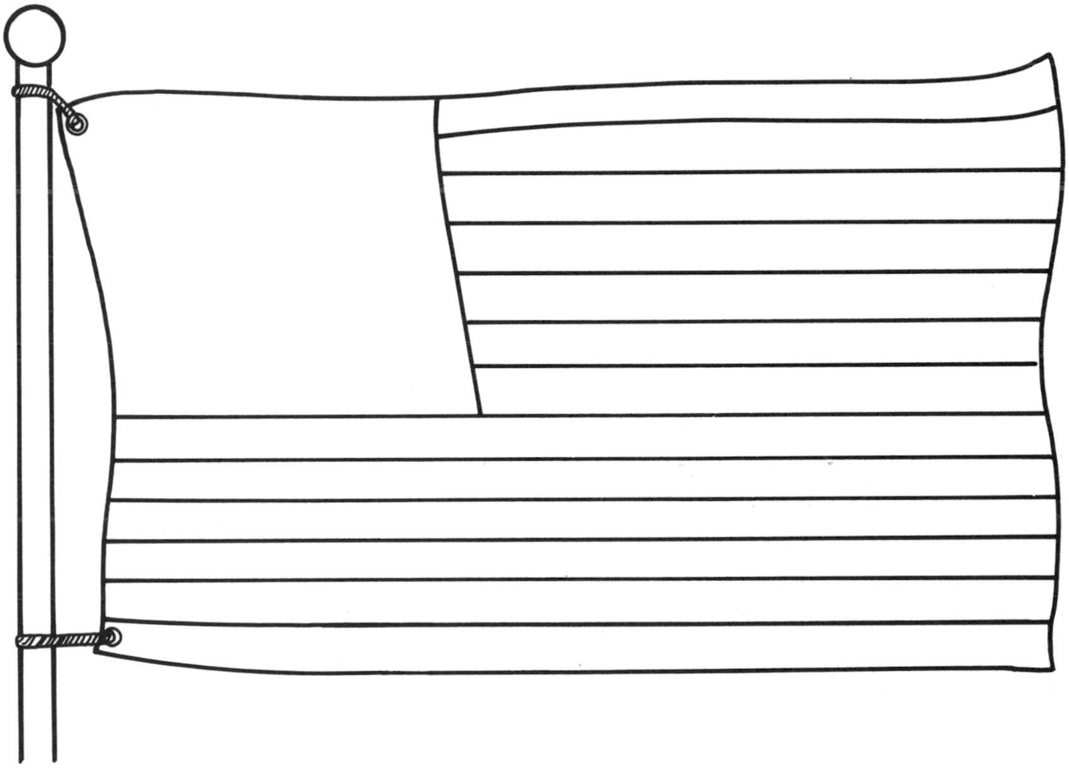

Vocabulary • 257

Activity Number and Title	Special Day
10-1 Father's Day	Father's Day
10-2 Flag Day	Flag Day

Vocabulary

The following two word lists will help develop your students' vocabularies in June.

Father's Day Word List	**Flag Day Word List**
special	government
day	stars
honor	displayed
June	selection
custom	officially
rose	congress
third	legal
celebration	organizations
speeches	holiday
father	public
promoted	anniversary
credit	patriotic
red	special
Sunday	requested
wearing	buildings
setting	homes
white	stripes
idea	country
permanently	parades
closest	flag

FATHER'S DAY

Directions: Fill in the blanks with words from the tie.

In 1972, President Richard M. Nixon permanently (1) ____________________ the third Sunday in June as Father's Day. Mr. Harry Meek and Mrs. John Bruce Dodd are given credit for (2) ____________________ the idea of setting aside a special day each (3) ____________________ to honor fathers.

Mr. Meek, a former (4) ____________________ of the Uptown Lion's Club of Chicago, promoted the (5) ____________________ in (6) ____________________. Members of the club chose the third Sunday in June for the (7) ____________________ because it was the Sunday (8) ____________________ to Mr. Meek's birthday.

Mrs. Dodd sent her (9) ____________________ of a Father's Day celebration to the Spokane Ministerial Association. They (10) ____________________ the idea. In 1910, Spokane became the first (11) ____________________ to honor fathers on a special day.

Mrs. Dodd also (12) ____________________ the custom of wearing a (13) ____________________ rose to honor a living father or a white rose to honor a father who is no longer (14) ____________________.

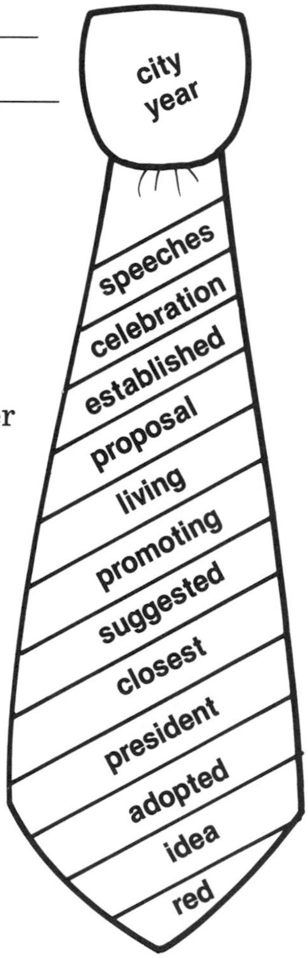

Name ________________________________

FLAG DAY

Directions: Fill in the blanks with words from the flag.

In 1777, the Continental Congress (1) ____________________ the Stars and Stripes as the (2) ________________ flag of the United States. Flag Day was first officially (3) ______________ on June 14, 1877 on the 100th (4) ______________ of the selection of the flag. Congress requested that all (5) ________________ buildings (6) ________________ the (7) ________________ on this day.

Flag Day is not a (8) ________________________ holiday in any state except (9) ____________________. (10) ____________________ says that Betsy Ross of (11) _______________ made the first flag according to the (12) ______________ adopted by the Continental Congress.

Although not a legal (13) __________________, special Flag Day observances are held throughout the (14) ________________. Flags are (15) ________________ on public buildings, businesses and (16) ______________________. Some patriotic (17) ________________ hold (18) ________________.

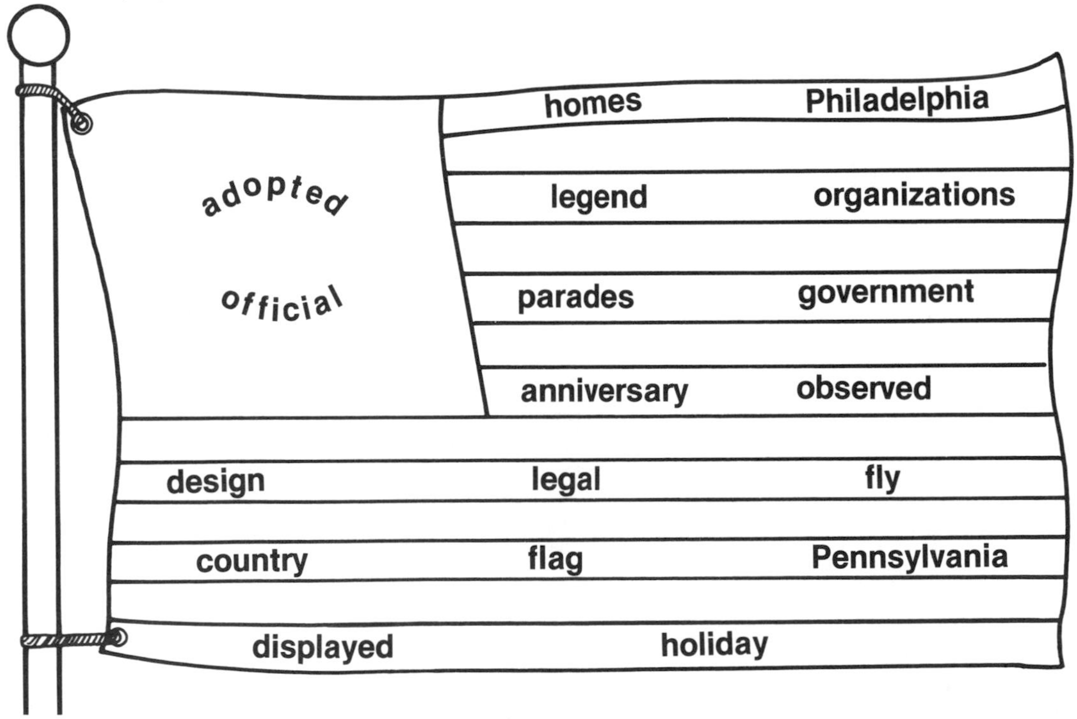

JULY

Vocabulary • 263

Activity Number and Title	Special Day
11-1 Independence Day	Independence Day
11-2 Independence Day Word Hunt	Independence Day

Vocabulary

The following word list will help develop your students' vocabularies in July.

Independence Day
Word List

independence
parades
fourth
providing
declaration
fireworks
speeches
adopted
services
July
people
special
music
birthday
military
fireworks
supervision
cities
celebrated
month

Name ______________________________

INDEPENDENCE DAY

Directions: Fill in the blanks with words from the cannon and cannonballs.

The (1) ______________________________ of the United States of America is (2) ____________________ on July 4 each year. The Declaration of Independence was (3) __________________ by the Continental Congress on July 4, 1776.

In the early (4) __________________, Independence Days were celebrated with (5) __________________, military parades, (6) __________________ of cannon fire, special church (7) __________________________________, bell ringing, military (8) __________________, and fireworks.

Hundreds of people were (9) __________________ or injured each year from the (10) ____________________. Many cities passed laws (11) ____________________ the sale of fireworks. Some (12) ______________________________________ began (13) ______________________ fireworks displays under the supervision of specially (14) __________________ people.

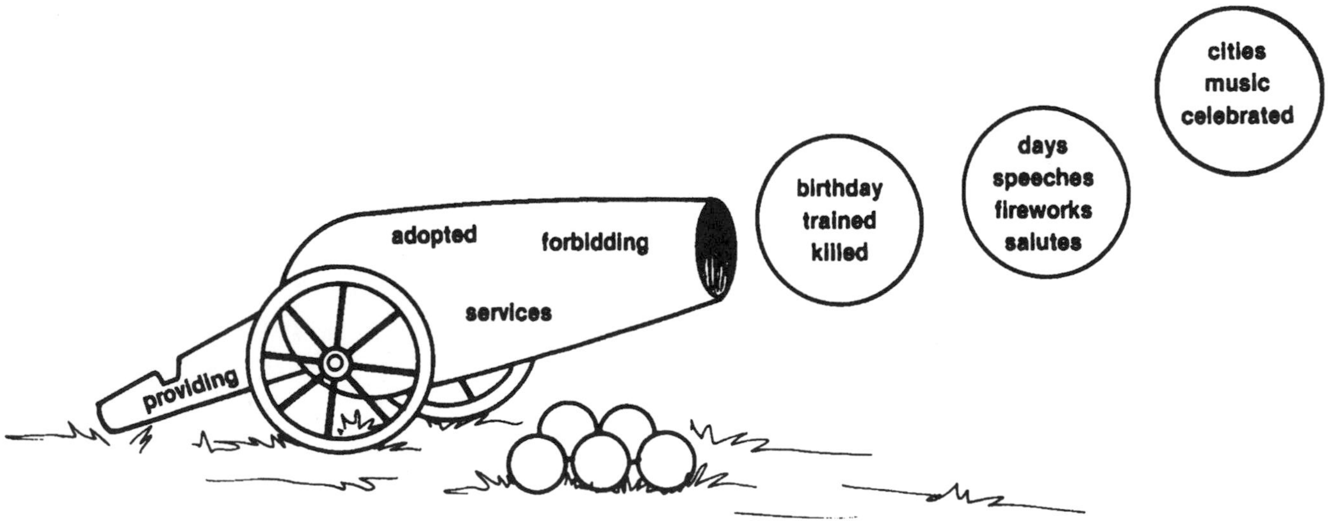

Name ______________________________ 11-2

INDEPENDENCE DAY WORD HUNT

Directions: Circle the hidden words. You may go across and down.

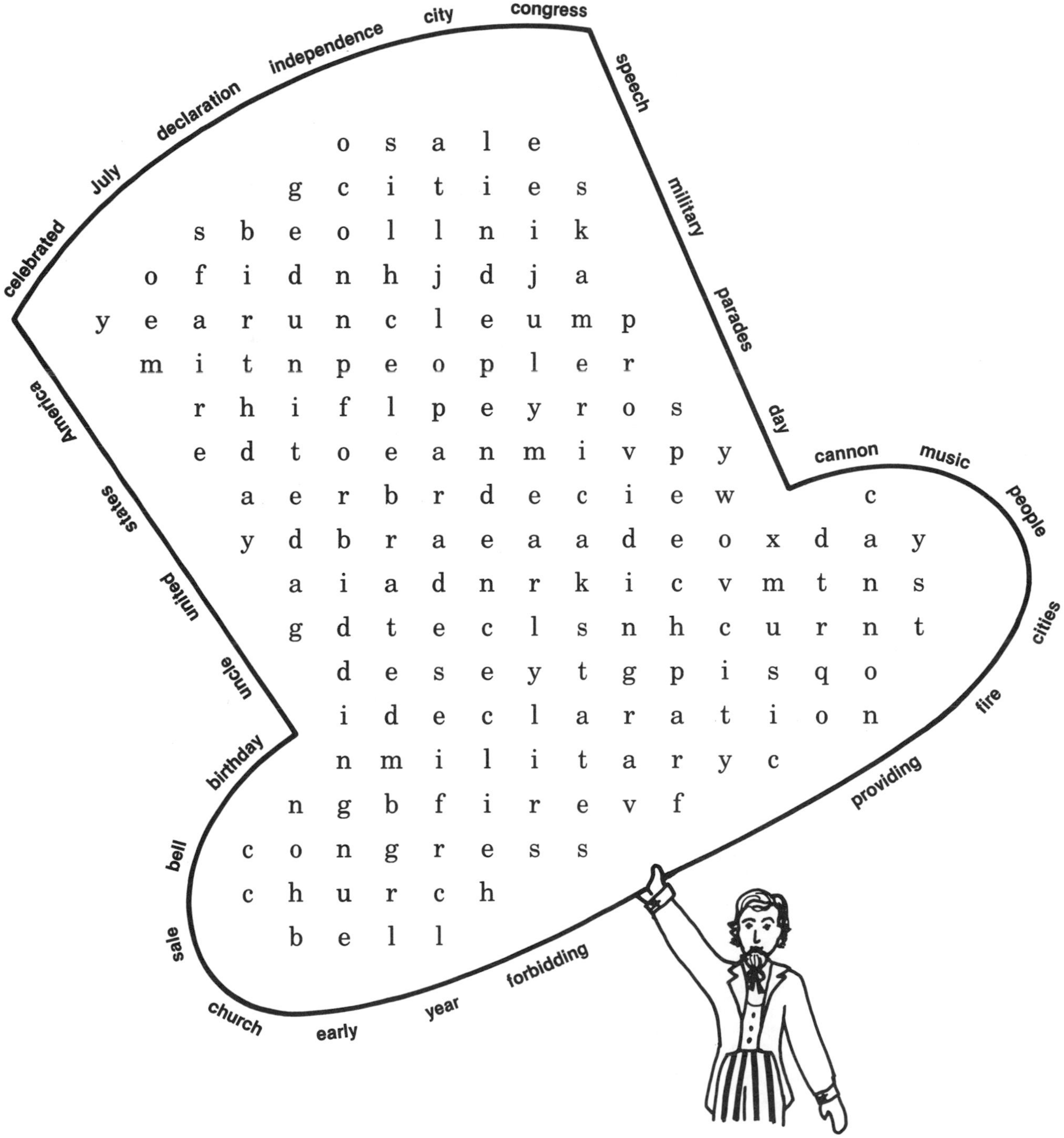

					o	s	a	l	e								
				g	c	i	t	i	e	s							
		s	b	e	o	l	l	n	i	k							
	o	f	i	d	n	h	j	d	j	a							
y	e	a	r	u	n	c	l	e	u	m	p						
	m	i	t	n	p	e	o	p	l	e	r						
		r	h	i	f	l	p	e	y	r	o	s					
		e	d	t	o	e	a	n	m	i	v	p	y				
			a	e	r	b	r	d	e	c	i	e	w			c	
			y	d	b	r	a	e	a	a	d	e	o	x	d	a	y
				a	i	a	d	n	r	k	i	c	v	m	t	n	s
				g	d	t	e	c	l	s	n	h	c	u	r	n	t
					d	e	s	e	y	t	g	p	i	s	q	o	
					i	d	e	c	l	a	r	a	t	i	o	n	
					n	m	i	l	i	t	a	r	y	c			
				n	g	b	f	i	r	e	v	f					
			c	o	n	g	r	e	s	s							
			c	h	u	r	c	h									
				b	e	l	l										

AUGUST

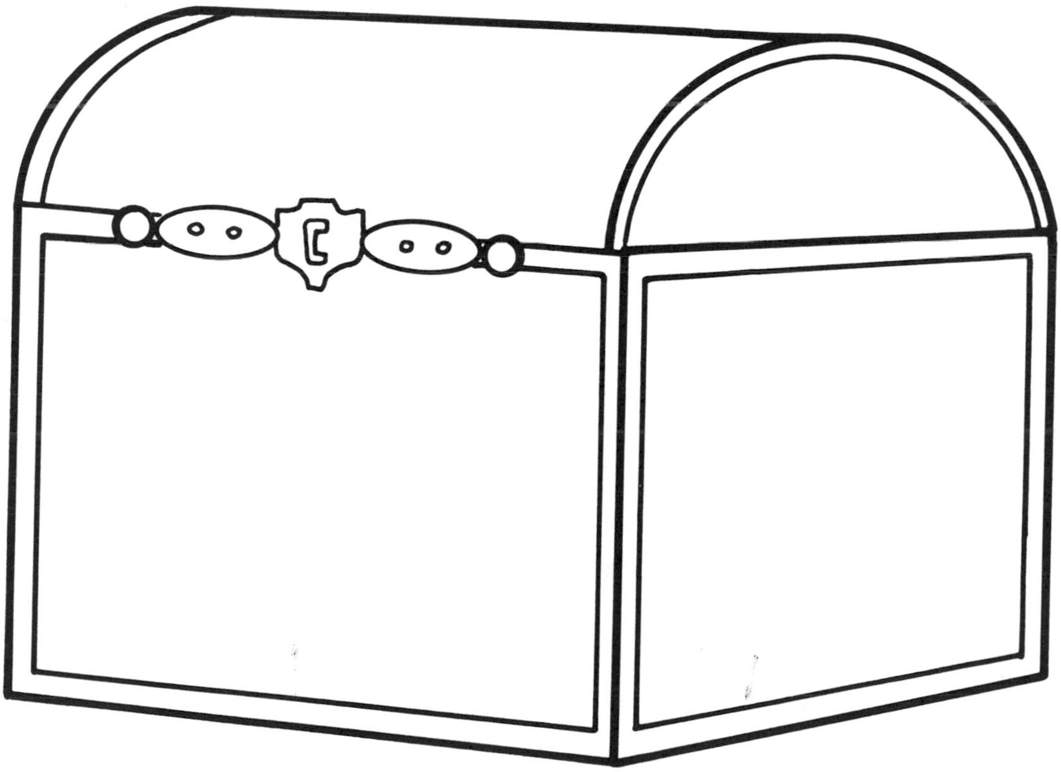

Vocabulary • 269

Activity Number and Title	Special Day
12-1 Columbus Sails	Columbus Sails

Vocabulary

The following word list will help develop your students' vocabularies in August.

Columbus Sails
Word List

sail
expensive
chance
refused
admiral
west
cheaply
money
land
rulers
sea
scarce
dangerous
wealthy
route
Spain
supplies
finance
rank
Asia

Name ______________________________

COLUMBUS SAILS

Directions: Fill in the blanks with words from the treasure chest.

Columbus had a dream. His dream was to reach Asia by sailing 3,000 miles (1) ________________. If he could reach (2) ________________ by sea, he could transport Asian spices, silks, and other valuable products by (3) ______________. At this time, the products had to be transported over a long and dangerous (4) ______________ route. This made the products scarce and (5) ______________. A sea route would mean that goods could be transported more (6) ______________ and in greater quantity. Anyone who could find this sea (7) ________________ would receive great honors and become very wealthy.

Columbus needed someone to help (8) ________________ the trip if he was to turn his dream into reality. He asked the (9) ____________________ of Portugal, Spain, and England for financial backing. They all (10) ____________________ to help. They thought the plan had little (11) ____________________ of success and would cost too much (12) ________________.

Finally, King Ferdinand and Queen Isabella of (13) ____________________ changed their minds. They provided Columbus with three ships and all the necessary (14) ______________. In addition, they promised to make him governor of any new lands that he discovered, to make him an (15) ______________, and to grant him a noble (16) __________________ if he was successful.

On August 3, 1492, Columbus set (17) ____________. On October 12, 1492, he landed in America. He was convinced that he had (18) __________________ the sea route from Europe to Asia. He believed this to his dying day.

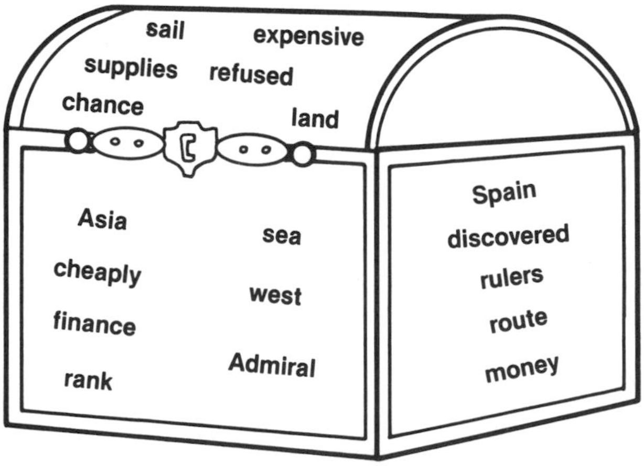

ANSWER KEY

1-1 Labor Day

1. observed
2. Monday
3. September
4. suggested
5. honor
6. working
7. celebration
8. city
9. state
10. National
11. President
12. legal
13. holiday
14. start
15. symbolize
16. summer
17. fall

1-2 A Picture to Color

Color according to color chart.

1-3 Same or Different

See exercise.

1-4 Alphabet Scramble

See exercise.

1-5 Who Is It?

The face of a young girl.

1-6 What Is It?

An apple.

1-7 The Lost Book

schoolmarm, teachers, desk, cook, library, cafeteria, lunch, recess, math, principal, book, science, students, reading, custodian, pen, ink, room, season, crayons, discipline, students, pass, grades, fall, graduate, librarian

1-8 Back to School Maze

students, schoolhouse, chalkboard, discipline, schoolmaster, graduate, quill, ink, punish, chalkstone, copybook, patience, hickory stick, custom, custodian, geography, subject, secretary, principal, ruler, eraser, art

1-9 Word Match

See exercise.

1-10 Word Hunt

p	h	y	s	i	c	a	l	e	d	u	c	a	l
m	g	h	e	t	e	d	u	c	a	t	i	o	n
q	r	e	w	y	a	e	n	s	r	a	z	r	i
w	r	i	t	i	n	g	c	p	i	l	a	t	g
a	s	v	o	s	r	p	h	e	t	q	l	s	h
m	u	s	i	c	p	s	t	l	h	i	a	p	e
r	e	a	d	i	n	g	x	l	m	w	n	e	a
e	w	c	m	e	o	s	b	i	e	r	g	l	l
c	f	g	k	n	h	n	w	n	t	x	u	l	t
e	d	e	y	c	t	m	a	g	i	n	a	i	h
s	u	l	j	e	s	v	r	d	c	z	g	n	c
s	o	c	i	a	l	s	t	u	d	i	e	s	e

1-11 Missing Consonant Puzzle

1. fall
2. season
3. school
4. football
5. principal
6. cafeteria
7. schedule
8. coach
9. students
10. game
11. lunch
12. rooms
13. desk
14. dictionary
15. education
16. encyclopedia
17. teacher

1-12 Missing Vowel Puzzle

1. book	11. music
2. pencils	12. paper
3. report card	13. principal
4. semester	14. writing
5. eraser	15. teacher
6. reading	16. geometry
7. art	17. basketball
8. grades	18. ruler
9. recess	19. test
10. science	20. math

1-13 Color Word Scramble

red, black, yellow, blue, brown, purple, green, orange, white, tan, pink, violet

1-14 Word Scramble

1. teachers	6. language
2. custodian	7. secretary
3. bus driver	8. reading
4. pupil	9. music
5. physical education	10. art

1-15 Scrambled Days

1. anSudy	Sunday
2. Mdoany	Monday
3. yTaudes	Tuesday
4. nesdayWed	Wednesday
5. rsThuyda	Thursday
6. driFya	Friday
7. yadrutaS	Saturday

1-16 Order! Order!

1. January	3. March
2. February	4. April
5. May	9. September
6. June	10. October
7. July	11. November
8. August	12. December

1-17 Sentence Completion

Answers will vary.

1-18 Make a Word

A few of the possible words:

back	best	cab	tool	hat
bat	act	cool	sat	oak
book	as	cot	so	look
black	cat	cloth	sob	lot
bath	cash	to	hot	lost

1-19 Crossword Puzzle

Across:	*Down:*
1. secretary	2. coach
3. teachers	6. custodian
4. books	8. pupils
5. bus driver	9. children
7. principal	11. counselor
10. nurse	

1-20 School Days

Answers will vary.

1-21 The New Student

Answers will vary.

1-22 Schoolmarms and Schoolmasters

1. female	3. formal
2. schoolmasters	4. graduate

5. examination
6. levels
7. custodian
8. lunchtime
9. recess
10. pay
11. family
12. received
13. month
14. goods
15. vegetables

1-23 Country Schoolhouse

1. schoolhouse
2. grades
3. chores
4. blackboard
5. water
6. fire
7. desk
8. roasted
9. froze
10. air
11. fresh
12. door
13. blasts
14. attended
15. farm
16. stove

1-24 The Hickory Stick

1. discipline
2. written
3. lesson
4. summer
5. docile
6. winter
7. rambunctious
8. patience
9. tricks
10. desk
11. punish
12. stick
13. corner
14. girls
15. preferred

1-25 School Tools

1. schoolhouse
2. board
3. blackened
4. paint
5. chalk
6. lumpy
7. sheepskin
8. tools
9. scratch
10. dirt
11. quill
12. ink
13. copybook
14. size
15. small
16. larger
17. accordion

1-26 Schoolhouse Word Hunt

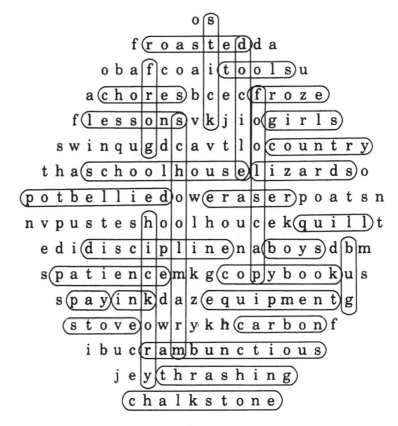

o s
f r o a s t e d d a
o b a f c o a i t o o l s u
a c h o r e s b c e c f r o z e
f l e s s o n s v k j i o g i r l s
s w i n q u g d c a v t l o c o u n t r y
t h a s c h o o l h o u s e l i z a r d s o
p o t b e l l i e d o w e r a s e r p o a t s n
n v p u s t e s h o o l h o u c e k q u i l l t
e d i d i s c i p l i n e n a b o y s d b m
s p a t i e n c e m k g c o p y b o o k u s
s p a y i n k d a z e q u i p m e n t g
s t o v e o w r y k h c a r b o n f
i b u c r a m b u n c t i o u s
j e y t h r a s h i n g
c h a l k s t o n e

1-27 Schoolhouse Scramble

1. schoolmarm
2. blackboard
3. eraser
4. foolscap
5. attended
6. discipline
7. lessons
8. hickory
9. thrashed
10. copybook

2-1 Columbus Day

1. discover
2. Queen
3. New
4. Sail
5. west
6. hard
7. finally
8. voyage
9. celebrated
10. October

2-2 Columbus Day Maze

discover, October, voyage, America, seaman, firelight, cabin, westward, history, fleet, inaugurated, sailing, west, King, west, October, Spain, voyage, land, sea, discovery, new, world, sailors, Columbus, landed, ocean, sea, ships, voyage, October, history, discoverer

2-3 Columbus Day Word Hunt

c	i	b	k	i	n	g	c	q	c	e	t	o	c	v
o	c	t	o	b	e	p	o	u	o	b	j	c	e	o
l	a	n	d	e	d	e	l	e	l	p	s	t	l	y
u	c	d	i	s	c	o	v	e	r	y	h	o	e	a
m	o	w	u	o	c	e	a	n	b	a	i	b	b	g
b	l	e	e	c	o	c	e	a	u	z	p	e	r	e
u	o	s	o	t	o	b	u	r	v	s	s	e	a	o
s	m	t	h	o	n	o	r	e	d	p	u	s	t	u
d	b	w	l	b	e	w	s	h	s	a	i	l	e	d
a	s	a	t	e	a	u	p	e	p	i	a	q	d	s
w	u	r	o	r	s	s	a	e	t	n	e	m	t	o
y	e	d	q	s	l	t	i	y	a	u	g	u	s	t

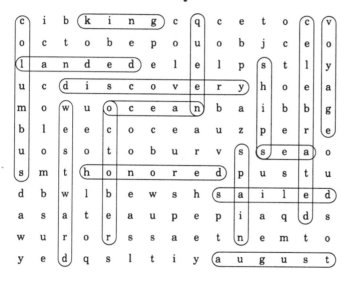

2-4 A Picture to Color

Colored pictures will vary.

2-5 Same or Different

See exercise.

2-6 Alphabet Scramble

See exercise.

2-7 Who Is It?

A witch.

2-8 The Lost Broomstick

with, scare, spooky, costume, trick-or-treat, Halloween, broom, black, cat, bat, night, afraid, pumpkin, trick, October, witch, afraid, goblins, skeleton, horror, treat

2-9 Halloween Maze

cauldron, frighten, witch, blood-chilling, skeleton, trick-or-treat, midnight, divining, terrifying, costumes, evil, demons, screech, haunted, house, goblins, broom, scream, mask, mean, nasty, ugly, fly, night, spell, bat, cat, monster, dress up, spirits, scared, afraid, Halloween, pumpkin, orange, black, afraid, screech, scared, haunted, Halloween, party, costumes, tricks, treats

2-10 Jack-O'-Lantern Puzzle

Vowels: a, i, o, a, e, u, o, u, i, i, e, a, a, a, e, e, o, i, u, e, u, a, i, o, u, i, e, a, u, i, u, e, u, e, i, u, o
Consonants: t, p, k, j, b, f, g, d, c, m, z

2-11 Halloween Word Match

See exercise.

2-12 Trick-or-Treat

Answers will vary.

2-13 Halloween Word Hunt

a	h	a	l	l	o	w	e	e	n	m	d
b	a	t	s	z	d	b	r	s	m	o	a
c	u	g	h	o	c	t	o	b	e	r	r
i	n	l	p	u	m	d	s	r	e	u	k
s	t	r	e	a	t	s	z	o	f	e	b
u	e	k	b	j	a	g	h	o	s	t	s
j	d	w	i	t	c	h	g	m	y	x	n
l	m	j	w	e	g	o	b	l	i	n	s

2-14 A Blood-Chilling Story

Answers will vary.

2-15 Sh! It's a Secret!

Look Out!
Here comes a wicked witch.
Run, run, run.

2-16 Missing Consonant Puzzle

1. haunted house
2. jack-o'-lanterns
3. trick-or-treat
4. witch
5. Halloween
6. dress-up

2-17 Missing Vowel Puzzle

1. Halloween
2. October
3. jack-o'-lantern
4. dress up
5. witch
6. ghost
7. haunted
8. dark
9. goblins
10. scary
11. house
12. candy
13. trick-or-treat
14. gloomy
15. monster
16. cauldron

2-18 Who Needs It?

1. Happy
2. Halloween
3. boys
4. and
5. girls

2-19 Make a Word

A few of the possible words:

he	heal	low	on	when
hen	all	lane	own	whale
hello	an	lean	whole	eel
hole	awe	owe	wheel	now
howl	lone	one	who	new

2-20 The Unfinished Spell

Answers will vary.

2-21 A Halloween Story

Answers will vary.

2-22 Look Who's Cooking?

Answers will vary.

2-23 Halloween Scramble

1. dark
2. spell
3. witch
4. horror
5. scream
6. ghosts
7. spooks
8. costume
9. pumpkin
10. Halloween

2-24 Halloween Divination

1. future
2. Halloween

3. divining
4. midnight
5. apple
6. slices
7. knife
8. mirror
9. sweetheart
10. slice
11. peeling
12. shoulder
13. floor
14. initial

2-25 Halloween Spirits

1. roamed
2. costumes
3. scare
4. weapon
5. torches
6. night
7. pumpkin
8. candle
9. doorsteps
10. house
11. iron
12. horseshoes
13. cross

2-26 Word Hunt

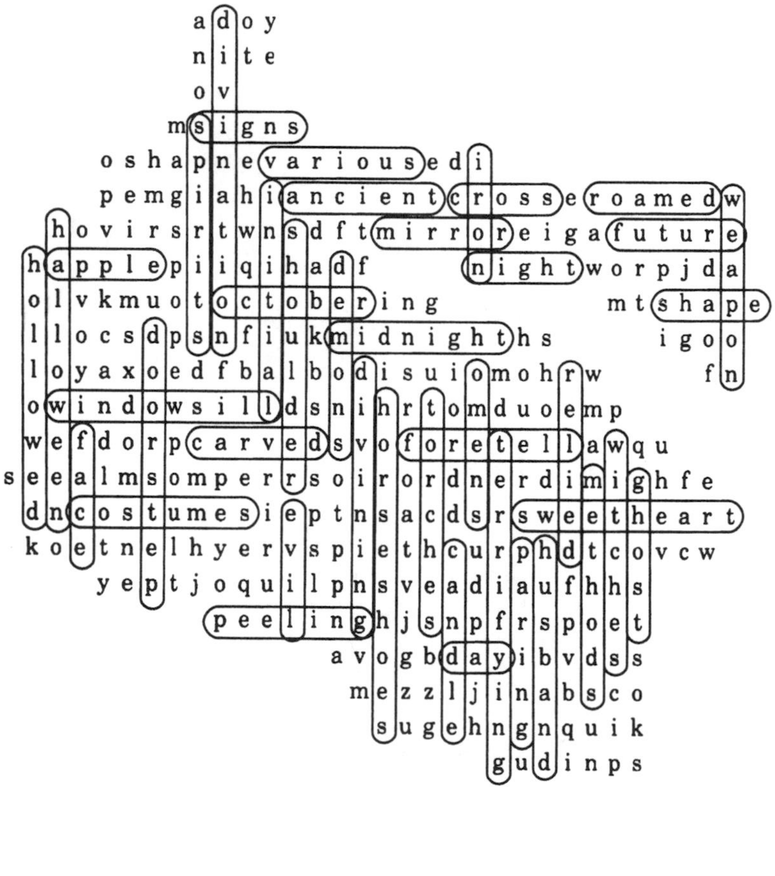

3-1 Veterans Day

1. known
2. armistice
3. ended
4. flashed
5. celebrations
6. ringing
7. weeping
8. streets
9. tape
10. proclaimed
11. remembrance
12. dead
13. honors
14. women
15. services
16. religious
17. ceremonies

3-2 Turkey Time

See exercise color directions.

3-3. Same or Different

See exercise.

3-4. Alphabet Scramble

See exercise.

3-5. Who Is It?

A pilgrim.

3-6 The Last Feast

pilgrims, cornucopia, thanks, bountiful, harvest, Mayflower, corn, cornstalk, pumpkin, pie, thankful, Indians, dinner, November, cranberry, mincemeat, dinner

3-7. Thanksgiving Maze

harvest, thanks, Indians, corn, feast, dinner, celebration, Pilgrims, cornucopia, Thanksgiving, November, Mayflower, cranberry, pumpkin, friendly, celebrate, holiday, fruit, fish, bountiful, acorn, hat, thankful, ship, friendly, fall, plenty, country, mincemeat, meal, football, proclamation, customs, floats, parades, football, games, church, services, Thursday, pie

3-8 Thanksgiving Puzzle

Consonants: b, m, t, r, p, z, y, g, s, f, f, k, v, d, n, v, g, q, c, s, l, w, t, b, m, r, j, h, p
Vowels: a, i, o, u, e, a, b, e, o, u, i, u, a, e

3-9 Thanksgiving Word Match

See exercise. Mayflower, pie, and acorn are not pictured.

3-10 Give Thanks

Answers will vary.

3-11 Thanksgiving Feast

Answers will vary.

3-12 Thanksgiving Word Hunt

t	h	a	n	k	s	g	i	v	i	n	g
h	o	l	i	d	a	y	c	x	z	o	f
u	z	p	n	c	o	r	n	g	i	v	e
r	t	u	d	q	r	o	v	d	w	e	a
s	u	m	i	s	h	i	p	i	e	m	s
d	r	p	a	n	p	m	b	n	x	b	t
a	k	k	n	z	l	o	l	n	p	e	z
y	e	i	c	r	a	n	b	e	r	r	y
h	y	n	i	q	s	t	m	r	n	x	s
g	j	m	e	k	t	h	a	n	k	s	a
p	i	l	g	r	i	m	s	t	f	d	i
u	m	a	y	f	l	o	w	e	r	a	l

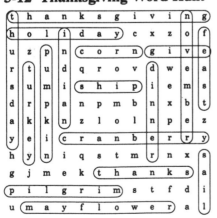

3-13 The First Thanksgiving Day

Answers will vary.

Possible answers:

1. turkey
2. corn
3. turkey, corn, pumpkin
4. surviving the winter

3-14 Sh! It's a Secret!

The Indians and Pilgrims celebrated the first Thanksgiving together.

3-15 Missing Consonant Puzzle

1. sail
2. celebrate
3. peace
4. fall
5. give
6. Mayflower
7. America
8. holiday
9. ship
10. thanks
11. help
12. Indians
13. month
14. country
15. plenty
16. harvest
17. bounty
18. Pilgrim
19. friendly
20. food

3-16 Missing Vowel Puzzle

1. Mayflower
2. feast
3. pumpkin pie
4. Thanksgiving
5. Indian
6. month
7. Pilgrim
8. holiday
9. November
10. turkey
11. cornucopia
12. hat
13. dinner
14. cranberry
15. mincemeat
16. thankful
17. hunt
18. corn

3-17 Thanksgiving Word Scramble

1. feast
2. holiday
3. ship
4. Thursday
5. Pilgrims
6. turkeys
7. Indians
8. Thanksgiving
9. Mayflower
10. November

3-18 Who Needs It?

1. Happy
2. Thanksgiving
3. boys
4. and
5. girls

Happy Thanksgiving, boys and girls.

3-19 Make a Word

A few of the possible words:

than	has	an	sing	is
think	hat	ash	sin	gang
thin	his	nag	sat	gas
this	ask	night	knit	vast
hint	ant	sign	it	van

3-20 My Thanksgiving Day

Answers will vary.

3-21 Thanksgiving Story

Answers will vary.

3-22 Thanksgiving

1. celebrated
2. centuries
3. parts
4. country
5. editor
6. magazine
7. campaign
8. holiday
9. articles
10. governors
11. support
12. proclaimed
13. Thursday
14. national

3-23 Thanksgiving Customs

1. customs
2. costumes
3. money
4. raffles
5. dinner
6. services
7. water
8. sauce
9. famous
10. season
11. relax

3-24 Word Hunt

p e i s d a t i m e n r t h k a g

r a s t t h u r s d a y o x p i c

m a d a y p   e s k e h n c f o k t u f a m t o

s p u m p k i n   d s s o l a m e o e d i t o r c u s t o m

s c k a y e c a c n i g i o t e n d l o c n o i v t p e c h s x

a o f p o s n d c m v k i e t p u n q u i r k e s u a

n s a a k g c e i n i s r b b s m a t n c o u n t r y

f o t m r i r o n a p s g u r a f f l e s l c i t e f h

b l v u o a s c m t t n i i m a l p l h d u e l m u b e r

u k o e m u d w h o d e k o v l t l i o o q p s a r r y t m r

w g a m e s e r u p s d h n i j e g l a l u p x i d i n n e r

a m b s o s e r v i c e s n u d a g t i v o w m s e f o z

t e l e v l c a m p a i g n j m r s d i r c e t s d

r e l a x h m a g a z i n e f i c a e t o d s g u

k p q i c k s g u a s m d y t

4-1 A Picture to Color

Results will vary.

4-2 Same or Different

See exercise.

4-3 Alphabet Scramble

See exercise.

4-4 Who Is It?

Santa Claus

4-5 What Is It?

A train engine.

4-6 Christmas Eve Maze

Santa, bells, reindeer, bake, wreath, father, holly, toys, bell, sleigh, Christmas, angel, package, holiday, cookie, stockings, decorate, December, candy cane, cards, fudge, noel, wreath, elf, gingerbread man, doll house, reindeer

4-7 Christmas Maze

Mrs. Santa, holiday, decorations, star, angel, bells, candy cane, December, Santa Claus, Christmas, sleigh, deliver, horn, holiday, toys, ball, drum, horn, candles, wreath, reindeer, presents, train, gingerbread man, elf, pudding

4-8 Christmas Puzzle

Food Words:

candy cane	pudding	popcorn
cake	cookies	salad
pie	pickle	bread
pretzels	corn	gravy
gingerbread	butter	tomato
doughnuts	jam	dressing
gumdrops	cranberry	peas
lollipops	mincemeat	relish
beans	ice cream	
carrots		

Toy Words:

bike	book
doll	ball
drum	train
horn	sled

Animal Words:

Vixen	Rudolph
Cupid	Donner
Dasher	

4-9 Christmas Match

See exercise.

4-10 A Christmas Wish

Answers will vary.

4-11 Christmas Word Hunt

c	a	r	o	l	k	m	o	z	b	p
h	o	l	l	y	u	s	t	j	e	r
r	e	d	k	q	c	a	n	d	l	e
i	x	r	s	t	a	r	u	w	k	s
s	a	c	a	n	d	y	c	a	n	e
t	d	b	n	o	c	s	n	o	w	n
m	e	f	t	e	h	i	g	i	f	t
a	g	m	a	l	t	b	e	l	l	s
s	t	o	c	k	i	n	g	k	l	o
j	n	p	c	o	o	k	i	e	s	q
t	r	e	e	r	s	f	u	d	g	e

4-12 Sh! It's a Secret!

Don't forget to leave a plate of cookies for Santa.

4-13 Christmas Consonant Puzzle

1. Christmas	6. stocking
2. decorations	7. cookies
3. snowman	8. candy cane
4. present	9. chestnuts
5. holiday	10. parties

4-14 Christmas Vowel Puzzle

1. elf	15. fudge
2. tree	16. holiday
3. decorate	17. candle
4. Santa Claus	18. pudding
5. Mrs. Santa	19. star
6. candy canes	20. angel
7. gingerbread man	21. carol
8. doll house	22. wreath
9. reindeer	23. package
10.snowflake	24. mittens
11.stocking	25. ball
12.present	26. drum
13.Christmas	27. train
14.dinner	28. horn

4-15 Christmas Word Scramble

1. December	6. candy cane
2. tree	7. holidays
3. decorate	8. Christmas
4. sleigh	9. parties
5. snowman	10. Santa

4-16 Who Needs It?

1. Merry	4. and
2. Christmas	5. girls
3. boys	

Merry Chistmas, boys and girls.

4-17 Make a Word

A few of the possible words:

car	his	in	stir	mat
cat	hit	it	tar	mar
cash	hair	star	trim	at
crash	rat	sat	miss	as
hat	rash	sir	match	arch

4-18 A Letter to Santa

Answers will vary.

4-19 A Christmas Story

Answers will vary.

4-20 What's Cooking?

Recipe: *cookies*

1-1/2 cups sugar
3-1/4 cups flour
2/3 cup butter
2 eggs
2-1/2 teaspoons baking powder
11 tablespoons milk
1 teaspoon vanilla
1/2 teaspoon salt

4-21 Saint Nicholas

1. bishop
2. saint
3. generosity
4. dowry
5. belief
6. Europe
7. shoes
8. horse
9. fireplace
10. straw
11. toys
12. word

4-22 Christmas

1. holiday
2. anniversary
3. services
4. scene
5. traditional
6. decorate
7. ornaments
8. wrap
9. desserts
10. cards
11. stockings
12. parties
13. dinner
14. family
15. happiest
16. adults

4-23 Word Hunt

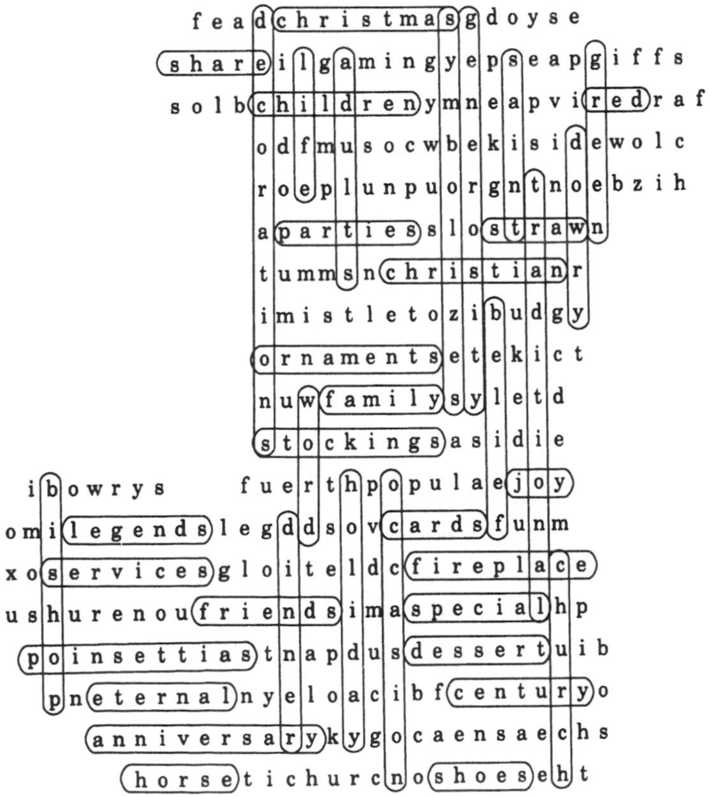

4-24 Hanukkah

1. Hebrew
2. begins
3. month
4. falls
5. eight
6. additional
7. candela-brum
8. commemo-rates
9. holy
10. consecrated
11. oil
12. traditions
13. festive
14. exchanged

5-1 A Picture to Color

Color as directed.

5-2 Find the Hidden Mitten

See exercise.
Coloring will vary.

5-3 Same or Different

See exercise.

5-4 Alphabet Scramble

See exercise.

5-5 What Is It?

An igloo.

5-6 The Hidden Sled

January, month, first, New Year, resolutions, parties, confetti, sled, sleet, slush, snowing, winter, mitten, snowman, ice, snow, sparkle, snowball, gloves, freezing, leader, black, rights, nonviolent, civil, birthday, equality

5-7 Guess What

See exercise.
A mitten.

5-8 New Year's Eve Puzzle

15 Consonants: b, j, t m v, p, q, c, x, k, d, f, z, h, q
15 Vowels: a, e, i, o, u, a, u, i, a, e, o, a, i, e, o
13 Consonants: f, w, s, r, g, k, l, d, h, y, b, r, n

5-9 Word Match

See exercise.

5-10 Winter Fun

Anwers will vary.

5-11 Word Hunt

a	m	n	o	v	e	m	b	e	r	j	s	t
u	w	o	c	t	o	b	e	r	a	u	a	h
f	e	b	r	u	a	r	y	i	p	l	t	u
r	d	e	c	e	m	b	e	r	r	y	u	r
i	n	a	u	g	u	s	t	r	i	t	r	s
d	e	s	u	n	d	a	y	l	l	m	d	d
a	s	e	p	t	e	m	b	e	r	a	a	a
y	d	x	n	p	j	a	n	u	a	r	y	y
m	a	v	q	s	u	y	i	g	h	c	e	d
i	y	f	m	o	n	d	a	y	j	h	k	l
s	u	n	t	u	e	s	d	a	y	m	u	a

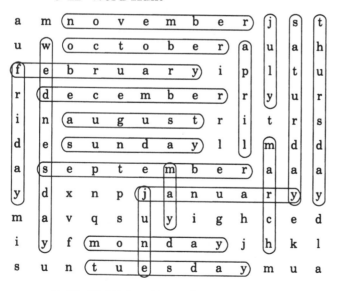

5-12 Sh! It's a Secret!

January is the first month of the year. It is one of the winter months.

5-13 Missing Consonant Puzzle

1. snow
2. cold
3. sled
4. snowman
5. happy
6. snowflake
7. mitten
8. January
9. month
10. season

5-14 Missing Vowel Puzzle

1. ice
2. wet
3. fall *or* fill
4. winter
5. January
6. season
7. snowstorm
8. sleet
9. freezing
10. slush *or* slash
11. rain
12. sneeze

5-15 Make a Word

A few of the possible words:

new	ewe	wave	are	say
near	ease	year	any	swan
never	war	yarn	rave	seven
eve	was	yew	raw	vase
ear	ware	an	ran	vane

5-16 Make a Word

nay	warm	year	read	seed
need	weed	yard	ray	sad
earn	way	yes	ram	day
end	wed	away	saw	deed
erase	were	awe	sew	less

5-17 Order! Order!

1. New Year's Eve
2. New Year's Day

3. Lincoln's Birthday
4. Valentine's Day
5. Washington's Birthday
6. St. Patrick's Day
7. Easter Sunday*
8. April Fool's Day
9. Mother's Day
10. Memorial Day
11. Father's Day
12. Fourth of July
13. Labor Day
14. Columbus Day
15. Halloween
16. Thanksgiving
17. Christmas Eve
18. Christmas

* Easter Sunday can fall from March 22 to April 25.

5-18 The Snowball Fight

Answers will vary.

5-19 Snow

Answers will vary.

5-20 Ice

Answers will vary.

5-21 Martin Luther King, Jr. Day

1. January
2. rights
3. equality
4. won
5. black
6. Nonviolent
7. assassinated
8. Tennessee
9. celebrated

5-22 Martin Luther King, Jr. Word Hunt

e	c	o	n	o	m	i	c	w	o	n	s	c
b	o	r	n	h	o	l	i	d	a	p	r	e
a	s	s	a	s	s	i	n	a	t	e	d	l
p	o	l	t	i	c	a	l	m	u	a	h	e
o	p	o	i	t	i	c	a	e	n	c	o	b
l	i	f	o	l	g	n	t	r	v	e	l	r
i	a	j	n	e	s	o	c	i	a	l	i	a
t	p	o	a	h	d	n	b	c	k	m	d	t
i	r	i	l	g	h	v	i	o	l	e	a	e
c	i	v	i	l	r	i	g	h	t	s	y	d
a	z	n	o	m	h	o	n	o	r	e	b	s
l	e	a	b	e	r	l	e	a	d	e	r	n
b	l	a	c	k	s	e	f	e	b	r	u	a
c	i	v	i	j	a	n	u	a	r	y	n	e
e	q	u	a	l	i	t	y	c	g	h	k	l

6-1 Groundhog Day

1. legend
2. groundhog
3. long
4. sleep
5. shadow
6. sunny
7. burrow
8. hibernate
9. winter
10. cloudy
11. spring

6-2 Ground Hog Day Word Hunt

g	c	l	o	u	d	y	l	s							
r	k	s	h	w	e	w	f	j	s	w					
o	u	t	s	i	d	e	g	t	h	v	f	w	b		
u	s	b	i	n	c	e	a	w	a	k	e	n	u		
n	p	u	x	t	s	k	y	g	d	f	b	h	r		
d	r	s	v	e	u	s	i	s	o	x	r	i	r	l	
h	i	b	e	r	n	a	t	e	w	l	u	j	o	o	m
o	n	c	t	s	n	d	s	c	z	b	a	k	w	o	e
g	g	o	l	l	y	m	q	o	k	w	r	o	g	k	a
	s	l	a	e	p	s	i	n	d	a	y	c	n	e	n
	e	d	l	e	g	e	n	d	d	r	w	o	i	t	s
			s	p	e	r	m	i	n	m	t	s	w	d	

6-3 A Picture to Color

Coloring will vary.

6-4 Same or Different

See exercise.

6-5 Alphabet Scramble

See exercise.

6-6 A Secret Pal

A witch. Facial features will vary.

6-7 What Is It?

A jug of flowers.

6-8 Valentine Maze

sweetheart, notes, love, February, cards, hearts, pink, red, hibernate, groundhog, shadow, sunshine, cloudy, overcast, winter, presidents, birthdays

6-9 Valentine Maze

Valentine, love, potion, friends, cards, flowers, candy, hearts, red, pink, party, February, month, second, gifts, love, mailbox, true, dear, kiss, truelove, Valentine, hearts, cards, love, pink, notes, mailman, send, letters, cards, mail, kiss, February, party, heart, sun, shadow, predict, flowers, heart, love, truelove

Drinker of potion: YOU

6-10 A Valentine Puzzle

Vowels: a, e, i, o, u, o, e, i, o, u, i, u, a, i, o, e, i, e, a, e, u, a, o, i, e, i, e, o, u, o, u, e, a, i, o, i, a, e, u, i
Consonants: c, p, d, s, m, b, r, f, q, g, y, n, c, h, w, k, t, v, x, l, z, f, p, x

6-11 Valentine Match

See exercise.

Words without corresponding pictures: love potion, party, ice cream, decorations, cake

6-12 Word Hunt

v	a	l	e	n	t	i	n	e	i	n	g
s	u	o	b	o	d	w	s	r	l	t	k
f	w	v	k	t	p	m	o	n	t	h	l
l	r	e	d	e	c	c	a	n	d	y	e
o	p	r	e	s	e	n	t	s	i	q	t
w	l	r	z	f	u	q	k	e	h	p	t
e	y	p	g	t	w	m	i	n	e	a	e
r	r	s	l	q	c	a	r	d	s	r	r
s	l	x	a	a	p	h	e	a	r	t	s
k	r	e	c	e	i	v	e	c	u	y	j
u	g	m	e	d	p	i	n	k	e	i	t
t	p	s	o	f	e	b	r	u	a	r	y

6-13 Sh! It's a Secret!

Dear Valentine,
please be mine
if you don't agree
I'll turn you
into a flea.

6-14 Word Scramble

1. love
2. dear
3. valentine
4. February
5. heart
6. party
7. kiss
8. red

6-15 Make a Word

A few of the possible words:

say sad sit stay salt
ant in nail veil eat
an it tidy van evil
aid idle tin lay day
idea nest tiny list dine

6-16 Valentine Puzzle

1. cards
2. valentines
3. February
4. party
5. flowers
6. candy
7. happy
8. love
9. kiss
10. red

6-17 Sentence Completion

1. Valentine's Day is *February.*
2. February is the second month of the *year.*
3. We give our *friends* pretty Valentine cards.
4. It's fun to get *more* Valentine cards than our friends
5. Some people *make* their own cards instead of buying them at the store.

6-18 A Valentine Party

Answers will vary.

6-19 A Love Note

Answers will vary.

6-20 Surprise! Surprise!

Answers will vary.

6-21 A Love Potion

Answers will vary.

6-22 What's Cooking?

Recipe: *cookies*

3/4 cup brown sugar
3/4 cup sugar
1 cup butter
2 eggs
11 tablespoons milk
2-1/2 teaspoons baking powder
1/2 teaspoon salt
1 teaspoon vanilla
1 teaspoon cinnamon
1/2 teaspoon cloves
1/2 teaspoon nutmeg

6-23 Saint Valentine

1. authorities
2. saints
3. merged
4. legend
5. secretly
6. couples
7. forbade
8. friends
9. prison
10. worship
11. love
12. cell
13. cured
14. signed

6-24 Love Story

1. name
2. brave
3. graveyard
4. chant
5. appear
6. pieces
7. water
8. rise
9. dream
10. leaves
11. riser
12. sunrise
13. window
14. future

6-25 Abraham Lincoln

1. truly
2. president
3. inaugurated
4. nation
5. preserve
6. union
7. split
8. separate
9. born
10. chores
11. formal
12. year
13. accomplished
14. education
15. scarce
16. distances
17. borrow
18. farm
19. firelight

6-26 Lincoln's Birthday

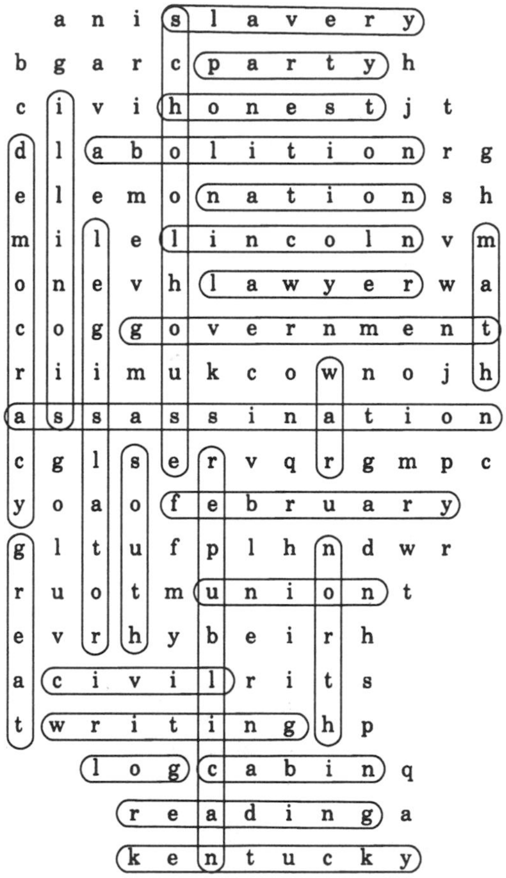

6-27 George Washington

1. Washington
2. independence
3. Britain
4. commander
5. president
6. convention
7. constitution
8. elected

9. first
10. stories
11. famous
12. chopped
13. trees
14. confessed

6-28 Washington's Birthday

		w	a	t	r	u	t	h	e	s	
	k	a	n	n	i	v	e	r	s	r	y
a	r	s	m	i	s	t	i	s	c	e	a
m	c	h	o	p	p	e	d	g	o	v	m
e	v	i	r	o	n	m	e	n	u	o	e
c	o	n	v	e	n	t	i	o	n	l	r
a	b	g	o	v	e	r	n	m	t	u	i
f	a	t	h	e	r	l	e	i	r	t	c
a	m	o	n	u	m	e	n	t	y	i	a
c	o	n	s	t	i	t	u	t	i	o	n
p	c	h	e	r	r	w	a	r	b	n	t
e	g	o	v	e	r	n	m	e	n	t	b
p	r	e	s	i	d	e	n	e	t	s	p
i	n	d	e	p	e	n	d	e	n	c	e
		f	e	b	r	u	a	r	y	f	a
		c	h	e	r	r	y	t	r	i	c
		h	o	l	i	d	a	l	y	r	e
		u	n	i	v	e	r	i	a	s	l
		p	r	e	s	i	d	e	n	t	d

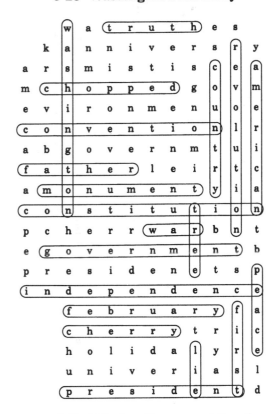

6-29 Missing Consonant Puzzle

first
war
won
father
country
great
independence
convention
president
constitution
cannot
wrote
states
through
chopped
February
cherry
united
years
story
elected

6-30 Missing Vowel Puzzle

independence
president
constitution
won
government
February
country
chopped
peace
Washington
convention
revolution
monument
elected
confessed
tree
lie
first
truth
American
cherry
war
army
commander

7-1 A Picture to Color

A shamrock. Color should be green.

7-2 Same or Different

See exercise.

7-3 Alphabet Scramble

See exercise.

7-4 Who Is It?

A leprechaun.

7-5 What Is It?

A pot of gold.

7-6 Shamrock Maze

leprechaun, shamrock, green, jig, Irish, pot of gold, wish, charm, Ireland, shillelagh, laddies, lassies, parade, island, luck, trick, coins

7-7 Saint Patrick's Day Puzzle

Vowels: e, i, o, a
Consonants: k, c, x, g q, t, b, p, w, j, v, f, r, h, s, k, v, z, f, p, t, h, b, y, m, h, d, x, l, g, n, z, n, r, s, j

7-8 Word Match

See exercise.

Words without corresponding pictures: parade, jig, trick, party

7-9 Shopping Spree

Answers will vary.

7-10 March Calendar

For year 2000.

Sunday	Monday	Tuesday	Wednesday	Thursday	Friday	Saturday
			1	2	3	4
5	6	7	8	9	10	11
12	13	14	15	16		18
19	20	21	22	23	24	25
26	27	28	29	30	31	

7-11 Word Hunt

l	e	p	r	e	c	h	a	u	n	q	c	s
u	b	p	a	r	a	d	e	g	r	e	e	n
c	h	a	r	m	i	n	p	w	u	t	l	b
k	e	i	r	i	s	h	k	i	h	h	e	a
y	d	f	k	j	p	i	g	s	c	i	b	n
i	p	u	l	m	a	r	c	h	o	r	r	d
s	t	p	a	t	r	i	c	k	s	d	a	y
h	o	m	o	n	t	h	r	s	t	u	t	w
g	h	a	p	p	y	m	n	o	p	q	e	i
p	o	u	p	o	t	o	f	g	o	l	d	s
z	d	c	e	f	s	h	a	m	r	o	c	k

7-12 Sh! It's a Secret!

People wear green on St. Patrick's Day and celebrate with parades.

7-13 Missing Consonant Puzzle

elf	blarney
jig	Ireland
pot of gold	lucky
leprechaun	holiday
island	stone
green	Irish
shillelagh	

Words not used: isle, wish, pinch, trick, (the second island)

7-14 Missing Vowel Puzzle

celebrate	laddies
lassies	charm
isle	parade

shillelagh	band
coin	wish
pinch	mushroom
trick	happy

Words not used: green, shamrock, island.

7-15 Word Scramble

1. Ireland	6. parade
2. lucky	7. charm
3. green	8. March
4. shamrock	9. shillelagh
5. leprechaun	10. wish

7-16 Rhyme Time

seen	green
big and bold	pot of gold
charade	parade
Bucky	lucky
big	jig
that	hat
dish	wish
shelf	elf
inch	pinch
slick	trick
alarm	charm
paint	saint
starch	March

Word not used: coin.

7-17 Make a Word

sand	an	it	trip	rat
spy	ant	is	trick	cat
sit	ask	ink	tin	car
sad	air	nay	pat	kind
sap	apt	nasty	pin	day

7-18 My Three Wishes

Answers will vary.

7-19 The Pot of Gold

Answers will vary.

7-20 Legend of the Leprechaun

Answers will vary.

7-21 Saint Patrick

1. authorities	9. shamrock
2. captured	10. schools
3. marauders	11. missionary
4. slavery	12. anniversary
5. escaped	13. national
6. monastery	14. ceremonies
7. returned	15. wearing
8. convert	

7-22 The Last Snake

1. famous	8. box
2. drove	9. size
3. snakes	10. small
4. ocean	11. argued
5. remained	12. prove
6. leave	13. slammed
7. trick	14. threw

8-1 April Fool's Day

1. first	7. custom
2. April	8. France
3. customary	9. calendar
4. jokes	10. changed
5. origin	11. time
6. lost	12. celebrated

13. tradition
14. continued
15. fools

8-2 Arbor Day

1. planting
2. children
3. conservation
4. man
5. treeless
6. erosion
7. moisture
8. legislature
9. birthday
10. recognized
11. tree
12. celebration
13. various
14. observe
15. between

8-3 Arbor Day Word Hunt

			t	r	e	e	l	e	s	s				
	c	o	n	s	e	r	v	a	t	i	o	n		
a	r	b	o	r	a	n	c	h	r	c	e	l	a	
m	i	s	d	e	c	e	m	b	e	r	p	l	v	
d	c	e	l	e	b	r	a	t	e	s	c	i	v	
a	p	r	i	l	p	o	p	r	o	c	l	a	i	m
y	i	v	e	r	l	s	n	v	a	r	i	o	u	s
l	s	e	p	c	a	i	e	m	e	b	m	e	s	k
a	o	g	n	z	i	o	b	c	h	i	a	n	f	
t	i	d	e	c	n	n	r	b	e	r	t	r	e	
i	l	e	g	i	s	l	a	t	u	r	e	i	s	
n	b	m	s	v	r	k	s	t	r	e	a	c		
p	g	a	n	i	v	e	k	s	a	r	y	h		
		y	w	c	i	m	a	r	c	h				
		p	e	r	s	u	a	d	e	d				

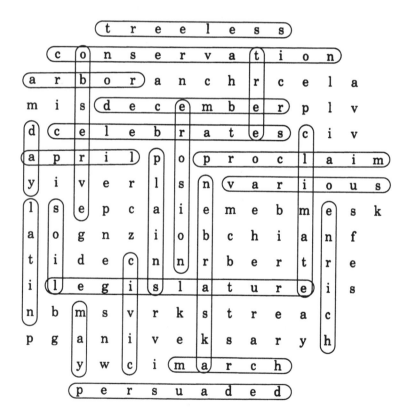

8-4 A Picture to Color

Results will vary.

8-5 Same or Different

See exercise.

8-6 Alphabet Scramble

See exercise.

8-7 Who Is It?

The Easter Bunny.

8-8 The Lost Bonnet

bunny, hare, eggs, clothes, flowers, crayons, new, rabbit, ink, Sunday, hide, lilies, Easter, candy, card, spring, decorate, cake, hunt, basket, April, chicks, March

8-9 Easter Maze

Easter, bunny, basket, eggs, hide, hare, April, new, card, candy, sunshine, clothes, hunting, spring, chicks, lilies, rain, sun, life, egg, hare, moon, March, symbol, relationship, outfits, candy, month, day, cake, flowers, showers, Easter, clothes, decorate, month, chick, card, cake, spring, bunny, happiness, Sunday, hide, eggs, March, sunrise, decorate, bunny, card, April, hare, Easter, church, Sunday, hide

8-10 Easter Puzzle

Vowels: a, a, o, u, i, e
Consonants: v, x, q, t, s, b, f, p, t, m, h, k, k, d, c, g, m, s, w, y, l, z

8-11 Easter Puzzle

Vowels: a, i, e, e, o, u, u, i, a, e, o, a, u, o, e, a, i, a, u, i, o, a, e, i
Consonants: b, q, l, y, s, t, z, n, m, v, v, q, t, d, x, w, j, c, m, g, k, s, l, f, m, p, d, k, w, l, q, p, z, j, h

8-12 Easter March

See exercise.

Words without corresponding pictures: showers, cake, candy, chicks, church

8-13 Easter Word Hunt

e	a	s	t	e	r	x	s	u	n	d	a	y
q	a	p	r	i	l	j	u	z	l	k	r	s
c	a	r	d	n	m	o	n	t	h	b	d	h
e	f	i	g	m	o	q	s	k	m	z	x	a
b	u	n	n	y	i	c	h	i	c	k	s	p
k	e	g	g	s	x	h	i	d	e	a	z	p
m	a	r	c	h	s	p	n	e	w	r	i	y
e	h	j	b	a	s	k	e	t	l	p	u	v
c	l	o	t	h	e	s	k	m	r	a	i	n
d	c	h	u	r	c	h	g	s	p	k	m	o
c	h	u	r	c	d	e	c	o	r	a	t	e

8-14 Easter Sentences

1. Easter is a special day.
2. It comes in the spring.
3. On Easter morning, we get an Easter basket filled with pretty eggs and candy.
4. It is fun to hide the Easter eggs and then have an Easter Egg Hunt.
5. For dessert we always have cake that looks like the Easter bunny.

8-15 Sh! It's a Secret!

All of the Easter eggs are hidden under the lilac bushes.

8-16 Easter Consonant Puzzle

1. happiness
2. month
3. showers
4. sunshine
5. clothes
6. Sunday
7. bunny
8. card
9. hide
10. eggs
11. rain
12. spring
13. warm
14. church
15. basket
16. chicks

Words not used: April, March, new

8-17 Easter Vowel Puzzle

1. bunny
2. card
3. eggs
4. decorate
5. flowers
6. Sunday
7. March
8. April
9. sunshine
10. basket
11. showers
12. spring

8-18 Word Scramble

Easter	candy
hide	chicks

basket bunny eggs hunt
decorate springtime Sunday

8-19 Word Scramble

1. flowers
2. dinner
3. sunshine
4. happiness
5. church
6. April
7. Sunday
8. playing
9. season
10. basket

8-20 Make a Word

A few of the possible words:

ease	ate	sea	steer	tar
east	at	see	seer	terse
eat	are	seat	tear	rest
ear	star	sear	tease	rate
as	sat	stare	tree	rat

8-21 An Easter Story

Answers will vary.

8-22 Easter Morning

Answers will vary.

8-23 New Clothes for an Old Witch

Answers will vary.

8-24 Easter

1. celebrate
2. sunrise
3. white
4. wearing
5. singing
6. basket
7. hidden
8. Santa
9. bunny
10. chickens
11. symbol
12. determined
13. moon
14. Easter
15. closely
16. chose

8-25 Word Hunt

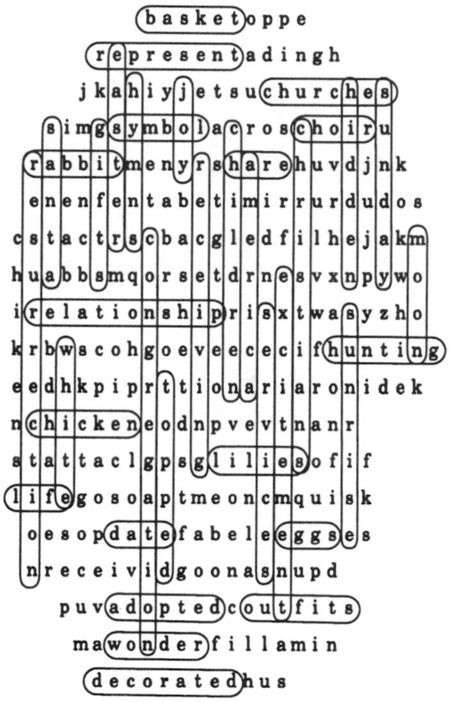

9-1 May Day Customs

1. customs
2. May
3. England
4. festivals
5. woods
6. decorate
7. churches
8. ribbons
9. danced
10. Maypole
11. girl
12. Queen
13. America
14. baskets
15. front
16. flowers
17. sweethearts

9-2 May Day Superstitions

1. magic
2. acts
3. predict
4. husband
5. sunrise
6. dew
7. rising
8. freckles

9. poem
10. marry
11. bottle
12. mirror
13. reflection
14. well
15. water

9-3 Mother's Day

1. recognized
2. founder
3. campaign
4. nationwide
5. first
6. honored
7. custom
8. carnation
9. white
10. dead
11. President
12. issued
13. proclamation
14. nation

9-4 Memorial Day

1. community
2. birthplace
3. honored
4. flowers
5. died
6. passed
7. engaged
8. patriotic
9. expanded
10. military
11. country
12. organizations
13. parades
14. citizens
15. loved
16. display

10-1 Father's Day

1. established
2. promoting
3. year
4. president
5. idea
6. speeches
7. celebration
8. closest
9. proposal
10. adopted
11. city
12. suggested
13. red
14. living

10-2 Flag Day

1. adopted
2. official
3. observed
4. anniversary
5. government
6. fly
7. flag
8. legal
9. Pennsylvania
10. legend
11. Philadelphia
12. design
13. holiday
14. country
15. displayed
16. homes
17. organizations
18. parades

11-1 Independence Day

1. birthday
2. celebrated
3. adopted
4. days
5. speeches
6. salutes
7. services
8. music
9. killed
10. fireworks
11. forbidding
12. cities
13. providing
14. trained

11-2 Independence Day Word Hunt

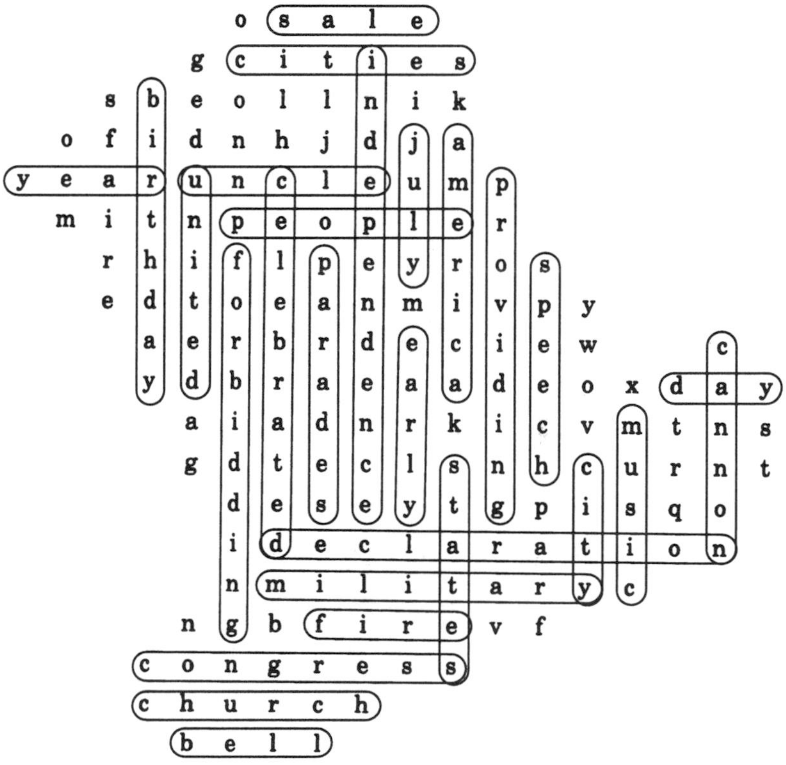

12-1 Columbus Sails

1. west	10. refused
2. Asia	11. chance
3. sea	12. money
4. land	13. Spain
5. expensive	14. supplies
6. cheaply	15. admiral
7. route	16. rank
8. finance	17. sail
9. rulers	18. discovered

NOTES

NOTES

NOTES

NOTES

NOTES

NOTES

NOTES